The Unfeigned Word

The Unfeigned Word

Fifteen Years of
New England Review

Edited by T. R. HUMMER

and DEVON JERSILD

Middlebury College Press

Published by University Press of New England / Hanover and London

MIDDLEBURY COLLEGE PRESS

Published by University Press of New England, Hanover, NH 03755

Printed in the United States of America   5 4 3 2 1

CIP data appear at the end of the book

Contents

Essays

Preface

$\mathbf{A}$s I consider this anniversary anthology of *New England Review,* I admit to feeling proud: thanks to the generosity of editors Hummer and Jersild, it consists in great measure of material published during my tenure, material that continues to delight by its energy and diversity. But my pride is as nothing against my astonishment to recall how naive I and my founding colleagues were as we set out to recruit such work.

The naiveté went far beyond the purely "literary." Around Labor Day of 1978, for example, just two weeks before publication of Volume I, number 1, it dawned on us that our magazine must not only be galleyed, proofed, and printed, but also *mailed* to subscribers. Casting wildly about for help, by happy accident we hooked onto the omnicompetent David Field of Post Mills, Vermont, who generated labels for us. Who guided us through frenetic eleventh-hour negotiations with the postal service. Who until his sad death in 1983 remained our unpaid mentor in all manner of odd ways, once for instance repairing an archaic answering maching with chewing gum for adhesive and vodka (left over from some profitless "fund raiser") for solvent.

Where would we have been without David or the many others who—perhaps touched by our bumbling, our enthusiasm, or both—stepped into the breaches?

Kate Emlen of Lyme, New Hampshire—*NER*'s original designer—taught us about manuscript preparation, layout, typeface, and so on, all for laughable compensation.

George Brady of Northlight Studio Press in Barre tolerated our trial-and-error efforts at putting actual books into printable shape.

Above all, Robin Barone of Norwich, Vermont, took over the business end of *NER* from the notoriously disorganized pair of Jay Parini and me; without her the magazine would have seen no first anniversary, let alone a fifteenth. How lucky that she should have been looking meagerly to supplement her bartender's income before setting off for law school; how downright lucky that she remained for five years as our managing editor.

And the downright luck endured in the persons of Robin's intelligent, hardworking, humane successors, Jim Schley and Maura High.

It endures today in Terry Hummer, Devon Jersild, and Toni Best, in Tom McFarland and his staff at the University Press of New England.

*

In the late seventies, this magazine's officers were as apt to be folding mailers or licking stamps or vacuuming its first headquarters in Norwich (just across the street from Dan & Whit's general store) as they were to be occupied by more demonstrably editorial chores. The distance therefore seems wide from that time—and its avatar of *New England Review*—to today—and the splendid, well established journal sponsored by Middlebury College. Yet as I read *NER* issue by issue, I detect in its pages the persistance of an original amateurism, if I may emphasize the part of love in that term's etymology. Obviously enough, *NER*'s current editors are far more professional than Robin, Jay, and I were when we launched the magazine; that forthright and catholic love for literature, however, surely prevails over mere professionalism in Terry and Devon's motives, just as it did in ours.

From the outset, I claimed that this magazine would be "beholden to no faction," that I'd be if anything more interested in the work of the unrecognized than in that of the already renowned, that—contrary to popular mythology about editors' indolence and/or hardness of heart—the so-called slush pile would be my chief resource.

However lustrous this anthology's collective authorship, then, I'm gratified that many of its writers appeared under *New England Review*'s aegis well before their reputations took on so apt a shine. In the 1990s, fledgling writers continue to be represented cheek by jowl with the often and lavishly praised, and it pleases me to know that the discovery of future Grahams, Clampitts, Erdrichs, and Wetherells remains as important to today's staff as it was to us when these fine authors' publishing careers were as young as our editorial ones.

It pleases me, in short, that a democratic spirit abides.

I can't help testifying as well to pleasure on finding that certain shiny names are *not* included in this retrospective . . . nor in any single past number of *New England Review*. Among my prouder boasts was always that I accepted no manuscript I wouldn't have accepted had it come in anonymously. My successors remain true to that side of democracy's spirit: one's connections count for nil; the work must, as ever, stand on its own.

In a world of rampant hype, to which literature is scarcely less given than politics or advertising, integrity will distinguish the amateur—again in the very best sense— from the hustler. I have suggested that this kind of integrity is finally a matter of the heart: by their unfeigned love for the unfeigned word shall such amateurs be known. And thus I end with a toast to their affection, which is the soul of *New England Review*.

Newbury, Vermont   SYDNEY LEA

The Unfeigned Word

Introduction

—————

Literary magazines often have a troubled relationship with history. The great ones, of course, *make* history; but the majority *become* history before they have one of their own.

New England Review, whose fifteenth anniversary this book has been assembled to celebrate, is a proven survivor; but its story consists of far more than simple endurance. Since its very first issue in the fall of 1978—presenting the work of such writers as Pablo Neruda, Anthony Hecht, Eleanor Clark, Robert Francis, Robert Penn Warren, Anne Stevenson, Charles Simic, and Ann Beattie—*New England Review* has been a magazine that matters, to writers and readers alike: an important part of the unfolding literary endeavor of this country and of the world.

I am in the luxurious position of being able to say these things without immodesty, since *New England Review*'s track record has little to do with me. When I became its editor in September of 1989, I inherited a strong and honorable tradition. I also inherited the responsibility that went along with that tradition. I take that responsibility seriously.

I went on record in The Bench Press's *Spreading the Word: Editors on Poetry* (1990) as saying that

this is what a good magazine does: it puts itself out on the ragged edge of what is going on and it hangs on desperately there, wide open and vulnerable as its editors' nerves can stand. This means searching out [writing] which take[s] ultimate risks; this means serving those writers who face down the darkness in the world and in themselves.

As editor of *New England Review* I have stood by this—and it is right and consistent that I should, since it is a position at which I arrived partly due to the example provided by *New England Review* itself.

My relationship with this magazine goes back to the publication of its first issue, of which I was a delighted reader but also a student. At that time, I was associate editor of *Quarterly West,* my first real venture in editing, and I was looking as much for paradigms of excellence in the field as I was for good reading. I wanted to know how to make a literary magazine, run on a shoestrong and read perhaps only by a few, exciting and important. *New England Review*—an absolutely independent journal in those days, funded more or less out of its editors' own pockets, plain but dignified in its production, startlingly distinguished in its list of contributors—set what still seems to me an impossibly high standard.

Years later, first as editor-in-chief of *Quarterly West* and then as editor of *Kenyon Review,* I received important advice and support from Sydney Lea, for whom the enterprise of editing was never a horse race but always a vital communal enterprise. By the time I became editor of *New England Review* in 1989, I had come to understand the full magnitude and burden of literary journal publication; I also understood the possibilities and rewards. My opportunity here has been, I take it, poetically just: I have had the chance to do all I can to give back to the magazine, and thus to its readers, the many important gifts it has given to me.

If *New England Review*'s story is a continuum of excellence and of generosity, it is also a story of change. In the fall of 1982, there appeared a large and impressive double issue celebrating the magazine's fifth anniversary and announcing its new affiliation with the Bread Loaf Writers' Conference; that issue also inaugurated changes in the magazine's production, and initiated its new title, *New England Review and Bread Loaf Quarterly,* or more familiarly *NER/BLQ.* The affiliation with Bread Loaf, as Sydney Lea wrote at the time,

in no way alters our usual editorial procedures, nor does it alter our commitment to discovering new or unestablished authors; it does broaden the range of our literary contacts, and it brings into consultative positions some very keen literary minds.

Spring of 1987 marked another change in the magazine's posture. In that issue, Sydney Lea announced *NER/BLQ*'s full association with Middlebury College. His confidence that Middlebury's sponsorship would strengthen the magazine has proved to be well-founded.

Changes in personnel naturally accompanied this evolution. Jay Parini, co-founder of the magazine, remained on the masthead as co-editor only for the first year, though as a member of the advisory board from that time to the present, he has remained one of its constant consultants and supporters. Robin Barone, the first managing editor, stayed on board until 1983, when she was replaced by Mary Moore, who was in turn replaced by Maura High in the following year. The redoubtable Jim Schley, who was to have an indelible influence on the character and direction of the operation, came on board in 1980 as an editorial assistant and exited from the position of full co-editor in 1987, having produced such important special issues as "Writers in the Nuclear Age" (Summer 1983) and "The Caribbean" (Summer 1985). After his departure, Maura High was promoted to the position of editor (at first understudy and eventually co-equal to Sydney Lea's senior editorship), a position she discharged with distinction until her departure in August of 1990; like Schley, Maura High put together strong special issues: "Writers of Wales" (Summer 1988) and "On Science" (Summer 1990).

I mention these names for two reasons: because they are part of the record, and in tribute. Everyone who has served this magazine has been part of it fully, out of loyalty and love—for the magazine, and for literature and those it serves. I am tempted to say that they are the secret of *New England Review*'s remarkable track record—but the truth is, it's no secret. Part of what the present staff inherited from the old was a tradition of simple, but radical, openness.

✳

This anthology promises to arrive at a dark moment in the history of the USA. As I write (October of 1992), it becomes increasingly clear that Saddam Hussein was indeed aided and abetted in his pursuit of power by the United States itself. The American economy is in what used to be called a depression—economists who fear the word call it a "triple-dip recession"—with millions out of work; the state of California faces bankruptcy; countless Americans are without health insurance, and the cost of health care is stratospheric; the country possesses more millionaires than at any moment in history, and more people live homeless on the streets.

The damage done to the USA, and to the world, in the fifteen years of *NER*'s existence will not be undone overnight. So much that is good and humane—and perhaps just barely beyond our grasp—has been either ignored or actually repudiated, that, at a time when hope should be at an historical peak, we tend instead toward cynicism and profound distrust of the forms of thought, of community, of being, for which we ourselves are responsible. Cultually, adrift, our government—on all sides—is calling for a "return to fundamental decency," to "family values" and the like, without defining those terms or describing how political policy can conjure them up from the past, assuming they ever existed at all. Government of, by, and for the privileged is familiar enough; in our time, it has been especially petty and therefore especially ugly and empty. And the populace, torn by bitter divisions of all kinds, seems unable to give rise to anything better.

In Mississippi, where I grew up, there is a story (probably apocryphal) about a corrupt governor who loved to give pompous speeches. Making a campaign address during half-time at a University of Mississippi football game, and encouraged by the concerted applause of an audience of fraternity boys who knew he would go on making a fool of himself as long as they went on applauding, the governor ran out of his usual repertoire of truisms and was reduced in the end to spouting, "And futhahmoah, Ah—Ah ahm—AGAINST EVIL!!!" Literary people discussing politics sometimes sound the same way—as if from the safety of the sidelines, good and evil are clear enough, and it's easy to say what's what. It cannot be denied that literary magazines in general, and *New England Review* in particular, are in a position of privilege, culturally speaking, and so must speak judiciously and self-consciously about the politics thereof.

As far as I can tell, *New England Review* has never gone on record as being against evil, and it's just as well; the history of this journal so far spans almost exactly the last half of the Carter administration, the whole of the Reagan era, and all of George Bush—years of insidious confusion and abuse. If we assume, as we must, that every individual and every institution in a culture are partly responsible for the actions of that culture, then *New England Review,* all its editors, and every one of its contributing authors, are complicit in what the USA has been and done, and what it is.

But there is another joke, which I also heard in the south, the punch line of which runs, "No, I'm not against evil—I wouldn't get that close to it." It is fair to say that *New England Review,* from its very earliest issues, has always been conscious of itself as part of the whole, and responsible to that whole. Far from stepping back from problems and issues, far from attempting to declare the aesthetic a realm separate from the social or political, *New England Review* has published work that attempts to address who we are, what we are, and why. This magazine has always recognized the fact that so-called literary people—writers, readers, editors—are not on the "sidelines" politically speaking because there are no sidelines—or, to shift the metaphor, that anyone who seeks to claim literature as a separate, immaculate, and privileged realm would hoard the riches of powerful writing for themselves as surely as an embezzling savings and loan vice-president hoards the rightful livelihood of others. Literary embezzling exists as surely as insider trading. The indifference of literary privilege is as real as Eisenhower's golf game.

Reviewing the work published in the first fifteen years of *New England Review,* we found ourselves discovering forgotten treasures—a Raymond Carver story not published in any of his collections; a chapter of Louise Erdrich's *Love Medicine,* which alerted me to her gift well before the novel appeared (and years before I was associated with this magazine); magisterial poems from Robert Penn Warren's last, great years; the title poem from Seamus Heaney's *Field Work* and Richard Kenney's *Evolution of the Flightless Bird*; Lucie Brock Broido's bizarre and magical long poem "Elective Mutes"; essays on all subjects by writers of a wide variety of persuasions—on and on. Back issues of *New England Review* are, we discovered, as full of mystery and power as the warehouses of the snow. What better way to begin our fifteenth anniversary volume than by opening the coffers, the bins, the vaults, and giving the treasure away?

In the 1988 presidential campaign, Jesse Jackson used to reply to critics who asked how he'd pay for his proposed social programs by saying, "You get the money from where it went." Wealth and power that belonged to the people had gone somewhere, Jackson was saying, and it wasn't enough to wait for trickle-down from the purchase of yachts to feed the hungry; it was necessary to find what had been stolen and give it back. This is not to suggest that *New England Review* has stolen poems, stories, and essays; the work is there, on the back shelves and in microfilm drawers of libraries—and in the many books in which much of this work has subsequently appeared—available to anyone who cares to seek it out and use it. Obviously, the economics of poetry are not the same as those of money; and yet the analogy is not meaningless. The gesture of *giving back* is essential to editing and publishing; that is why *New England Review* is not a profit-making enterprise. We are one conduit of the wealth of a nation—its literary wealth, the wealth of its language and of whatever we mean when we say *spirit.* This is how its current editors see it, and how all its editors—Sydney Lea, Jay Parini, James Schley, Maura High, to whose vision and skill this anniversary is in part a tribute—have seen it.

"Give beauty back," Gerard Manley Hopkins wrote in one of his splendid poems. He meant that we must give beauty back to God. My suspicion is that God has less need of beauty than humans do—God, I imagine, has all the beauty she needs. But we, being only what we are, have an endless hunger for it. That is why writers write; that is why literary magazines go on publishing: against poverty of spirit; against that kind of homelessness, that kind of starvation.

And that is why we have assembled the anthology you are holding—*The Unfeigned World: Fifteen Years of New England Review*—to give back at least this much of what has been given to us.

T. R. HUMMER

Charles Baxter

Gershwin's Second Prelude

While Kate practiced the piano in the tiny third-floor apartment, Wiley cooked dinner, jogging in place in front of the stove. His feet made the pans clatter, and after twenty minutes of exercise, he began to hyperventilate. He stopped, took his pulse, then continued, jogging to the spice rack, to the refrigerator's butter shelf, then back to the stove. The air smelled of cumin, chicken stock, and tomatoes—something Mexican. The noise was terrible. He knocked over a spatula. A bottle of soda fell into the catfood dish. Worse yet, he hummed stupid tunes from his high school prom days, melodies like "Call Me Mister Blue" and "Dream Lover," in a nasal, plaintive whine. The noise diverted Kate's attention and broke her Schubert sonatas into small pieces of musical trash.

That day at lunch, Kate's friend Sarah had told her to put an end to her passivity in the face of this uproar. "Tell him to shut up," she said. "Wiley's a narcissist. You have to tell him everything twice. I introduced you to him, so I know."

Kate nodded.

She went on. "It was probably a mistake. Wiley has sinister friends. If I were you, I'd get rid of him fast, before those creeps show up in their Halloween masks. Besides, have you ever watched him comb his hair? Of course you have. He stands for half an hour in front of the mirror. I've seen him put aftershave *into* his hair. Nobody does that. I'm sorry, but he's disgusting. He'll never love you."

"I know," Kate said. She couldn't afford to eat out and was taking her omelette in tiny bites.

"He's just living in your apartment because you gave him a bed to flop in." Sarah stopped for a minute, took a long sip of water, and then bit down on an ice cube. "I'm sorry to be crude, but that's how it is. I shouldn't have introduced you two. I feel terrible about it. Will you forgive me?"

Kate nodded. "Of course. You know, I don't mind Wiley. You know why? He makes me laugh."

"Makes you laugh? Watch *The Flintstones* if you want to laugh. But don't keep that loser around."

"He's a good cook."

"He's a chef, for heaven's sake. That's his *job*. That's why he's a good cook." She stopped. "You love him, don't you?"

Kate shrugged. "I know he's a loser, but losers make me laugh. Things don't matter to them anymore, and they treat life like a joke." She put her fork down. "Winners make ugly lovers," she said with finality. "I don't want that."

"No more Schubert," said Madame Gutowski in her studio, one flight up from Buster's Subs 'n' Suds. Madame Gutowski was an old woman and her voice came out in a breathy rattle. In her studio the paint was flaking off the ceiling; mice, or worse, were inside the walls. Kate had finished the second movement of the Schubert B-flat sonata while the old woman had scowled and tapped her fingers on the edge of the chair. "No more Schubert," she repeated irritably. "You play like an American. You speed up the tempo to make a climax. This is Schubert, not Las Vegas. Too much, too much effort to please the customers. The score does not say to accelerate. You make it too pathetic. Also, you make it silly. Has been played like this." Madame rolled her hand into a tight fist, shaking it in Kate's face. "Should be played like this." She relaxed her hand and waved goodbye. "Schubert stands at the door, lends handkerchief, gives good wishes, says, 'Farewell, farewell.' But he knows the sky is getting dark. Always he knows this. This is Schubert." She shook her head. "You seem unable to learn the style."

"Maybe I could learn some new Chopin," Kate suggested. "Chopin instead of Schubert. The impromptus or the—"

"—Chopin?" Madame whispered, before making a clucking sound. "No no no no no no. He is not ready for you. He waits up ahead, is standing inside summer house, head down, listening to sky and grass, thinking about love and anger." She continued to whisper. "I consider Chopin all the time. He is very close to me. *He talks.*" Madame leaned back and stared at Kate, pretending surprise at this revelation. She returned to her normal voice. "You are too young for him. You have some growing to do. Maturing. He is not for you. Not while you are playing this way, in this girlish American style."

"I'm not a girl," Kate sighed. "But you could teach me to play Chopin. Your style."

"No. You must learn how to be calm as you sit at piano first. Chopin will wait for you. I will wait for you. I will introduce you to him. But not yet! He likes quickness but not quite so much push."

Kate leaned back and looked out of the window at the grime-streaked traffic. It, too, had a great deal of push. Then, inside, her gaze fell first on Madame's cane leaning against the over-stuffed chair, then on the lady's bony fingers. Long-term arthritis made the knuckles look like popcorn. "What do you suggest?" she asked. "Beethoven? Beethoven has a lot of push."

"No," Madame said. "Gershwin."

"Gershwin?" Kate frowned. "That's trash."

"No. Is *not* trash. Get 'Three Preludes,' learn number two. It is a good piece for Americans. Is hard, requires wizard, but teaches tenderness from first bar to end. You

Americans have such trouble learning tenderness, I don't understand. Learn to relax into calm. We start next week." Madame glared angrily at her watch.

Kate stood up and bowed, as instinctively she always had. "Thank you, Madame," she said.

The old woman nodded without looking at Kate. "Gershwin, a nice boy. You two will adore each other."

Kate left, annoyed as usual that Madame never looked her in the eye.

At the institute, Kate sat in front of her telephone, collecting data, or "social research" as it was called. Each day's work list included a list of numbers to dial, chosen with guaranteed randomness by a computer, and a small pile of questionnaires. An electric clock the size of a large pizza hummed on the wall above her. The clock obsessed her in an unhealthy way. She considered it her enemy. In a nearby glassed-in office, her supervisor monitored all the calls to make sure that the interviews were both discreet and successful. The other women at the institute were all younger than Kate and had taken the job interviewing people they didn't know as a diversion until the job they really wanted came along. For some reason, the institute didn't like to hire men; they had tried it, but the men hadn't stayed for more than three days or so. Something about the job was intolerable to people with ambitions. The average employee stayed around for about three months. Kate had set a record at the institute: she had been there four years.

"You know," Wiley said, picking his teeth with a pocketknife after dinner, "I once worked as a circus clown. I may again."

"What?"

"A circus clown. You didn't know that, did you?"

"No," Kate said. "There's a lot I don't know about you."

"You said the truth," Wiley agreed. "But the fact is, I always liked to hang around with those show people, you know, the carnival types. I'll tell you how I got to be a clown. It was in my Joe College days, when I was so straight that I thought people were real. It was one of those junior-year-abroad deals and I was in Amsterdam. I was supposed to be working in a Dutch mental hospital, and I was, with part of my brain, but with the other part I'd gotten mixed up with some lowdown importer-exporters." He stopped, leaned his head back, and laughed. "I guess I wasn't so straight. Anyway, I was headed downtown one day for a meeting with a guy I didn't want to see, and I passed by a large brown door with a sign next to it. The sign said that the place was the one and only School for Fools."

"School for Fools?"

"Yup. A clown college. Biggest in the world. They teach makeup, pratfalls, balancing, and all sort of routines. I tried it out for a while. When I got back to the states, I worked as a clown for a couple of weeks during the summer on a state fair midway. In Minnesota." He nodded. "The land of ten thousand lakes." He nodded again. "I never got my college diploma. But I learned about crowds."

"What's it like, being a clown?"

"Well, working as a salad chef is easier. They pay you more. By the way, I need to borrow some money from you. I almost forgot. But, as I was saying, a circus clown needs timing, which is essentially the hard part. He's usually taught first how to tumble, how to take falls, then how to do pratfalls and stand on his hands. Like I say, though, it's mostly timing."

"You never told me this."

"We're strangers, Kate."

"I know, but it seems so interesting." She smiled. "Can you still do a pratfall? Is it painful?"

Wiley got up from the dinner table. "Of course it's not painful. You just have to know how to do it." As he stood, he let his body go loose in an effort to relax. As he lit a cigarette, he said, "All right. Suppose you're in the audience. Now imagine I've just been kicked real hard from behind."

Kate nodded, feeling shy.

"Okay," Wiley said. "Watch."

All at once, his mouth opened in an expression of clown-shock, his eyebrows flew up, and his legs shot out in front of him, his body hanging there momentarily as if held by invisible wires before it dropped to the floor, making the dinner dishes rattle.

"Good God, Wiley," Kate said, laughing. "Jesus. You *are* a clown. That's terrific. Can you walk on your hands?"

"Not only can I walk on my hands," Wiley said, "but I can walk on my hands and play your piano with my feet. Are you going to lend me fifty bucks or not?"

"Of course, of course."

Wiley jumped, stood on his hands, his change falling out of his pockets, and walked on his hands out of the dining room, into the living room, where he lowered his feet to hit the piano keys. He stood up and walked back to the table.

"See?" he asked. "A real clown. Kate, I need that money tonight, before I go off to work."

In the bedroom, Kate searched through her dresser drawer where she thought she had stashed seventy dollars. She could only find forty of it, but she picked it up and clenched it in her right hand.

"Here," she said. "It's all I've got left."

"Forty?" He sighed. "Oh, all right." He made a face. "I've got to go to work." He squatted down, put his hands under her arms to lift her up, and when she was standing, he put his arms around her and held her for a long time, kissing her mouth and her forehead. When he was finished, Kate felt her heart's rhythms beginning to pick up, along with her breath rate. She leaned herself hard against him.

"Oh don't leave yet," she said, trying to whisper. "Stay for a few minutes."

"Later, Kate," he said. "Good love takes time."

"I can't sit around waiting for you," she said as he drew away. "I can't."

"You will."

She understood that despite his passionate embrace and kiss, he wasn't physically aroused at all. His responses were unpredictable: he could stay physically indifferent to her as he managed, simultaneously, to lead her into the greatest sexual feelings she had ever experienced. She sometimes felt as if he treated her body as if he were a scientist, experimenting to see what he could do to it.

After he left, Kate sat at the dinner table for an hour, imagining that Wiley had walked down to the drugstore at the corner to buy some antihistamine. "I've lived with different guys," she said aloud to herself, "but never with a circus clown." She was collecting the dirty dishes and putting them to soak in the kitchen sink when the phone rang.

"Hi, Kate," Wiley said. "It's me. I'm under arrest."

"Wiley, what happened?"

"They said I was shoplifting."

Gershwin's second prelude is marked "Andante con moto e poco rubato," and as soon as she tried to play it, later that week, Kate discovered that she would have to tinker with the rhythms in order to project the feeling Madame would expect. Her own feelings of nervousness about Wiley she kept out of the music. The prelude sounded like the blues—white urban blues—and as she worked through the cross-over fingerings, she imagined a fitting scene for the melody: a well-tailored man standing on a penthouse balcony gazes over a city just after sunset. His building's empty elevators rise and descend automatically throughout the early evening. He thinks of a joke that fails to amuse him. Lights in the other buildings come on. F. Scott Fitzgerald appears, Zelda drunk on his arm.

Wiley was out on bail. That afternoon, Kate had discovered a hypodermic needle in the medicine cabinet, hidden behind Wiley's electric shaver.

"Posture!" Madame Gutowski snapped, knocking once on the side of the piano bench with her cane. "Remember always posture! Be relaxed but alert. You sit like killer in electric chair. Stiff, guilty of crimes. Remember to let hands rest on keys, relaxed but alert. And *lean forward*! Music leans forward."

Kate looked down at her hands, trying to make them more alert than they were. They felt like sea slugs, unable to achieve anything like consciousness. Perhaps they knew, in their dumb animal way, that Madame wouldn't care for what they were about to do.

"Play," Madame commanded. "Demonstrate Gershwin."

The left hand stretched out and began. Together it and the right hand did what they could, while Kate tried to imagine that lonely soul in the penthouse overlooking the city park, but as she played, she felt herself losing that image as another one took its place: a semitrailer truck unloading a ton of damp saltines.

"Concentrate," Madame whispered. "Do not fight with your mind."

Then she pictured Wiley shooting up a small, discrete quantity of junk before he walked—no, *sailed*—off to his evening chores as a salad chef.

"Play notes on page," Madame instructed. "Do not swing the rhythm. Do not try to jazz it."

Kate worked her way to the last chord and waited, hands in lap, for Madame to speak. From downstairs she heard the cook in Buster's Subs 'n' Suds calling an order of two chili dogs to the kitchen. Madame stared at her, then said, "You have not met Gershwin yet. He is still inside the piano trying to get out. Play the piece again for me. Remember that the goal of prelude is not to arrive at doublebar line, like a train pulling into a depot. The goal is to express tenderness, as landscape flows past."

Kate repeated the piece as Madame's jaw worked with what Kate thought might be senile anger.

Kate had been on the phone to Sarah again.

"You didn't tell me that Wiley's a junky," she said.

"Oh Jesus. Is he? I didn't know that. Christ. But you can't blame me, Kate. I only lived with him for two weeks."

"He's been arrested for shoplifting," Kate announced, her voice creeping toward tonelessness. "Why did you introduce us?" She stopped. "Why did you bring him over here?"

"Well, he *is* so funny. At first. You know Wiley. I wanted to get him off my back, I guess. Sorry, Kate. Really, you've got to dump him."

"How?"

"Introduce him to somebody else."

Wiley's ideas about music were superficial and narrative: he enjoyed putting Kate's recording of Mahler's second symphony on the phonograph and explaining what the music meant, minute by minute. "Here," Wiley droned, "Mahler is trying to put on his overshoes. But they won't fit. Mahler goes into the kitchen and has a big argument with Mrs. Mahler." (Here the orchestra played *fortissimo*.) "But Mrs. Mahler resists! She tells Gustav that overshoes aren't her department! 'Liebchen,' she says, 'leave me alone with my strudel.' Mahler exits to conduct the Vienna State Opera Orchestra in his French Shriners." (The music's level went down to *mezzoforte*.) "But on the way, Mahler falls into a mud puddle."

Despite herself, Kate was amused by this patter; she liked to have music humiliated occasionally. Making music look cheap was Wiley's line, and Kate enjoyed it.

"Wiley," Kate interrupted, "I found something a few days ago that I wanted to ask you about."

"Yeah? What?"

"A hypodermic in the medicine chest."

Wiley nodded. "I know about it."

"What's it doing there?"

"It's mine."

"What are *you* doing with it?"

"Engine tune-ups."

"No, really." She had to shout to be heard about the music.

"What do you think it's for?" He smiled. "A diabetic condition?"

"You're not diabetic. Do you shoot up?"

He turned the music off. Then he nodded. "Sometimes," he said. "When I'm in the mood. You aren't going to be American and get all hysterical about this, are you? Because there's nothing to be hysterical about. When they talk about it on television, it's all lies. How do I know? I know because I know."

"Why do you do it?"

"I like to feel like God," Wiley said. "I like to have the sun explode and then spray over my face." He stood up and walked over to her. "And I think you should try it. I honestly honestly do. If anyone is ready for a little taste of shit, Kate darling, that person is Kate."

"No."

Wiley sank to his knees and clasped his hands in her lap. "I can turn your whole spine into a Christmas tree. Colored lights, Kate, and blue and red ornaments hanging on your heart. Listen to me. You could be a bright star. You could make your brains into a success."

"Wiley, where do you get this stuff?"

"You don't want to know them." He shuddered. "The pleasure gets to you by way of riffraff."

"I don't get it," Kate said. "You jog and you eat health foods. But you shoot up this stuff? What's the connection?"

"The body," Wiley said without hesitation. "The body is the theater, the scene. I like to experiment with it. Sometimes I get a little bored with the theater of life, so I do the theater of death. The theater of death is a pleasure. Still silent solitary pleasure. It's not like anything happens in pure pleasure. Nothing does. It's the pleasure of death, you understand?" He looked at his watch and stood up. "Oooops. Time to go to work." He bent down to kiss her, and she felt his tongue flick against her ear lobe. "Bye, kitten."

Kate usually woke up when Wiley came in at two o'clock, but when the door didn't open and Wiley failed to drop his boots in the foyer, failed to go to the refrigerator for a beer, and failed to turn on Dr. Tormento's All Night Terror Theater, she lay awake with the light burning. The digital clock glowed. She watched the numbers attentively. Three o'clock had no funny stories. Four o'clock, the worst hour in the day, had character but no tenderness. Five o'clock was the alarm going off for the sun; its light glowed like an infection in the east. At six all was not well. At seven she knew Wiley was in trouble, and at eight he walked in, his face bloody. He collected his clothes and records, would not say anything, smiled at her, then left. Kate grabbed onto his shirt as he walked down the stairs.

"Oh no," he said. "No. I don't ever explain."

Kate had turned thirty that month. With Wiley gone, she thought of her past, of the music scholarships, the lost jobs, the men, the empty bank accounts. She thought of her parents. They didn't like to call her because she just gave them bad news. "Success is counted sweetest / By those who ne'er succeed," wrote Emily Dickinson, poet of the dormouse experience, and Kate's favorite writer. Kate's mind was full of questions but the mind refused to answer them. She stared at Wiley's pencil lifestudy of her, where her body had been drawn with specific tenderness.

"He left me," she told Sarah.

"Good riddance."

"You don't understand. I'm alone."

"So?"

"I don't like it."

"Learn to live with it. He was a creep."

"That's easy for you to say. You're married. I never had sex before the way I had it with him. He broke through to something in me."

"I'm not married, I'm separated. There's a difference. Why'd he leave?"

"I asked him about the hypodermic. He left the next day."

"You're better off than you were before."

"And you have children, too. So don't tell me how wonderful it is being alone. You haven't been alone for seven years. You don't know anything about it."

"Kate, I *do* understand. I am lonely sometimes."

"Also," Kate continued, "you've never failed at having a career. You have kids, a husband who may come back to you, and for two weeks you had Wiley. He wasn't good enough for you. He was just a piece of male trash, a piece of garbage you threw out. Okay, he wasn't good enough for you, but he looked all right to me. You've never lost out on anything, Sarah, so don't go sermonizing to me." She swallowed. "Because you don't know what you're talking about."

The bus having arrived fifteen minutes too early in front of Madame's studio, Kate went into Buster's Subs 'n' Suds and ordered a torpedo sandwich and a glass of red wine. It was her sixth glass of wine since noon: she had left work, claiming illness, and had walked to a cafe to read Doris Lessing and to drink wine. She had succeeded at both. Now, realizing she was drunk, she studied the other diners until they noticed her; then she turned away. From upstairs, filtered through the grease-flecked ceiling, came music from Madame's baby grand Mason and Hamlin: chords and passages with bizarre contours, the luminously structural madness of Scriabin. Kate thought that the sandwich would sober her up, but when two identical waitresses came toward her, carrying the check, she knew it hadn't.

At exactly four o'clock she walked upstairs, tripping on one step, and knocked. Madame shouted, "Come in!" and Kate entered. Madame was seated at the piano, bent over the keyboard as if weeping, her long thin fingers rushing up and down in a grotesque way. Kate shivered. Madame had known Enesco and Bartók. She had once played for Ravel. Ravel hadn't just applauded; Ravel stood up. Arthritis had put an end to Madame's career in the 1940s. Without knowing what Madame was playing, Kate knew it wasn't being played correctly, that it was being damaged, that Ravel would no longer applaud.

Madame stopped, turned, and looked at Kate. She pointed one bent finger at Kate's mouth. "Food. Please wipe it off." Kate took a tissue from her purse and licked it before cleaning the mustard stains on her chin. The wine made her feel both drunk and sleepy. She hardly knew where she was. She rubbed and rubbed at her chin until the skin felt raw.

Madame lifted herself off the piano bench with her cane, half-sat, half-fell into her usual chair, and barked at Kate. "Sit. Play Gershwin, correctly. It is a new day today, I know it. Concentrate on tenderness this time."

Though she had double-vision, Kate had been practicing the piece regularly, and at first the wine gave her courage. She was halfway through when Madame sat up. "No!" she said. "It is *worse* than before! Incredible! Is much worse! You are not reading notes on page. *Poco* rubato, little one, not *molto*! Pedal use is very poor: all clear notes turning indistinct. Too much slurring. Whining and pausing and stopping for breath. Why do you insist on playing this way? This style of self-pity? Why must you be so terrible?"

Kate stopped. Her hands went limp. She absent-mindedly took out a cigarette, lit it, inhaled, and with it between her fingers she started the piece again. Before she remembered that she was at her weekly piano lesson, and not at home, Madame exploded. "What is that?"

"Oh shit," Kate said, instantly blushing. She tried to stub the cigarette out on the wood floor near the pedals. The cigarette stuck to her sandal and she had to pick it off with her fingers before throwing it out of the window. "Madame," she said. "I'm sorry. I forgot you were there. I've been smoking lately."

"I smell wine also," the old woman said, her teeth chattering.

"Yes, I'm drunk." Coming back from the window, Kate sat on the bench and looked Madame in the eye. "You know, Madame," she said in an undertone, "I'm a nitwit."

"A what?"

"A nitwit." She pointed at her head. "Nothing but cotton up here. I have a silly job. I fall in love with ridiculous men. I fill myself up with nicotine and alcohol. No talent. I'm not a serious woman."

Madame's eyes stared at her, clear and hawk-like. "What? What is this nicotine? You mean morphia?"

"No, that's Wiley. Wiley does that. Me, I just smoke cigarettes. Oh, and the wine."

"Who is Wiley?"

"This man. He just left me."

"You have tried morphia also?"

"No. Never."

There was a long pause. Then Madame leaned back. "Now listen. You children think you are so new with your misery, with your morphia. Pain always seems new when you have it. And I admit: grief gets in the way of playing piano. It mixes you up. But listen." She tilted her head back and closed her eyes. "Imagine Paris in 1928. I was studying and playing. *Very* young. You have heard the names of people I knew. I will not mention them. Ravel, many others. For a time, possibility was everywhere. We had been through the war and that was that."

"So much talent around," Kate said.

Madame waved her hand like a broken flag. "Yes, yes. But they were busy all day, working. You do not see artists in bars drinking wine. They are busy in their rooms, they have *schedules*!" Madame scowled for a moment. "But do not interrupt me. As I said, there was much happiness then, with the war gone away and hundred of new ideas coming into practice. I was then your age, maybe younger. Like you, very talented. A small bit more talented, but the difference is not important. Basically I sat at piano five, six hours a day.

"So, a beautiful place. Everyone said so. 'Aren't you lucky to be here, Clara?' they said to me. I always said, 'Yes.' And I had a friend." Madame closed her eyes and nodded. "A beautiful young man, a painter: oils, watercolors, ex-cubist. He was given attention in galleries and salons. The critics noticed him. For one year we had each night a rendezvous before dinner, when the light was useless for painting and piano practice time was over. We took walks in the Bois. We made dinner for friends. Attended concerts and openings. We talked often, often, about future. Then, the end." Madame stopped and waited.

"Why?"

Madame nodded, pleased that Kate was listening. "I will tell you. Remember what you have read about Paris. Now the books say there was only happiness and creative fire. I arrived, a little girl from Poland. I was introduced to groups. Then, a girl, I discover what everyone has always known. Joy is infected. Joy for too long is infection. Cannot last. My painter disappears, then turns up to see me with his face all cloudy. I ask him why, and he says, 'Opium.' Well. Some it doesn't hurt. But others, the weak little happy ones get it but do not get over it. They don't come up. More joy. *Too much joy!* You have heard maybe of Cocteau?"

Kate nodded.

"Talented, but oh, he was silly. He had a weakness for happiness, that one. Clutched at it all the time. He thought boredom was not real, Cocteau. A big mistake. So my painter who like Cocteau is finding this opium, he tries to stop but does *not* stop. He loses his vision for painting. His ideas go away. What does he spend his day thinking about? I don't know. He won't tell me. He says there are no more pictures. He says: 'Color is too much work.' Too much work! To me, he looks more and more like a man turning around, on his way back to his mother. One afternoon, we drink champagne together. We walk together by Seine to Notre Dame. He says maybe he will convert, be a Catholic as I am, safe in God's arms. Maybe he will solve problems of soul. We walk up stairs to the top of the cathedral, to see Paris to the west. Then he lifts himself up, says, 'Au futur,' and puts his foot on top of a gargoyle face. He takes a leap, aaiiee, into space. He just broke like an egg below. He lived for three hours, speaking to ghosts."

"I'm sorry."

"Do *not* be sorry. Congratulate me for living in Paris for ten more years, alone. Congratulate me for coming here, for losing career, for opening a studio over a restaurant. Congratulate me for teaching slow clucks and dumb bunnies. Congratulate me for avoiding infection, for having not too much happiness."

"Congratulations," Kate said.

"Boredom has its own tenderness, its own mercy," Madame said softly. "Now tell me. Will you not celebrate with wine constantly, from now on? Will you not try to be happy, always?"

"I promise. Cross my heart."

"Then give me my cane."

Kate reached over to where the cane leaned against the Mason and Hamlin's shiny black wood and gave it to Madame. The old woman put both hands over it and lifted herself up. Standing, her shoulders bent, she said, "Already you are learning. You will become a hero. You will learn to face losses of great size. That requires ceremony. It requires champagne. We will drink."

"Do you have champagne here?" Kate asked. The studio was bare except for the piano and Madame's chair.

"Of course not. It will have to be imagined. Raise glass."

"What about my piece? What about Gershwin?"

"Poor boy. He died of a brain tumor when young. Do as I say!"

Kate watched the old woman prop herself on her cane, as her right hand lifted into the air, the thumb and forefingers holding an invisible glass. If there had been a glass, a real one, it would have been shaking, because the old woman trembled with anger and passion, and the champagne would have spilled out over Madame's thin veiled wrist.

"Raise glass!" Madame shouted. "Stand!"

Kate stood and after a moment hoisted her right hand, thumb and forefinger in a half-circle broken by a gap for the invisible stem, until the glass that was not there had reached the level of her shoulder. The old woman, seeing that she had done so, suddenly shot at her an utterly fierce and impersonal smile.

"Cheers!" she commanded. Kate drank.

—Summer 1982

Ann Beattie

Octascope

We live in a house divided into five rooms, heated by a wood stove. When Carlos finished building his house, a friend gave him furniture: three beds, so there are three bedrooms and a living room and a bathroom. In one of the bedrooms is a refrigerator and a sink and a hotplate on top of cinder blocks.

The marionette-maker, Carlos, supports us. His friends Nickel and Dime come by and leave cigarettes and fiddle strings and Jordan almonds (lint-specked from the pockets of their flannel shirts). The baby puts all of these things in her mouth, and when she has nothing else sucks her fingers until the corner of her mouth is raw. She sleeps on a mat by the wood stove, far enough away so that the cats are closest to the warmth. The cats, five of them, belonged to Dime, but one by one Dime brought them to live with us. There is also an old mutt, thirteen years old, part hound and part coyote, legend has it, with a missing tail. This dog is devoted to the baby, as is the sleek gray cat, who looks too noble to be in this house, but whose specialty is killing bats.

Nickel's real name is Nick. His best friend, Dominic, had been nicknamed Dime before he met Nick. Because they were best friends, the rest of the joke seemed inevitable.

Nickel brought me here to live. I was living with my aunt, and the baby, and waitressing the night shift at a restaurant. I lived with her when I was pregnant and for nearly a year after the baby was born, with her caring for the baby while I worked, until she told me she was getting married.

Nick came for me in his old Mercedes, with a velvet-covered, foam-padded board for a front seat, and drove us to Carlos's house. All the time I was hoping he'd tell me to come to his house—that his large, scarred hand would shyly slip into mine, and that I would go with him. The wind chimes dangled from the handle of the glove compartment and the baby kept lunging for them. Our cat was in the back seat, pacing, meowing. She didn't like living with the gray cat and ran away our first week at Carlos's house. Inside the car were little square mirrors. There was a full moon and when the trees were not dense along the road I could cock my head and see my profile in the mirror glued on the passenger side window, or bend forward to take the chimes out of the baby's sticky fist and see my eyes in the mirror on the dashboard. Nick was grumbling about what a bad thing it was that the Mass was no longer said in Latin.

The front left headlight had burned out, and he smoked grass and drove seventy all the way there. No cop had ever stopped the car.

I first met Nick at the restaurant about a month before. He was there trying to sober up Dominic. It was the end of my shift. When I got off I went out to my aunt's car that I parked in the field behind the place and saw the two of them, in the Mercedes, doors thrown open, weeping. Dominic was alcohol sick, and Nick was sick of being called from bars to round him up. I talked to them, and pretty soon we started to laugh. Dominic passed out in the back seat, and Nick and I drove for hours, going in circles, because he was a strange man I had just met and I was afraid to go anywhere with him. I told him about my baby, my aunt. He told me that he had lived with a woman named Julie for seven years. He had met her when he went to college in the Hudson Valley in 1965. Her father gave them money. They always had money. Every Valentine's day she cut hearts out of red paper and wrote love messages on them and glued them together in a circle, points touching. He took his hands off of the wheel, curling his fingers and looking into the empty circle between them. We went to a bar, had three drinks apiece and danced. We went back to the car and he opened the door for me. I sat down and put my hands beside me, bracing myself already for his fast driving, and it shocked me to feel the material: I was confused and thought that it was something living that I was sitting on—soft, chilly moss. The dome light came on again when his door opened, and I looked down to see the royal blue velvet. In the back seat Dominic was very still, no expression on his face, his hand cupped over his fly.

We drove a long way without speaking, until a big black dog ran in front of the car.

"Do you have a dog?" I said.

He shook his head no. "Dime's got five cats."

"Does she really love you?"

"I don't know. I guess so."

"Should I stop asking questions?"

"I'm not giving very good answers."

"Aren't you afraid to drive so fast?"

"I used to work in the pits, repair race cars." He turned his scarred hand toward me. "I don't have any awe of cars."

"There," he said, pointing across a field. "That's where I live."

The silhouette of a big barn, no house nearby. No lights on in the barn.

"I could take you in," he said.

"No," I said, afraid for the first time. "I don't want to go in there."

"Neither do I," he said.

We drove to the end of that road and turned and began to climb a mountain. There were more stars, suddenly. Out of habit, I looked for the Big Dipper. It was as though the small mirror was a magnet—I kept looking into my own eyes.

We went to Dominic's house. There was no phone to call my aunt, and in my sleepy confusion, as I watched Nick load logs into the wood stove, I held my hand over my heart and sent her telepathic messages that I was all right. He put on a light and we helped Dominic to bed and pulled the cold covers over him. I saw the scar clearly then—a thick, jagged scar still deep pink and not very old, from thumb to fourth finger.

"You want to know about my life?" he said. "I was born in China. No kidding. My father was with the Embassy—you don't believe me? I don't remember anything about it, though. We left before I was three."

My eyes moved from Dominic's bed in the corner of the room to a row of vacuum cleaners lined as straight as soldiers, and from there to the only table in the room where there was a mannequin head with a wide-brimmed black hat.

"He repairs vacuum cleaners," Nick said. "He's been my friend since we were twelve years old. Really. Don't you believe that?" He struck a long wooden match on the side of the stove and held the flame over the bowl of a small ivory pipe.

When I woke up it was getting dark. Nick was breathing into my hair. Dominic was sitting on the floor surrounded by his tools, repairing a vacuum cleaner, able to concentrate as though he'd never passed out the night before.

"I thought you should wake up," Nick said, his hand on mine as though he was consoling a patient. I was sprawled in a pile of blankets and quilts that seemed about three feet high. "You've been asleep for almost fourteen hours."

When I told him my aunt was getting married, he told me I should go live with the marionette-maker. They call him that instead of calling him by his real name because his profession interests them. Formerly he was in medical school. Formerly a fiddle player.

His marionettes are made of cherry wood and peach wood, some of birch. They are unicorns and bears and huntsmen. He has passed some on to a friend, a silver-smith, to sink eyes of silver into them. There is a green-jacketed huntsman with silver eyes, and there is a shapeless cow with a ridge of fox fur down its back and amber beads for eyes. Sometimes he hangs them on strings from the ceiling beams and the slits and circles of eyes glow at night like the eyes of nightmare demons. The baby is not afraid of any of them. She has broken pieces of some of them and understands their fragility—a bit of unicorn horn, a sliver of claw.

It is sad when Kirk comes the last Saturday of every month and collects them for the drive to New York. The ones that have been around a long time seem like friends, and it reminds me of a funeral when they are laid in layers of white towel in boxes and carried to Kirk's VW bus.

"It would be good if you could make more people and less animals," Kirk says. But he knows that Carlos will carve whatever he pleases. He lingers by our stove, accepts a mug of tea with cloves and honey.

"What do I want to drive to New York for?" he always says. It is his mother's shop that sells the marionettes.

Carlos's father was Mexican, his mother Scandinavian. Carlos does not look like he belongs to any nationality. He is 6'3", almost too tall for his house, with thick, curly red hair and a blond beard streaked with gray. The baby watches him move around the house, watches him carving and painting. It is clear from her expression that she already understands that men are to be respected. He is fond of her and will sometimes call her "my baby," although he has never asked who her father is.

We came to Carlos's because Nick told me Carlos was a kind person who wanted a woman to live with him. I went feeling like a prostitute, but it was weeks before he touched me. The cats and the dog were more affectionate—and he tried to keep the animals away, afraid that they would overwhelm us. The baby missed her cat when it ran away, though, and quickly befriended all of them.

I looked for clues about him in the old cabinet above the bathroom sink that he used for a medicine cabinet. I found gauze and adhesive, tweezers, aspirin, a jar of crystalized clover honey, a pair of socks folded small, and a card decorated with a pressed yellow field flower—the sort of card you'd scotch tape to a gift—with nothing written inside. There was a box of Cepacol throat lozenges. There was a paperback book about megavitamin therapy.

That was the end of my first week in his house, and it frightened me the way I felt about him, as though I could love any man.

Kirk is apologetic. I have heard people described as shrinking before, but this is the first time I have understood what a person who is shrinking looks like. He opens his mouth, clenching his teeth; his neck disappears into his sweater like a turtle's neck.

He has not been to New York. Before he got ten miles down the road, his bus was stopped by the cops. At first he is so funny, cringing, hating the cops, that Carlos is amused. There were all those bumper stickers: NO NUKES; I AM A COON HUNTER; HONK IF IT'S MY BIRTHDAY. And on the side of his bus Kirk's brother had painted Gypsy women, dancing in a field with blue smoke blowing through it. Kirk's headlight was burned out. The cops went mad looking for drugs, with Kirk telling them his rights all along; they couldn't search the bus unless they saw something, or they had a warrant (cocky because he had nothing with him).

They lifted the lid of the cardboard box and smiled to each other as they saw the packages of white towels. The tall, old cop was furious when he unwrapped the towel and saw a smirking bear in a painted vest. His partner smelled it. Nothing. They make Kirk walk—to see if he could walk a straight line. He thought then that they would pretend that he had failed and run him in. But when he turned, they were huddled together, no longer even watching. The tall old cop stayed where he was and the other—who looked to Kirk like he was a little stoned himself—went to the cop car and opened the trunk and came back with an axe. They placed the bear between them as Kirk watched. Then the young, funny-faced cop whomped the axe through the center of it. The bear split into two halves, exposing the pale peach wood inside, where it had not been oiled. The funny-faced cop bent over it, squinted, and picked up one half, sniffed again. They gave him a warning ticket to get the headlight fixed and drove away.

Carlos listened, transfixed as if a Guru was speaking, the expression on his face somewhere between joy and wonder. That expression never meant that he was feeling good.

We followed Kirk out of the house, walking single-file on the shovelled path, the baby taking clumsy baby steps beside me. They had not disturbed the swathed marionettes in the rest of the box. On the front seat of the bus, along with a horseshoe-shaped mirror Kirk was taking his mother and an unopened bag of licorice, lay the bear. It had been neatly chopped, exactly in the middle. The pieces lay side by side. Before I saw that, I hadn't been as awed by Carlos's profession as the others, but when I saw it destroyed, I was as moved as if he had created something that was living, that they had cut open.

Kirk's teeth were chattering. He wanted both of them to sue the cops. Cops couldn't axe your possessions at will—.

Carlos stared through the window sadly. He didn't open the door or touch the bear.

Kirk, neck still hunched into his shoulders, said he couldn't get it together to go to New York now.

We sat by the stove, as lost in our own silences as if we were stoned.

When the baby cried, Kirk went out to the bus and got the licorice. She sucked a piece and spit it out. He took a circle of licorice from the bag and skipped it across the floorboards. She watched it and smiled. He flipped another out of his fingers and she smiled and went for it.

It has made Carlos more sure that he is right: there is nowhere in the United States safe to bring up a baby.

He is so good to us that I hardly ever think about Nick anymore, though tonight Nick is coming to the house, and they are going to shoot pool at the bar where Nick and I once danced.

I am reading a book about ant societies. I am learning to type on a tall Royal typewriter lent to me by Kirk's brother. The baby, asleep in the cocoon of Carlos's coat, with Bat the Cat curled against her, sucks her first finger (she has never sucked her thumb). I part the material because she is too warm, her forehead pale pink and sweaty. She has a small blue vein just at her temple. When we lived at my aunt's house, I could hear, at night, her whispered prayers: "Please God, please King Christ, she's a girl—make the vein in her face go away." Her voice at night was nice to listen to— the prayers were so logical, all the things I would have forgotten to ask for, and she breathed them in a rhythm that came fast and slow, like a music-box song.

Carlos made my aunt two marionettes: a bride and a groom, with pointed silk shoes on the bride and rabbit fur slippers on the groom. They both wrote letters to thank him. They have never asked us, since I came here, to come to visit.

At dusk Nick comes, a bottle of beer in his hand, his gray knit stocking cap lowered over his eyebrows. I am always happy to see him. I never see him alone, and I have never properly thanked him for bringing me here. The last time he came, when he got a sliver of wood in his thumb from stroking an unfinished marionette and I tweezed it out, I wanted to hold his hand longer than necessary to tweeze; I thought that I'd close the bathroom door and say thank you, but he was eager to be back in the living room, embarrassed to have cried out.

From the front window I watch them go down the plank from door to field, and over to Nick's car. The baby waves, and they wave back. The car starts and fishtails out of the snowy driveway. The baby looks to me for amusement. I settle us by the fire, baby on my lap, and do what she likes best: I seat her facing me and bend my head until my lips graze the top of her head and softly sing songs into her hair.

He does not know what childhood diseases he has had. He thinks he remembers itching with the measles.

He has lost his passport, but has extra passport photographs in a jar that once was filled with Vaseline.

With Nick and Dominic he plays Go on Mondays.

He washes his own sweaters, and shapes them.

He can pare radishes into the shape of rosebuds.

The woman he lived with five years ago, Marguerite, inspired him to begin making the marionettes because she carved and painted decoys. Once he got furious with her and pulled all her fennel out of the garden before it was grown, and she came at him screaming, punching him and trying to push him over with the palms of her hands.

I practice typing by typing these facts about him. He nods his head only—whether to acknowledge that these are facts (some told to me by Nick) or because my typing is improving, I don't know. Sometimes I type lies—or what I think are lies—and that usually makes him laugh:

He secretly likes Monopoly better than Go.
He dreams of lactobacilli.
He wants a Ferrari.

I have typed a list for him that says I was born to parents named Toni and Tony, and that they still live in Virginia, where I grew up. That I have no brothers or sisters who can console them for their wild child who wanted to run away to New York at seventeen. At eighteen, they sent me to live with my aunt in Vermont, and I went through a year and a half of college at Bennington. I fell in love with a musician. We skied cross-country (I was more timid than my parents knew), and in the spring he taught me to drive a car. I learned to like Mexican food. I learned to make cheese, and to glaze windows. I ended the list here; I wanted him to ask if this man was the baby's father, where he went, what my life was really like before I met that man, if I was happy or sad living in my aunt's house. I have told him a lot about myself. Sometimes I've talked for so long that we are both left exhausted. He is so good to us that I want him to remember these facts: height and weight and age, and details of my childhood, color preferences, favorite foods. Sometimes, in his quiet way, he'll ask a question, say he understands. Last week, after I had rambled on for hours, I stopped abruptly. He knew he had to give something. He was painting a unicorn white; it was suspended from the beam with fish-line, so he could paint it all at once and let it air-dry, steadying it only at the last beneath a hoof, then dabbing paint on the last spot of bare wood. He took a deep breath, sighed, and began: Should he raise chickens? Do we want our own eggs, so we will not have to rely on Dime?

Tonight, or tomorrow, or the next day or night, we have to talk.

I have to know if we are to stay always, or for a long time, or a short time.

When he talked to me about eggs, I went along with his conversation. I said we should get another hive, make more honey.

We are thinking about the spring.

I pick up the baby's Christmas present from Nick: an Octascope (a kaleidoscope without the colored glass), which she uses as a toy to roll across the floor. I hold it and feel as powerful raising it to my eye as a captain with his periscope. I aim it at the two toys suspended from the beams, a camel and a donkey, and watch them proliferate into a circular zoo. I put on my jacket and go to the door and open it. It closes behind me with a tap. I have never before lived where there is no lock on the door. I thought that a baby would make demands until I was driven crazy. When I step out, she is silent inside, dog curled beside her, waiting. I raise the Octascope to eye level, and in floods the picture: the fields, spread white with snow, the palest ripple of pink at the horizon—eight triangles of the same image, as still as a painted picture when my hand is steady on the Octascope.

Bat the Cat darts from under the Juniper bush to crouch between my legs. It will rain, or snow. Pink blurs to pearly gray.

This is the dead of winter.

—Autumn 1978

Robert Olen Butler

_____

A Good Scent from a Strange Mountain

Ho Chi Minh came to me again last night, his hands covered with confectioners' sugar. This was something of a surprise to me, the first time I saw him beside my bed, in the dim light from the open shade. My oldest daughter leaves my shades open, I think so that I will not forget that the sun has risen again in the morning. I am a very old man. She seems to expect that one morning I will simply forget to keep living. This is very foolish. I will one night rise up from my bed and slip into her room and open the shade there. Let *her* see the sun in the morning. She is sixty-four years old and she should worry for herself. I could never die from forgetting.

But the light from the street was enough to let me recognize Ho when I woke, and he said to me, "Dao, my old friend, I have heard it is time to visit you." Already on that first night there was a sweet smell about him, very strong in the dark, even before I could see his hands. I said nothing, but I stretched to the nightstand beside me and I turned on the light to see if he would go away. And he did not. He stood there beside the bed—I could even see him reflected in the window—and I knew it was real because he did not appear as he was when I'd known him but as he was when he'd died. This was Uncle Ho before me, the thin old man with the dewlap beard wearing the dark clothes of a peasant and the rubber sandals, just like in the news pictures I studied with such a strange feeling for all those years. Strange because when I knew him, he was not yet Ho Chi Minh. It was 1917 and he was Nguyen Ai Quoc and we were both young men with clean-shaven faces, the best of friends, and we worked at the Carlton Hotel in London where I was a dishwasher and he was a pastry cook under the great Escoffier. We were the best of friends and we saw snow for the first time together. This was before we began to work at the hotel. We shoveled snow and Ho would stop for a moment and blow his breath out before him and it would make him smile, to see what was inside him, as if it was the casting of bones to tell the future.

On that first night when he came to me in my house in New Orleans, I finally saw what it was that smelled so sweet and I said to him, "Your hands are covered with sugar."

He looked at them with a kind of sadness.

I have received that look myself in the past week. It is time now for me to see my family, and the friends I have made who are still alive. This is our custom from Vietnam. When you are very old, you put aside a week or two to receive the people of your life so that you can tell each other your feelings, or try at last to understand each other, or simply say good-bye. It is a formal leave-taking, and with good luck you can do this before you have your final illness. I have lived almost a century and perhaps I should have called them all to me sooner, but at last I felt a deep weariness and I said to my oldest daughter that it was time.

They look at me with sadness, some of them. Usually the dull-witted ones, or the insincere ones. But Ho's look was, of course, not dull-witted or insincere. He considered his hands and said, "The glaze. Maestro's glaze."

There was the soft edge of yearning in his voice and I had the thought that perhaps he had come to me for some sort of help. I said to him, "I don't remember. I only washed dishes." As soon as the words were out of my mouth, I decided it was foolish for me to think he had come to ask me about the glaze.

But Ho did not treat me as foolish. He looked at me and shook his head. "It's all right," he said, "I remember the temperature now. Two hundred and thirty degrees, when the sugar is between the large thread stage and the small orb stage. The Maestro was very clear about that and I remember." I knew from his eyes, however, that there was much more that still eluded him. His eyes did not seem to move at all from my face, but there was some little shifting of them, a restlessness that perhaps only I could see, since I was his close friend from the days when the world did not know him.

I am nearly one hundred years old but I can still read a man's face. Perhaps better than I ever have. I sit in the overstuffed chair in my living room and I receive my visitors and I want these people, even the dull-witted and insincere ones—please excuse an old man's ill temper for calling them that—I want them all to be good with each other. A Vietnamese family is extended as far as the blood line strings us together, like so many paper lanterns around a village square. And we all give off light together. That's the way it has always been in our culture. But these people that come to visit me have been in America for a long time and there are very strange things going on that I can see in their faces.

None stranger than this morning. I was in my overstuffed chair and with me there were four of the many members of my family: my son-in-law Thang, a former colonel in the Army of the Republic of Vietnam and one of the insincere ones, sitting on my Castro convertible couch; his youngest son Loi, who had come in late, just a few minutes earlier, and had thrown himself down on the couch as well, youngest but a man old enough to have served as a lieutenant under his father as our country fell to the communists more than a decade ago; my daughter Lam, who is Thang's wife, hovering behind the both of them and refusing all invitations to sit down; and my oldest daughter, leaning against the door frame, having no doubt just returned from my room where she had opened the shade that I had closed when I awoke.

It was Thang who gave me the sad look I have grown accustomed to, and I perhaps seemed to him at that moment a little weak, a little distant. I had stopped listening to the small talk of these people and I had let my eyes half close, though I could still see them clearly and I was very alert. Thang has a steady face and the quick eyes of a man who is ready to come under fire, but I have always read much more there, in spite of his efforts to show nothing. So after he thought I'd faded from the room, it was with slow eyes, not quick, that he moved to his son and began to speak of the killing.

You should understand that Mr. Nguyen Bich Le had been shot dead in our community here in New Orleans just last week. There are many of us Vietnamese living in New Orleans and one man, Mr. Le, published a little newspaper for all of us. He had recently made the fatal error—though it should not be that in America—of writing that it was time to accept the reality of the communist government in Vietnam and begin to talk to them. We had to work now with those who controlled our country. He said that he remained a patriot to the Republic of Vietnam, and I believed him. If anyone had asked an old man's opinion on this whole matter, I would not have been afraid to say that Mr. Le was right.

But he was shot dead last week. He was forty-five years old and he had a wife and three children and he was shot as he sat behind the wheel of his Chevrolet pick-up truck. I find a detail like that especially moving, that this man was killed in his Chevrolet, which I understand is a strongly American thing. We know this in Saigon. In Saigon it was very American to own a Chevrolet, just as it was French to own a Citroen.

And Mr. Le had taken one more step in his trusting embrace of this new culture. He had bought not only a Chevrolet but a Chevrolet pick-up truck, which made him not only American but a man of Louisiana, where there are many pick-up trucks. He did not, however, also purchase a gun rack for the back window, another sign of this place. Perhaps it would have been well if he had, for it was through the back window that the bullet was fired. Someone had hidden in the bed of his truck and had killed him from behind in his Chevrolet and the reason for this act was made very clear in a phone call to the newspaper office by a nameless representative of the Vietnamese Party for the Annihilation of Communism and for the National Restoration.

And Thang my son-in-law said to his youngest son Loi, "There is no murder weapon." What I saw was a faint lift of his eyebrows as he said this, like he was inviting his son to listen beneath his words. Then he said it again, more slowly, as if it was code. "There is *no weapon*." My grandson nodded his head once, a crisp little snap. Then my daughter Lam said in a very loud voice, with her eyes on me, "That was a terrible thing, the death of Mr. Le." She nudged her husband and son, and both men turned their faces sharply to me and they looked at me squarely and said, also in very loud voices, "Yes, it was terrible."

I am not deaf, and I closed my eyes further, having seen enough and wanting them to think that their loud talk had not only failed to awaken me but had put me more completely to sleep. I did not like to deceive them, however, even though I have already spoken critically of these members of my family. I am a Hoa Hao Buddhist and I believe in harmony among all living things, especially the members of a Vietnamese family.

After Ho had reassured me, on that first visit, about the temperature needed to heat Maestro Escoffier's glaze, he said, "Dao, my old friend, do you still follow the path you chose in Paris?"

He meant by this my religion. It was in Paris that I embraced the Buddha and disappointed Ho. We went to France in early 1918, with the war still on, and we lived in the poorest street of the poorest part of the Seventeenth Arrondissement. Number nine, Impasse Compoint, a blind alley with a few crumbling houses, all but ours rented out for storage. The cobblestones were littered with fallen roof tiles and Quoc and I each had a tiny single room with only an iron bedstead and a crate to sit on. I could see my friend Quoc in the light of the tallow candle and he was dressed in a dark suit and a bowler hat and he looked very foolish. I did not say so, but he knew it himself and he kept seating and re-seating the hat and shaking his head very slowly, with a loudly silent anger. This was near the end of our time together, for I was visiting daily with a Buddhist monk and he was drawing me back to the religion of my father. I had run from my father, gone to sea, and that was where I had met Nguyen Ai Quoc and we had gone to London and to Paris and now my father was calling me back, through a Vietnamese monk I met in the Tuileries.

Quoc, on the other hand, was being called not from his past but from his future. He had rented the dark suit and bowler and he would spend the following weeks in Versailles, walking up and down the mirrored corridors of the Palace trying to gain an audience with Woodrow Wilson. Quoc had eight requests for the Western world concerning Indochina. Simple things. Equal rights, freedom of assembly, freedom of the press. The essential things that he knew Wilson would understand, based as they were on Wilson's own Fourteen Points. And Quoc did not even intend to ask for independence. He wanted Vietnamese representatives in the French Parliament. That was all he would ask. But his bowler made him angry. He wrenched out of the puddle of candlelight, both his hands clutching the bowler, and I heard him muttering in the darkness, and I felt that this was a bad sign already, even before he had set foot in Versailles. And as it turned out, he never saw Wilson, or Lloyd George either, or even Clemenceau. But somehow his frustration with his hat was what made me sad, even now, and I reached out from my bedside and said, "Uncle Ho, it's all right."

He was still beside me. This was not an awakening, as you might expect, this was not a dream ending with the bowler in Paris and me awaking to find that Ho was never there. He was still beside my bed, though he was just beyond my outstretched hand and he did not move to me. He smiled on one side of his mouth, a smile full of irony, as if he too was thinking about the night he'd tried on his rented clothes. He said, "Do you remember how I worked in Paris?"

I thought about this and I did remember, with the words of his advertisement in the newspaper *La Vie Ouvriere*: "If you would like a lifelong momento of your family, have your photos retouched at Nguyen Ai Quoc's." This was his work in Paris; he retouched photos with a very delicate hand, the same fine hand that Monsieur Escoffier had admired in London. I said, "Yes, I remember."

Ho nodded gravely. "I painted the blush into the cheeks of Frenchmen."

I said, "A lovely portrait in a lovely frame for forty francs," another phrase from his advertisement.

"Forty-five," Ho said.

I thought now of his question that I had not answered. I motioned to the far corner of the room where the prayer table stood. "I still follow that path."

He looked and said, "At least you became a Hoa Hao."

He could tell this from the simplicity of the table. There was only a red cloth upon it and four Chinese characters: Bao Son Ky Huong. This is the saying of the Hoa Haos. We follow the teachings of a monk who broke away from the fancy rituals of the other Buddhists. We do not need elaborate pagodas or rituals. The Hoa Hao believes that the maintenance of our spirits is very simple, and the mystery of joy is simple too. The four characters mean "A good scent from a strange mountain."

I had always admired the sense of humor of my friend Quoc so I said, "You never did stop painting the blush into the faces of Westerners."

Ho looked back to me but he did not smile. I was surprised at this but more surprised at my little joke seeming to remind him of his hands. He raised them and studied them and said, "After the heating, what was the surface for the glaze?"

"My old friend," I said, "you worry me now."

But Ho did not seem to hear. He turned away and crossed the room and I knew he was real because he did not vanish from my sight but opened the door and went out and closed the door behind him with a loud click.

I rang for my daughter. She had given me a porcelain bell and after allowing Ho enough time to go down the stairs and out the front door, if that was where he was headed, I rang the bell, and my daughter, who is a very light sleeper, soon appeared.

"What is it, father?" she asked with great patience in her voice. She is a good girl. She understands about Vietnamese families and she is a smart girl.

"Please feel the doorknob," I said.

She did so without the slightest hesitation and this was a lovely gesture on her part, a thing that made me wish to rise up and embrace her, though I was very tired and did not move.

"Yes?" she asked after touching the knob.

"Is it sticky?"

She touched it again. "Ever so slightly," she said. "Would you like me to clean it?"

"In the morning," I said.

She smiled and crossed the room and kissed me on the forehead. She smelled of lavender and fresh bedclothes and there are so many who have gone on before me into the world of spirits and I yearn for them all, yearn to find them all together in a village square, my wife there smelling of lavender and our own sweat, like on a night in Saigon soon after the terrible fighting in 1968 when we finally opened the windows onto the night and there were sounds of bombs falling on the horizon and there was no breeze at all, just the heavy stillness of the time between the dry season and the wet, and Saigon smelled of tar and motorcycle exhaust and cordite, but when I opened the window and turned to my wife, the room was full of a wonderful scent, a sweet smell that made her sit up, for she sensed it too. This was a smell that had nothing to do with flowers but instead reminded us that flowers were always ready to fall into dust while this smell was as if a gemstone had begun to give off a scent, as if a mountain of emerald had found its own scent. I crossed the room to my wife and we were already old, we had already buried children and grandchildren that we prayed waited for us in that village square at the foot of the strange mountain, but when I came near the bed she lifted her silk gown and threw it aside and I pressed close to her and our own sweat smelled sweet on that night. I want to be with her in that square and with the rest of those we'd buried, the tiny limbs and the sullen eyes and the gray faces of the puzzled children and the surprised adults and the weary old people who have gone before us, who know the secrets now. And the sweet smell of the glaze on Ho's hands reminds me of others that I would want in the square, the people from the ship, too, the Vietnamese boy from a village near my own who died of a fever in the Indian Ocean and the natives in Dakar who were forced by colonial officials to swim out to our ship in shark-infested waters to secure the moorings and two were killed before our eyes without a French regret. Ho was very moved by this, and I want those men in our square and I want the Frenchman, too, who called Ho "monsieur" for the first time. A man on the dock in Marseilles. Ho spoke of him twice more during our years together and I want that Frenchman there. And, of course, Ho. Was he in the village square even now, waiting? Heating his glaze fondant? My daughter was smoothing my covers around me and the smell of lavender on her was still strong.

"He was in this room," I said to her to explain the sticky doorknob.

"Who was?"

But I was very sleepy and I could say no more, though perhaps she would not have understood anyway, in spite of being the smart girl that she is.

The next night I left my light on to watch for Ho's arrival, but I dozed off and he had to wake me. He was sitting in a chair that he'd brought from across the room. He said to me, "Dao. Wake up, my old friend."

I must have awakened when he pulled the chair near to me, for I heard each of these words. "I am awake," I said. "I was thinking of the poor men who had to swim out to our ship."

"They are already among those I have served," Ho said. "Before I forgot." And he raised his hands and they were still covered with sugar.

I said, "Wasn't it a marble slab?" I had a memory, strangely clear after these many years, as strange as my memory of Ho's Paris business card.

"A marble slab," Ho repeated, puzzled.

"That you poured the heated sugar on."

"Yes." Ho's sweet-smelling hands came forward but they did not quite touch me. I thought to reach out from beneath the covers and take them in my own hands, but Ho leaped up and paced about the room. "The marble slab, moderately oiled. Of course, I am to let the sugar half cool and then use the spatula to move it about in all directions, every bit of it, so that it doesn't harden and form lumps."

I asked, "Have you seen my wife?"

Ho had wandered to the far side of the room, but he turned and crossed back to me at this. "I'm sorry, my friend. I never knew her."

I must have shown some disappointment in my face, for Ho sat down and brought his own face near mine. "I'm sorry," he said. "There are many other people that I must find here."

"Are you very disappointed in me?" I asked. "For not having traveled the road with you?"

"It's very complicated," Ho said softly. "You felt that you'd taken action. I am no longer in a position to question another soul's choice."

"Are you at peace, where you are?" I asked this knowing of his worry over the recipe for the glaze, but I hoped that this was only a minor difficulty in the afterlife, like the natural anticipation of the good cook expecting guests when everything always turns out fine in the end.

But Ho said, "I am not at peace."

"Is Monsieur Escoffier over there?"

"I have not seen him. This has nothing to do with him, directly."

"What is it about?"

"I don't know."

"You won the country. You know that, don't you?"

Ho shrugged. "There are no countries here."

I should have remembered Ho's shrug when I began to see things in the faces of my son-in-law and grandson this morning. But something quickened in me, a suspicion. I kept my eyes shut and laid my head to the side, as if I was fast asleep, encouraging them to talk more.

My daughter said, "This is not the place to speak."

But the men did not regard her. "How?" Loi asked his father, referring to the missing murder weapon.

"It's best not to know too much," Thang said.

Then there was silence. For all the quickness I'd felt at the first suspicion, I was very slow now. In fact, I did think of Ho from that second night. Not his shrug. He had fallen silent for a long time and I had closed my eyes, for the light seemed very bright. I listened to his silence just as I listened to the silence of these two conspirators before me.

And then Ho said, "They were fools but I can't bring myself to grow angry anymore."

I opened my eyes in the bedroom and the light was off. Ho had turned it off, knowing that it was bothering me. "Who were fools?" I asked.

"We had fought together to throw out the Japanese. I had very good friends among them. I smoked their lovely Salem cigarettes. They had been repressed by colonialists themselves. Did they not know their own history?"

"Do you mean the Americans?"

"There are a million souls here with me, the young men of our country, and they are all dressed in black suits and bowler hats. In the mirrors they are made ten million, a hundred million."

"I chose my path, my dear friend Quoc, so that there might be harmony."

And even with that yearning for harmony I could not overlook what my mind made of what my ears had heard this morning. Thang was telling Loi that the murder weapon had been disposed of. Thang and Loi both knew the killers, were in sympathy with them, perhaps were part of the killing. The father and son had been airborne rangers and I had several times heard them talk bitterly of the exile of our people. We were fools for trusting the Americans all along, they said. We should have taken matters forward and disposed of the infinitely corrupt Thieu and done what needed to be done. Whenever they spoke like this in front of me there was soon a quick exchange of sideways glances at me and then a turn and an apology. "We're sorry, grandfather. Old times often bring old anger. We are happy our family is living a new life."

I would wave my hand at this, glad to have the peace of the family restored. Glad to turn my face and smell the dogwood tree or even smell the coffee plant across the highway. These things had come to be the new smells of our family. But then a weakness often came upon me. The others would drift away, the men, and perhaps one of my daughters would come to me and stroke my head and not say a word and none of them ever would ask why I was weeping. I would smell the rich blood smells of the afterbirth and I would hold our first son, still slippery in my arms, and there was the smell of dust from the square and the smell of the South China Sea just over the rise of the hill and there was the smell of the blood of the inner flesh from my wife as my son's own private sea flowed from this woman that I loved, flowed and carried him into the life that would disappear from him so soon. In the afterlife would he stand before me on unsteady child's legs, would I have to bend low to greet him, or would he be a man now?

My grandson said, after the silence had nearly carried me into real sleep, troubled sleep, my grandson Loi said to his father, "I would be a coward not to know."

Thang laughed and said, "You have proved yourself no coward."

And I wished then to sleep, I wished to fall asleep and let go of life somewhere in my dreams and seek my village square. I have lived too long, I thought. My daughter was saying, "Are you both mad?" And then she changed her voice, making the words very precise. "Let grandfather sleep."

So when Ho came tonight for the third time, I wanted to ask his advice. His hands were still covered with sugar and his mind was, as it had been for the past two nights, very much distracted. "There's something still wrong with the glaze," he said to me in the dark and I pulled back the covers and swung my legs around to get up. He did not try to stop me, but he did draw back quietly into the shadows.

"I want to pace the room with you," I said. "As we did in Paris, those tiny rooms of ours. We would talk about Marx and about Buddha and I must pace with you now."

"Very well," he said. "Perhaps it will help me remember."

I slipped on my sandals and I stood up and Ho's shadow moved past me, through the spill of streetlight and into the dark near the door. I followed him, smelling the sugar on his hands, first before me and then moving past me as I went on into the darkness he'd just left. I stopped as I turned and I could see Ho outlined before the window and I said, "I believe my son-in-law and grandson are involved in the killing of a man. A political killing."

Ho stayed where he was, a dark shape against the light, and he said nothing, and I could not smell his hands from across the room. I smelled only the sourness of Loi as he laid his head on my shoulder. He was a baby and my daughter Lam retreated to our balcony window after handing him to me and the boy turned his head and I turned mine to him and I could smell his mother's milk, sour on his breath, he had a sour smell and there was incense burning in the room, jasmine, the smoke of souls, and the boy sighed on my shoulder, and I turned my face away from the smell of him. Thang was across the room and his eyes were quick to find his wife and he was waiting for her to take the child from me.

"You have never done the political thing," Ho said.

"Is this true?"

"Of course."

I asked, "Are there politics where you are now, my friend?"

I did not see him moving toward me but the smell of the sugar on his hands grew stronger, very strong, and I felt Ho Chi Minh very close to me, though I could not see him. He was very close and the smell was strong and sweet and it was filling my lungs as if from the inside, as if Ho was passing through my very body, and I heard the door open behind me and then close softly shut.

I moved across the room to the bed. I turned to sit down but I was facing the window, the scattering of a streetlamp on the window like a nova in some far part of the universe. I stepped to the window and touched the reflected light there, wondering if there was a great smell when a star explodes, a great burning smell of gas and dust. Then I closed the shade and slipped into bed, quite gracefully, I felt, I was quite wonderfully graceful, and I lie here now waiting for sleep. Ho is right, of course. I will never say a word about my grandson. And perhaps I will be as restless as Ho when I join him. But that will be all right. He and I will be together again and perhaps we can help each other. I know now what it is that he has forgotten. He has used confectioners' sugar for his glaze fondant and he should be using granulated sugar. I was only a washer of dishes but I did listen carefully when Monsieur Escoffier spoke. I wanted to understand everything. His kitchen was full of such smells that you knew you had to understand everything or you would be incomplete forever.

—Spring/Summer 1991

Raymond Carver

If It Please You

Edith Packer had the tape cassette cord plugged into her ear and was smoking one of his cigarettes. The TV played without any volume as she sat on the sofa with her legs tucked under her and turned the pages of a news magazine. James Packer came out of the guest room which he'd fixed up as an office. He was wearing his nylon windbreaker and looked surprised when he saw her, and then disappointed. She saw him and took the cord from her ear. She put the cigarette in the ashtray and wiggled the toes of one stockinged foot at him.

"Bingo," he said. "Are we going to play bingo tonight or not? We're going to be late, Edith."

"I'm going," she said. "Sure. I guess I got carried away." She liked classical music, and he didn't. He was a retired accountant, but he did tax returns for some old clients and he'd been working tonight. She hadn't wanted to play her music so that he'd hear it and be distracted.

"If we're going, let's go," he said. He looked at the TV, and then went to the set and turned it off.

"I'm going," she said. "Just let me go to the bathroom." She closed the magazine and got up. "Hold your old horses, dear," she said and smiled. She left the room.

He went to make sure the back door was locked and the porch lamp on, then came back to stand in the living room. It was a ten-minute drive to the community center, and he could see they were going to be late for the first game. He liked to be on time, which meant a few minutes early, so he'd have a chance to say hello to people he hadn't seen since last Friday night. He liked to joke with Frieda Parsons as he stirred sugar into his styrofoam cup of coffee. She was one of the club women who ran the bingo game on Friday nights and during the week worked behind the counter of the town's only drugstore. He liked getting there with a little time to spare so he and Edith could get their coffee from Frieda and take their places at the last table along the wall. He liked that table. They'd occupied the same places at the same table every Friday night for months now. The first Friday night that he'd played bingo there, he'd won a forty-dollar jackpot. He'd told Edith afterwards that now he was hooked forever. "I've been looking for another vice," he'd said and grinned. Dozens of bingo cards were piled on each table, and you were supposed to pick through and find the cards you wanted, the cards that might be winning cards. Then you sat down, scooped a handful of white beans from the bowl on the table, and waited for the game to get under way, for the head of the women's club, stately, white-haired Eleanor Bender, to commence turning her basket of numbered poker chips and begin calling numbers. That's the real reason you had to get there early, to get your place and pick out your particular cards. You had cards you favored and even felt you could recognize from week to week, cards whose arrangements of numbers seemed more inviting than those of other cards. Lucky cards, maybe. All of the cards had code numbers printed in the upper right-hand corner, and if you'd won a bingo on a certain card in the past, or even came close, of if you just had a feeling about certain cards, you got there early and went through the piles of cards for your cards. You started referring to them as your cards, and you'd look for them from week to week.

Edith finally came out of the bathroom. She had a puzzled expression on her face. There was no way they were going to be on time.

"What's the matter?" he said. "Edith?"

"Nothing," she said. "Nothing. Well, how do I look, Jimmy?"

"You look fine. Lord, we're just going to a bingo game," he said. "You know about everybody there anyway."

"That's the point," she said. "I want to look nice."

"You look nice," he said. "You always look nice. Can we go now?"

There seemed to be more cars than usual parked on the streets around the center. In the place where he normally parked, there was an old van with psychedelic markings on it. He had to keep going to the end of the block and turn.

"Lots of cars tonight," Edith said.

"There wouldn't be so many if we'd gotten here earlier," he said.

"There'd still be as many, we just wouldn't have seen them," she corrected, teasing. She pinched his sleeve.

"Edith, if we're going to play bingo we ought to try to get there on time," he said. "First rule of life is get where you're going on time."

"Hush," she said. "I feel like something's going to happen tonight. You watch and see. We're going to hit jackpots all night long. We're going to break the bank," she said.

"I'm glad to hear it," he said. "I call that confidence." He finally found a parking space near the end of the block and turned into it. He switched off the engine and cut the lights. "I don't know if I feel lucky tonight or not. I think I felt lucky earlier this evening for about five minutes when I was doing Howard's taxes, but I don't feel very lucky right now. It's not lucky if we have to start out walking half a mile just to play bingo."

"You stick close to me," she said. "We'll do fine."

"I don't feel lucky," he said. "Lock your door."

They began walking. There was a cold breeze and he zipped the windbreaker to his neck. She pulled her coat closer. He could hear the surf breaking on the rocks at the bottom of the cliff down behind the community center.

She said, "I'll take one of your cigarettes, Jimmy, before we get inside."

They stopped under the streetlamp at the corner. The wires supporting the old streetlamp swayed in the wind, and the light threw their shadows back and forth over the pavement. He could see the lights of the center at the end of the block. He cupped his hands and held the lighter for her. Then he lit his own cigarette. "When are you going to stop?" he said.

"When you stop," she said. "When I'm ready to stop. Maybe just like when you were ready to stop drinking. I'll just wake up some morning and stop. Like that. Like you. Then I'll find a hobby."

"I can teach you to knit," he said.

"I guess I don't think I have the patience for that," she said. "Besides, one knitter in the house is enough."

He smiled. He took her arm and they kept walking.

When they reached the steps in front of the center, she threw down her cigarette and stepped on it. They went up the steps and into the foyer. There was a sofa in the room, along with a scarred wooden table and several folding chairs. On the walls of the room hung old photographs of fishing boats and a naval vessel, a frigate from before the First World War, that had capsized off the point and been driven ashore onto the sandy beaches below the town. One photograph that always intrigued him showed a boat turned upside down on the rocks at low tide, a man standing on the keel and waving at the camera. There was a sea chart in an oak frame, and several paintings of pastoral scenes done by club members: rugged mountains behind a pond and a grove of trees, and paintings of the sun going down over the ocean. They passed through the room, and he took her arm again as they entered the hall. Several of the club women sat to the right of the entrance behind a long table. There were thirty or so other tables set up on the floor, along with folding chairs. Most of the chairs were filled. At the far end of the hall was a stage where Christmas programs were put on, and sometimes amateur theatrical productions. The bingo game was in progress. Eleanor Bender, holding a microphone, was calling numbers.

They didn't stop for coffee but walked quickly along the wall toward the back, toward their table. Heads bent over the tables. No one looked up at them. People watched their cards and waited for the next number to be called. He headed them toward their table, but tonight starting out the way it had already, he knew someone would have their places, and he was right.

It was a couple of hippies, he realized with a start, a man and a young woman, a girl really. The girl had on an old faded jeans outfit, pants and jacket, and a man's denim shirt, and was wearing rings and bracelets and long, dangling earrings that moved when she moved. She moved now, turned to the long-haired fellow in the buckskin jacket beside her and pointed at a number on his card, then pinched his arm. The fellow had his hair pulled back and tied behind his head, and a scruffy bunch of hair on his face. He wore little steelframe spectacles and had a tiny gold ring in his ear.

"Jesus," James said and stopped. He guided them to another table. "Here's two chairs. We'll have to take these places and take our chances. There's hippies in our place." He glared over in their direction. He took off his windbreaker and helped Edith with her coat. Then he sat down and looked again at the pair sitting in their place. The girl scanned her cards as the numbers were called. Then she leaned over next to the bushy fellow and looked his cards over, as if, James thought, she were afraid he might not have sense enough to mark his own numbers. James picked up a stack of bingo cards from the table and gave half to Edith. "Pick some winners for yourself," he said. "I'm just going to take these first three on top. I don't think it matters tonight which cards I choose. I don't feel very lucky tonight, and there's nothing I can do to change the feeling. What the hell's that pair doing here? They're kind of off their beaten path, if you ask me."

"Don't pay them any attention, Jimmy," she said. "They're not hurting anybody. They're just young, that's all."

"This is regular Friday night bingo for the people of this community," he said. "I don't know what they want here."

"They want to play bingo," she said, "or they wouldn't be here. Jimmy, dear, it's a free country. I thought you wanted to play bingo. Let's play, shall we? Here, I've found the cards I want." She gave him the stack of cards, and he put them with the other cards they wouldn't use in the center of the table. He noticed a pile of discards in front of the hippie. Well, he'd come here to play bingo and by God he was going to play. He fished a handful of beans from the bowl.

The cards were twenty-five cents each, or three cards for fifty cents. Edith had her three. James peeled a dollar bill from a roll of bills he kept for this occasion. He put the dollar next to his cards. In a few minutes one of the club women, a thin woman with bluish hair and a spot on her neck—he knew her only as Alice—would come around with a coffee can picking up quarters, dollar bills, dimes and nickels, making change from the can when necessary. It was this woman, or another woman named Betty, who collected the money and paid off jackpots.

Eleanor Bender called "I 25," and a woman at a table in the middle of the room yelled, "Bingo!"

Alice made her way between the tables. She bent over the woman's card as Eleanor Bender read out the winning numbers. "It's a bingo," Alice said.

"That bingo, ladies and gentlemen, is worth twelve dollars," Eleanor Bender said. "Congratulations to you!" Alice counted out some bills for the woman, smiled vaguely, and moved away.

"Get ready now," Eleanor Bender said. "Next game in two minutes. I'll set the lucky numbers in motion right now." She began turning the basket of poker chips.

They played four or five games to no purpose. Once James was close on one of his cards, one number away from a bingo. But Eleanor Bender called five numbers in succession, none of them his, and even before someone else in the hall had found the right number and called out, he knew she wouldn't be calling the number he needed. Not for anything, he was convinced, would she have called his number.

"You were close that time, Jimmy,"

"Close doesn't count," he said. "It may as well have been a mile. She was teasing me, that's all." He turned the card up and let the beans slide into his hand. He closed his hand and made a fist. He shook the beans in his fist. Something came to him about a kid who'd thrown some beans out of a window. It had something to do with a carnival, or a fair. A cow was in there too, he thought. The memory reached to him from a long way and was somehow disturbing.

"Keep playing," Edith said. "Something's going to happen. Change cards, maybe."

"These cards are as good as any others," he said. "It just isn't my night, Edith, that's all."

He looked over at the hippies again. They were laughing at something the fellow had said. He could see the girl rubbing his leg under the table. They didn't seem to be paying attention to anyone else in the room. Alice came around collecting money for the next game. But just after Eleanor Bender had called the first number, James happened to glance in the direction of the hippies again. He saw the fellow put a bean down on a card he hadn't paid for, a card that was supposed to be with the discard pile. But the card lay so that the fellow could see it and play it along with his other cards. Eleanor Bender called another number, and the fellow placed another bean on the same card. Then he pulled the card over to him with the intention of playing it. James was amazed at the act. Then he got mad. He couldn't concentrate on his own cards. He kept looking up to see what the hippie was doing. No one else seemed to have noticed.

"James, look at your cards," Edith said. "Watch your cards, dear. You missed number thirty-four. Here." She placed one of her beans on his number. "Pay attention, dear."

"That hippie over there who has our place is cheating. Doesn't that beat all?" James said. "I can't believe my eyes."

"Cheating? What's he doing?" she said. "How's he cheating at bingo, Jimmy?" She looked around, a little distracted, as if she'd forgotten where the hippie was sitting.

"He's playing a card that he hasn't paid for," he said. "I can see him doing it. My God, there's nothing they won't stop at. A bingo game! Somebody ought to report him."

"Not you, dear. He's not hurting us," Edith said. "One card more or less in such a room full of cards and people. Let him play as many cards as he wants. There're some people here playing six cards." She spoke slowly and tried to keep her eyes on her cards. She marked a number.

"But they've paid for them," he said. "I don't mind that. That's different. This damned fellow is cheating, Edith."

"Jimmy, forget it, dear," she said. She extracted a bean from her palm and placed it on a number. "Leave him alone. Dear, play your cards. You have me confused now, and I've missed a number. Please play your cards."

"I have to say it's a hell of a bingo game when they can get away with murder," he said. "I resent that. I do."

He looked back at his cards, but he knew he might as well write this game off. The remaining games as well, for that matter. Only a few numbers of his cards had beans. There was no way of telling how many numbers he'd missed, how far behind he'd fallen. He clenched the beans in his fist. Without hope, he squeezed a bean out onto the number just called, G 60. Someone yelled, "Bingo!"

"Christ," he said.

Eleanor Bender said they would take a ten-minute break for people to get up and move around. The game after the break would be a blackout, one dollar a card, winner take all. This week's pot, Eleanor announced, was ninety-eight dollars. There was whistling and clapping. He looked over at the hippies. The fellow was touching the ring in his ear and looking around the room. The girl had her hand on his leg again.

"I have to go to the bathroom," Edith said. "Give me your cigarettes. Maybe you'd get us one of those nice raisin cookies we saw, and a cup of coffee."

"I'll do that," he said. "And, by God, I am going to change cards. These cards I'm playing are born losers."

"I'll go to the bathroom," she said. She put his cigarettes into her purse and stood up from the table.

He waited in line for cookies and coffee. He nodded at Frieda Parsons when she made some light remark, paid, then walked back to where the hippies were sitting. They already had their coffee and cookies. They were eating and drinking and conversing like normal people. He stopped behind the fellow's chair.

"I see what you're doing," James said to him.

The man turned around. His eyes widened behind his spectacles. "Pardon me?" he said and stared at James. "What am I doing?"

"You know," James said. The girl seemed frightened. She held her cookie and fixed her eyes on James. "I don't have to spell it out for you," James said to the man. "A word to the wise, that's all. I can see what you're doing."

He walked back to his table. He was trembling. Damn all the hippies in the world, he thought. It was enough of an encounter so that it made him feel he'd like to have a drink. Imagine wanting to drink over something happening at a bingo game. He put the coffee and cookies down on the table. Then he raised his eyes to the hippie, who was watching him. The girl was watching him too. The hippie grinned. The girl took a bite of her cookie.

Edith came back. She handed him the cigarettes and sat down. She was quiet. Very quiet. In a minute James recovered himself and said, "Is there anything the matter with you, Edith? Are you all right?" He looked at her closely. "Edith, has something happened?"

"I'm all right," she said and picked up her coffee. "No, I guess I should tell you, Jimmy. I don't want to worry you, though." She took a sip of her coffee and waited. Then she said, "I'm spotting again."

"Spotting?" he said. "What do you mean, Edith?" But he knew what she meant, that at this age and happening with the kind of pain she'd said it did, it might mean what they most feared. "Spotting," he said quietly.

"You know," she said, picking up some cards and beginning to sort through them. "I'm menstruating a little. Oh dear," she said.

"I think we should go home. I think we'd better leave," he said. "That isn't good, is it?" He was afraid she wouldn't tell him if the pain started. He'd had to ask her before, watching to see how she looked. She'd have to go in now. He knew it.

She sorted through some more cards and seemed flustered and a little embarrassed.

"No, let's stay," she said after a minute. "Maybe it's nothing to worry about. I don't want you to worry. I *feel* all right, Jimmy," she said.

"Edith."

"We'll stay," she said. "Drink your coffee, Jimmy. It'll be all right. I'm sure. We came here to play bingo," she said and smiled a little.

"This is the worst bingo night in history," he said. "I'm ready to go any time. I think we should go now."

"We'll stay for the blackout, and then it's just forty-five minutes or so. Nothing can happen in that time. Let's play bingo," she said, trying to sound cheerful.

He swallowed some coffee. "I don't want my cookie," he said. "You can have my cookie." He cleared away the cards he was using and took two cards from the stack of bingo cards that weren't in use. He looked over angrily at the hippies as if they were somehow to blame for this new development. But the fellow was gone from the table and the girl had her back to him. She had turned in her chair and was looking toward the stage.

They played the blackout game. Once he glanced up and the hippie was still at it, playing a card he hadn't paid for. James still felt he should call the matter to someone's attention, but he couldn't leave his cards, not at a dollar a card. Edith's lips were tight. She wore a look that could have been determination, or worry.

James had three numbers to cover on one card and five numbers on another card, a card he'd already given up on, when the hippie girl began screaming. "Bingo! Bingo! Bingo! I have Bingo!"

The man clapped and shouted with her. "She's got a bingo! She's got a bingo, folks! A bingo!" He kept clapping.

Eleanor Bender herself went to the girl's table to check her card against the master list of numbers. Then she said, "This young woman has just won herself a ninety-eight-dollar jackpot. Let's give her a round of applause. Let's hear it for her."

Edith clapped along with the rest of the players, but James kept his hands on the table. The hippie fellow hugged the girl. Eleanor Bender handed the girl an envelope. "Count it if you want to," she said with a smile. The girl shook her head.

"They'll probably use the money to buy drugs," James said.

"James, please," Edith said. "It's a game of chance. She won fair and square."

"Maybe she did," he said. "But her partner there is out to take everyone for all he can get."

"Dear, do you want to play the same cards again?" Edith said. "They're about to start the next game."

They stayed for the rest of the games. They stayed until the last game was played, a game called Progressive. It was a bingo game whose jackpot was increased each week if no one had bingoed on a fixed amount of numbers. If no one had hit a bingo when the last number was called, that game was declared closed and more money, five dollars, was added to the pot for the next week's game, along with another number. The first week the game had started, the jackpot was seventy-five dollars and thirty numbers. This week it was a hundred and twenty-five dollars and forty numbers. Bingoes were rare before forty numbers had been called, but after forty numbers you could expect someone to bingo at any time. James put his money down and played his cards without any hope or intention of winning. He felt close to despair. It wouldn't have surprised him if the hippie had won this game.

When the forty numbers had been called and no one had cried out, Eleanor Bender said, "That's bingo for tonight. Thank you all for coming. God bless you, and if He's willing we'll see you again next Friday. Good night and have a nice weekend."

James and Edith filed out of the hall along with the rest of the players, but somehow they managed to get behind the hippie couple who were still laughing and talking about her big jackpot. The girl patted her coat pocket and laughed again. She had an arm around the fellow's waist under his buckskin jacket, fingers just touching his hip.

"Let those people get ahead of us, for God's sake," James said to Edith. "They're a plague."

Edith kept quiet, but she hung back a little with James to give the couple time to move ahead.

"Good night, James. Good night, Edith," Henry Kuhlken said. Kuhlken was a graying, heavy-set man who'd lost a son in a boating accident years before. His wife had left him for another man not long afterwards. He'd turned to serious drinking after a time and later wound up in AA where James had first met him and heard his stories. Now he owned one of the two service stations in town and sometimes did mechanical work on their car. "See you next week."

"Night, Henry," James said. "I guess so. But I feel pretty bingoed out tonight."

Kuhlken laughed. "I know just exactly what you mean," he said and moved on.

The wind was up and James thought he could hear the surf over the sound of automobile engines starting. He saw the hippie couple stop at the van. He might have known. He should have put two and two together. The fellow pulled open his door and then reached across and opened the door on the woman's side. He started the van just as they walked by on the shoulder of the road. The fellow turned on his headlamps and James and Edith were illumined against the walls of the nearby houses.

"That dumbbell," James said.

Edith didn't answer. She was smoking and had the other hand in her coat pocket. They kept walking along the shoulder. The van passed them and shifted gears as it reached the corner. The streetlamp was swinging in the wind. They walked on to their car. James unlocked her door and went around to his side. Then they fastened the seat belts and drove home.

Edith went into the bathroom and shut the door. James took off his windbreaker and threw it across the back of the sofa. He turned on the TV and sat down and waited.

In a little while Edith came out of the bathroom. She didn't say anything. James waited some more and tried to keep his eyes on the TV. She went to the kitchen and ran water. He heard her turn off the faucet. In a minute she came to the kitchen doorway and said, "I guess I'll have to see Dr. Crawford in the morning, Jimmy. I guess something's happening down there." She looked at him. Then she said, "Oh damn it, the lousy, lousy luck," and began to cry.

"Edith," he said and moved to her.

She stood there shaking her head. She covered her eyes and leaned into him as he put his arm around her. He held her.

"Edith, dearest Edith," he said. "Good Lord." He felt helpless and terrified. He stood with his arms around her.

She shook her head a little. "I think I'll go to bed, Jimmy. I am just exhausted, and I really *don't* feel well. I'll go see Dr. Crawford first thing in the morning. It'll be all right, I think, dear. You try not to worry. If anyone needs to worry tonight, let me. Don't you. You worry enough as it is. I think it'll be all right," she said and stroked his back. "I just put some water on for coffee, but I think I'll go to bed now. I feel worn out. It's these bingo games," she said and tried to smile.

"I'll turn everything off and go to bed too," he said. "I don't want to stay up tonight either, no sir."

"Jimmy, dear, I'd rather be alone right now, if you don't mind," she said. "It's hard to explain. It's just that right now I want to be alone. Dear, maybe that doesn't make any sense. You understand, don't you?"

"Alone," he repeated. He squeezed her wrist.

She reached up to his face and held him and studied his features for a minute. Then she kissed him on the lips. She went into the bedroom and turned on the light. She looked back at him, and then she shut the door.

He went to the refrigerator. He stood in front of the open door and drank tomato juice while he surveyed its lighted interior. Cold air blew out at him. The little packages and cartons of food-stuffs on the shelves, a chicken covered in plastic wrap, the neat foil-wrapped bundles of leftovers, all of this suddenly repelled him. He thought for some reason of Alice, that spot on her neck, and he shivered. He shut the door and spit the last of the juice into the sink. Then he rinsed his mouth and made himself a cup of instant coffee which he carried into the living room where the TV was still playing. It was an old western. He sat down and lit a cigarette. After watching the screen for a few minutes, he felt he'd seen the movie before, years ago. The characters seemed faintly recognizable in their roles, and some of the things they said sounded familiar, as things to come often did in movies you'd forgotten. Then the hero, a movie star who'd recently died, said something—asked a hard question of another character, a stranger who'd just ridden into the little town; and all at once things fell into place, and James knew the very words that the stranger would pick out of the air to answer the question. He knew how things would turn out, but he kept watching the movie with a rising sense of apprehension. Nothing could stop what he had set in motion. Courage and fortitude were displayed by the hero and the townsmen-turned-deputies, but these virtues were not enough. It took only one lunatic and a torch to bring everything to ruin. He finished the coffee and smoked and watched the movie until its violent and inevitable conclusion. Then he turned off the set. He went to the bedroom door and listened, but there was no way of telling if she were awake. At least there was no light showing under the door. He hoped she was asleep. He kept listening. He felt vulnerable and somehow unworthy. Tomorrow she'd go to Dr. Crawford. Who knew what he would find? There'd be tests. Why Edith? he wondered. Why us? Why not someone else, why not those hippies tonight? They were sailing through life free as birds, no responsibilities, no doubts about the future. Why not them then, or someone else like them? It didn't add up. He moved away from the bedroom door. He thought about going out for a walk, as he did sometimes at night, but the wind had picked up and he could hear branches cracking in the birch tree behind the house. It'd be too cold anyway, and somehow the idea of a solitary walk tonight at this hour was dispiriting.

He sat in front of the TV again, but he didn't turn on the set. He smoked and thought of the way the hippie had grinned at him across the room. That sauntering, arrogant gait as he moved down the street toward his van, the girl's arm around his waist. He remembered the sound of the heavy surf, and he thought of great waves rolling in to break on the beach in the dark at this very minute. He recalled the fellow's earring and pulled at his own ear. What would it be like to want to saunter around like that fellow sauntered, a hippie girl's arm around your waist? He ran his fingers through his hair and shook his head at the injustice. He recalled the way the girl looked as she yelled her bingo, how everyone had turned enviously to look at her in her youth and excitement. If they only knew, she and her friend. If he could only tell them.

He thought of Edith in there in bed, the blood moving through her body, trickling, looking for a way out. He closed his eyes and opened them. He'd get up early in the morning and fix a nice breakfast for them. Then, when his office opened, she would call Dr. Crawford, set a time for seeing him, and he would drive her to the office and sit in the waiting room and page through magazines while he waited. About the time Edith came out with her news, he imagined that the hippies would be having their own breakfast, eating with appetite after a long night of lovemaking. It wasn't fair. He wished they were here now in the living room, in the noontime of their lives. He'd tell them what they could expect, he'd set them straight. He would stop them in the midst of their arrogance and laughter and tell them. He'd tell them what was waiting for them after the rings and bracelets, the earrings and long hair, the loving.

He got up and went into the guest room and turned on the lamp over the bed. He glanced at his papers and account books and at the adding machine on his desk and experienced a welling of dismay and anger. He found a pair of old pajamas in one of the drawers and began undressing. He turned back the covers on the bed at the other end of the room from his desk. Then he walked back through the house, turning off lights and checking doors. For the first time in four years he wished he had some whiskey in the house. Tonight would be the night for it, all right. He was aware that twice now in the course of this evening he had wanted something to drink, and he found this so discouraging that his shoulders slumped. They said in AA never to become too tired, or too thirsty, or too hungry—or too smug, he might add. He stood looking out the kitchen window at the tree shaking under the force of the wind. The window rattled at its edges. He recalled the pictures down at the center, the boats going aground on the point, and hoped nothing was out on the water tonight. He left the porch lamp on. He went back to the guest room and took his basket of embroidery from under the desk and settled himself into the leather chair. He raised the lid of the basket and took out the metal hoop with the white linen stretched tight and secured within the hoop. Holding the tiny needle to the light, he threaded the eye with one end of the blue silk thread. Then he set to work where he'd left off on the floral design a few nights before.

When he'd first stopped drinking he'd laughed at the suggestion he'd heard one night at AA from a middle-aged businessman who said he might want to look into needlework. It was, he was told by the man, something he might want to do with the free time he'd now have on his hands, the time previously given over to drinking. It was implied that needlework was something he might find good occupation in day or night, along with a sense of satisfaction. "Stick to your knitting," the man had said and winked. James had laughed and shaken his head. But after a few weeks of sobriety when he did find himself with more time than he could profitably employ, and an increasing need for something to do with his hands and mind, he'd asked Edith if she'd shop for the materials and instruction booklets he needed. He was never all that good at it, his fingers were becoming increasingly slow and stiff, but he had done a few things that gave him satisfaction after the pillowcases and dishcloths for the house. He'd done crocheting too—the caps and scarves and mittens for the grand-children. There was a sense of accomplishment when a piece of work, no matter how commonplace, lay finished in front of him. He'd gone from scarves and mittens to create little throw-rugs which lay on the floor of every room in the house now. He'd also made two woolen ponchos which he and Edith wore when they walked on the beach; and he'd knitted an afghan, his most ambitious project to date, something that had kept him busy for the better part of six months. He'd worked on it every evening, piling up the small squares, and had been happy with the feeling of regular industry. Edith was sleeping under that afghan right now. Late nights he liked the feel of the hoop, its taut holding of the white cloth. He kept working the needle in and out of the linen, following the outline of the design. He tied little knots and clipped off bits of thread when he had to. But after a while he began to think about the hippie again, and he had to stop work. He got mad all over again. It was the principle of the thing, of course. He realized it hadn't helped the hippie's chances, except maybe by a frac-tion, just by cheating on a single card. He hadn't won, that was the point, the thing to bear in mind. You couldn't win, not really, not where it counted. He and the hippie were in the same boat, he thought, but the hippie just didn't know it yet.

James put the embroidery back into the basket. He stared down at his hands for a minute after he did so. Then he closed his eyes and tried to pray. He knew it would give him some satisfaction to pray tonight, if he could just find the right words. He hadn't prayed since he was trying to kick the drink, and he had never once imagined then that the praying would do any good, it just seemed to be one of the few things he could do under the circumstances. He'd felt at the time that it couldn't hurt any-way, even if he didn't believe in anything, least of all in his ability to stop drinking. But sometimes he felt better after praying, and he supposed that was the important thing. In those days he'd prayed every night that he could remember to pray. When he went to bed drunk, especially then, if he could remember, he prayed; and some-times just before he had his first drink in the morning he prayed to summon the strength to stop drinking. Sometimes, of course, he felt worse, even more helpless and in the grip of something most perverse and horrible, after he'd say his prayers and then find himself immediately reaching for a drink. He had finally quit drinking, but he did not attribute it to prayer and he simply hadn't thought about prayer since then. He hadn't prayed in four years. After he'd stopped drinking, he just hadn't felt any need for it. Things had been fine since then, things had gotten good again after he'd stopped drinking. Four years ago he'd awakened one morning with a hangover, but instead of pouring himself a glass of orange juice and vodka, he decided he wouldn't. The vodka had still been in the house, too, which made the situation all the more remarkable. He just didn't drink that morning, nor that afternoon or evening. Edith had noticed, of course, but hadn't said anything. He shook a lot. The next day and the next were the same: he didn't drink and he stayed sober. On the fourth day, in the evening, he found the courage to say to Edith that it had been several days now since he'd had a drink. She had said simply, "I know that, dear." He remembered that now, the way she'd looked at him and touched his face, much in the manner she'd touched his face tonight. "I'm proud of you," she'd said, and that was all she'd said. He started going to AA meetings, and it was soon after that he took up needlework.

Before the drinking had turned bad on him and he'd prayed to be able to stop, he'd prayed on occasions some years before that, after his youngest son had gone off to Vietnam to fly jet planes. He'd prayed off and on then, sometimes during the day if he thought about his son in connection with reading something in the newspaper about that terrible place; and sometimes at night lying in the dark next to Edith, turning over the day's events, his thoughts might come to rest on his son. He'd pray then, idly, like most men who are not religious pray. But nevertheless he'd prayed that his son would survive and come home in one piece. And he had returned safely too, but James hadn't ever for a minute really attributed his return to prayer—of course not. Now he suddenly remembered much farther back to a time when he'd prayed hardest of all, a time when he was twenty-one years old and still believed in the power of prayer. He'd prayed one entire night for his father, that he would recover from his automobile accident. But his father had died anyway. He'd been drunk and speeding and had hit a tree, and there was nothing that could be done to save his life. But even now he still remembered sitting outside the emergency room until sunlight entered the windows and praying and praying for his father, making all kinds of promises through his tears, if only his father would pull through. His mother had sat next to him and cried and held his father's shoes which had unaccountably come along in the ambulance beside him when they'd brought him to the hospital.

He got up and put his basket of embroidery away for the night. He stood at the window. The birch tree behind the house was fixed in the little area of yellow light from the back porch lamp, the treetop lost in the overhead darkness. The leaves had been gone for months, but the bare branches switched in the gusts of wind. As he stood there he began to feel frightened, and then it was on him, a real terror welling in his chest. He could believe that something heavy and mean was moving around out there tonight, and that at any minute it might charge or break loose and come hurtling through the window at him. He moved back a few steps and stood where a corner of light from the porch lamp caused the room to brighten under him. His mouth had gone dry. He couldn't swallow. He raised his hands toward the window and let them drop. He suddenly felt he had lived nearly his whole life without having ever once really stopped to think about anything, and this came to him now as a terrible shock and increased his feeling of unworthiness.

He was very tired and had little strength left in his limbs. He pulled up the waist of his pajamas. He barely had energy to get into bed. He pushed up from the bed and turned off the lamp. He lay in the dark for a while. Then he tried praying again, slowing at first, forming the words silently with his lips, and then beginning to mutter words aloud and to pray in earnest. He asked for enlightenment on these matters. He asked for help in understanding the situation. He prayed for Edith, that she would be all right, that the doctor wouldn't find anything seriously wrong, not, please not, cancer, that's what he prayed for strongest. Then he prayed for his children, two sons and a daughter, scattered here and there across the continent. He included his grand-children in these prayers. Then his thoughts moved to the hippie again. In a little while he had to sit up on the side of the bed and light a cigarette. He sat on the bed in the dark and smoked. The hippie woman, she was just a girl, not much younger or different-looking than his own daughter. But the fellow, him and his little specta-cles, he was something else. He sat there for a while longer and turned things over. Then he put out his cigarette and got back under the covers. He settled onto his side and lay there. He rolled over onto his other side. He kept turning until he lay on his back, staring at the dark ceiling.

The same yellow light from the back porch lamp shone against the window. He lay with his eyes open and listened to the wind buffet the house. He felt something stir inside him again, but it was not anger this time. He lay without moving for a while longer. He lay as if waiting. Then something left him and something else took its place. He found tears in his eyes. He began praying again, words and parts of speech piling up in a torrent in his mind. He went slower. He put the words together, one after the other, and prayed. This time he was able to include the girl and the hippie in his prayers. Let them have it, yes, drive vans and be arrogant and laugh and wear rings, even cheat if they wanted. Meanwhile, prayers were needed. They could use them too, even his, especially his, in fact. "If it please you," he said in the new prayers for all of them, the living and the dead.

—Spring 1981

Jennifer Egan

Sacred Heart

In ninth grade I was a great admirer of Jesus Christ. He was everywhere at Sacred Heart: perched over doorways and in corners, peering from calendars and felt wall hangings. I liked his woeful eyebrows and the way his thin, delicate legs crossed at the ankles. The stained-glass windows in our chapel looked like piles of wet candy to me, and from the organ came sounds which seemed to rise from another world, a world of ecstasy and violence. I longed to visit that place, wherever it was, and when they told us to pray for our families I secretly prayed for the chance.

We had a new girl in class that year whose name was Amanda. She had short red hair and wore thin synthetic kneesocks tinted different colors from the wash. She wore silver bracelets embedded with chunks of turquoise, and would cross her legs and stare into space in a way that gave the impression she lived a dark and troubled life. We had this in common, I thought, though no one else knew it.

During Mass I once saw her scrape something onto the pew with the sharp end of a pin she was wearing. Later I sneaked back when the chapel was empty to see what it was, and found her single first initial, "A." To leave one's mark on a church pew seemed a wondrous and terrible thing, and I found myself watching Amanda more often after that. I tried talking to her once, but she twirled her pen against her cheek and fixed her gaze somewhere to my left. Close up her eyes looked cracked and oddly lifeless, like mosaics I'd seen pictures of in our religion class.

Though we were only girls at Sacred Heart, there were boys to contend with. They came from St. Pete's, our companion school three blocks away, and skulked relentlessly at the entrances and exits of our building. Unlike Christ, who was gentle and sad, these boys were prone to fits of hysterical laughter without cause. I was disturbed by stories I had heard of them tampering with the holy wafers and taking swigs of the sacred wines Father Damian kept in his cabinet. They reminded me of those big dogs that leap from nowhere and bark convulsively, stranding young children near fences. I kept my distance from these boys, and when the girls began to vie for their attention, I avoided them too.

Late in the fall of that ninth grade year I saw Amanda cutting her arm in the girls' room. I pretended not to notice, but when I left the stall and began washing my hands she was still there with her wrist laid out on the wood box which covered the radiator. She was jamming a bobby pin into the skin of her forearm, bunching it up.

"What are you doing?" I said.

Amanda glanced at me without expression, and I moved a step closer. She was working her arm in the fierce, quiet way she might work a splinter from her foot.

"It's not sharp enough," she said, raising the bobby pin. It was straightened, and the plastic nubs at its ends had been removed. Amanda seemed unembarrassed by my presence, as though trying to cut her arm were no different from braiding her hair with ribbons. This amazed me, and her urgency drew me in.

I was wearing a pin, a white goat my mother's husband Julius had bought me on a trip to Switzerland. I wore it to please my mother, for although it was hard to imagine a nicer man than Julius, I just couldn't like him. It was as if my not liking him had been decided beforehand by someone else, and I were following orders. Now as I touched this present from him I wanted Amanda to use it—I craved it like you crave a certain taste. It was wrong and bad and yet perfect, somehow. I felt a pleasant twisting in my stomach, and my hands shook as I unhooked the pin from my dress.

"Here," I said, holding it up, "this might work."

Amanda's face looked softer than normal and puffy, as if she had been sleeping. She held me with her eyes while I looked for a match to sterilize the pin. A lot of furtive smoking went on in that bathroom, and I found a book wedged behind the mirror. I clasped my goat's head and held the pin in the flame until it turned black. Then I held it out to Amanda, but she shook her head.

"You," she said.

I stood there a moment, the goat between my fingers. Although I was frightened, there was something raw and splendid in the sight of Amanda's arm against the chipped paint of the radiator cover. Her skin was white and smooth. Gently I held her wrist and touched the pin to the scratch she had already made. Then I pulled it away. "I can't," I said.

Her face went slack. When I tried to give her the pin she turned away from me, embarrassed. I felt like a coward, and I knew that unless I helped Amanda now, she would never be my friend.

"Wait," I said.

I took her wrist and held it. I scraped the pin hard this time and made a thin, bleeding scratch along her skin. I kept going, no longer afraid, and was surprised to find that the point made a sound against her as though I were scraping a piece of thick fabric. It was hard work, and soon my arms were shaking. Sweat gathered on my forehead. I did not look once at Amanda until I had finished an "A" like the one she carved on the pew. When I did look I found her eyes squeezed shut, her lips drawn back as if she were smiling.

"It's finished," I told her, and let go.

When Amanda opened her eyes, tears ran from them, and she rubbed them away with her other hand. I found that I was crying too, partly with relief at having finished, partly from some other sadness I didn't understand. In silence we watched her arm, which looked small and feverish under its bright tattoo. I was aware of the hot light overhead, a smell of chalk in the air and my own pounding heart. Finally Amanda smoothed her hair and pulled her sweater-sleeve down. She smiled at me—

a thin smile, and kissed me on the cheek. For an instant I felt her weight against me, the solidness of her, then she was gone.

Alone in the bathroom I noticed her blood on my fingers. It was reddish-orange, sticky and thin like the residue of some sweet. A wave of sadness made me shut my eyes and lean against the sink. Slowly I washed my hands and my goat pin, which I stuck in my pocket. Then I stood for a while and looked at the radiator, trying to remember each thing, the order of it all. But already it had faded.

From that day on when I looked at Amanda a warm feeling rose from my stomach to my throat. When I walked into class the first place I looked was at her desk, and if she were talking to somebody else I felt almost sick. I knew each detail of Amanda: her soiled-looking hands with their bitten nails, the deep and fragile cleft at the base of her neck. Her skin was dry and white around the kneecaps, and this got worse as fall wore on. I adored these imperfections—each weakness made Amanda seem more tender, more desperate for my help. I was haunted by the thought that I had seen her blood, and would search her distracted eyes for some sign of that event, some hint of our closeness. But her look was always vague, as if I were someone she had met once, a long time ago, and couldn't quite place.

At that time I lived in a tall apartment building with my mother and Julius, her husband of several months. Julius was a furrier, and the Christmas before he had given me a short fox coat which still draped a padded hanger in my closet. I hadn't worn it. Now that it was fall I worried my mother would make me put it on, saying Julius's feelings would be hurt. His lips seemed unnaturally wet, as though he'd forgotten to swallow for too long. He urged me to call him Dad, which I avoided by referring to him always as "you" and looking directly at him when I spoke. I would search the apartment until I found him, rather than have to call out. Once, when I was tele-phoning from school, Julius answered the phone. I said, "Hello . . ." and then pan-icked over what to call him. I hung up and prayed he hadn't recognized my voice. He never mentioned it.

It was getting near Christmas. Along the wind-beaten streets of downtown the windows were filled with cotton-bearded Santas and sleighs piled high with gifts. It was darker inside our chapel, and candles on thin gold saucers covered the stone walls with halos of light. During Mass I would sit and imagine the infant Christ on his bale of straw, the barn animals with burrs and bits of hay caught in their soft fur. I would gaze at our thin Jesus perched above the altar and think of what violence he had suffered since his day of birth, what pity he deserved. And I found to my confusion that I was jealous of him.

Amanda grew thinner as winter wore on. Her long kneesocks slipped and pooled in folds around her ankles. Her face was drawn to a point and often feverish, so her eyes seemed glossy as white marbles against its flush. Sister Wolf let her wear a tur-quoise sweater studded with yellow spots after Amanda explained that neither one of her parents was home and she had shrunk her uniform. That same day her nose began to bleed in science class, and I watched Sister Donovan stand for thirty minutes be-hind her desk, cupping Amanda's small head in her palm while another girl caught the dark flow of blood in a towel. Amanda's eyes were closed, the lids faintly moist.

As I stared at her frail hands, the blue chill which marbled the skin of her calves, I felt that nothing mattered more to me than she did. My mouth filled with a salty taste I couldn't swallow and my head began to ache. I knew that I would do anything for her. And sitting there, in the familiar dull surroundings of my classroom, I was suddenly afraid.

Later that day I found her resting outside on a bench, and forced myself to sit beside her.

"Are your parents on vacation?" I asked. It made me nervous, approaching her like this. I glanced at her arm, but her sweater-sleeves reached the tops of her wrists.

"They're getting a divorce," she said.

Uttered by Amanda the word sounded splendid to me, like a chain of bright railway cars sliding over well-oiled tracks. Divorce.

"My parents are divorced," I told her, but it hissed when I said it, like something being stepped on.

Amanda looked at me directly for the first time since that day in the girls' room, weeks before. Her irises were piles of broken glass in clean, still water. "They are?" she asked.

"My father lives in California."

I felt an urge to describe my entire life to Amanda, beginning with the "Devil's Paint Pots" I had seen with my father at Disneyland when I was six. These were craters filled with thick, bubbling liquid, each a different color. They gave off steam. My father and I had ridden past them on the backs of donkeys. I hadn't seen him since.

"I have a brother," Amanda said.

In my mind the Devil's Paint Pots bubbled lavishly, but I said nothing about them. Amanda crossed her legs and rapidly moved the foot which hung suspended. She fiddled with her bracelets.

"Why do you watch me all the time," she asked.

A hot blush flooded my face and neck. "I don't know," I told her.

Our silence filled with the shouts of younger children swinging on the rings and bars. I thought of the days when I, too, used to hang upside down from those bars, their cold metal stinging the backs of my knees. I hadn't cared if my dress flopped past my head and flaunted my underwear. But it was ninth grade now, and nothing was the same.

"If you could have one wish," said Amanda, looking at me sideways with her broken eyes, "what would it be?"

I considered this. I wanted plenty of things: to poke freely through the cupboards of our altar, to eat communion wafers by the fistful and take a swig of the sacred wine. But I told Amanda, "I'd wish I were you."

I had never seen her really smile before. Her teeth were slightly discolored, and her gums seemed redder than most people's. "You're crazy," she said, shaking her head. "You're really nuts."

She hunched over and made a high, thin sound like a damp cloth wiping a mirror. I thought at first that her nose was bleeding again, but when I leaned over, I saw she was only laughing.

Each morning, as the arc of frost on my windowpane grew wider, I worried about the coat. It hung in my closet, like an eager pet I knew would have to feed eventually. When I touched the soft fur it swung a little. I had an urge sometimes to stroke it.

While I was dressing for school my mother came into my room. Her face was puffed with sleep, her lips very pale. It still amazed me to think that she and Julius shared the big bed where she had slept alone for so many years, where I had slept too when I had nightmares. I imagined an extra room back there where Julius slept, an inner door where he and my mother kissed goodnight and did not meet again until morning.

"It's cold outside," my mother said.

I nodded, scanning my closet for a sweater. I could feel her watching the coat. She was quiet while I unrolled my kneesocks over my legs.

"You know," she said, "Julius really likes you. He thinks you're terrific." Her voice was filled with irrepressible pleasure, as if just saying his name felt good.

"I know it," I said, and I did—he fixed me pancakes in the morning and had offered many times to take me to his warehouse, where I pictured row after row of soft, beckoning furs. So far I'd refused.

"Sarah," my mother said, waiting for me to look at her. "Please won't you wear it?"

She had flat hair and an open, pleading face. When she was dressed up and wearing her makeup my mother could look beautiful to me, but now, in the early white light of a winter day as she balanced her cup on her kneecap, she looked as if she had been badly damaged once, a long time ago, and never fully recovered.

"I will," I said, meaning it now. "I'll wear the coat when it's freezing."

Two weeks before the start of Christmas vacation, Amanda wasn't in school. When I saw her empty chair I felt a flicker of dread. I came inside the classroom and sat at my desk, but without Amanda to hook my attention to, the room felt baggy. I worried, before the teacher had even called her absent, that she would not be back.

A special assembly was called. Our headmistress, Sister Brennan, announced to the school that Amanda had run away from home with her brother, a high school dropout who worked at Marshall Fields. As she spoke there, I felt a vast stirring around me, the same I remembered from the day when we learned that Melissa Shay, two years below me with long gold braids, had died of leukemia during summer vacation. That stirring was laced with collective delight, a jittery pleasure at news so shocking that it briefly banished all traces of normal life. I twisted around with the other girls, exchanging pantomimed amazement. It comforted me to feel like one of them, to pretend that the news of Amanda meant no more than a shorter math class. By the time Sister Brennan was finished an invisible mist of awe had risen among us, frail and delicate as steam, at the terrible thing Amanda had dared to do.

After that I found it hard to concentrate. I was obsessed with the thought that she had left me behind with the rest: Father Damian in his robes, the old chalkboards and desks, the solemn chapel. I felt physical pain in my stomach and arms as I walked through the doors to Sacred Heart, this place Amanda had discarded. The chapel stank of old lint and damp stone, the same words endlessly repeated. As Father Damian lectured to us on Amanda's sin, I noticed how the clerical collar squashed and wrinkled his neck to look like a turkey's, how his eyes were thick and clouded as fingernails. I looked at Jesus and saw, where his crossed ankles should have been, the neatly folded drumsticks on a roasting chicken. After that I kept my eyes averted.

What compelled me instead was her desk. For weeks and weeks—who knew how long?—Amanda had sat before it, twirling her pen against her cheek and planning her escape. After school sometimes when the shadowy halls had emptied, I would sit in her chair and feel the ring of her absence around me. I opened the desk and fingered her chewed pencils, the grimy stub of her eraser, a few haphazard notes she had taken in class. One by one I took these items home with me, lined them carefully along my windowsill and watched them as I went to sleep. I imagined Amanda and her brother walking through thick dunes of sand or climbing the turrets of castles. In my thoughts this brother bore a striking resemblance to Jesus. As for Amanda, she grew more unearthly with every day, until what amazed me was not that she had vanished, but that she had ever really been here.

One night when my mother had gone to a meeting and Julius was reading, I took a razor blade from the pack he kept in his cabinet. I held it between my fingers and brought it to my room, where I sat on the edge of my bed and took off my sweater. I was still in my school jumper with the short-sleeved blouse underneath, and I lay a pillow across my lap and placed my bare arm on top of it. My forearm was white as milk, smooth, full of pale, snaking veins. I touched it with the blade and found that I was terrified. Around me were my childhood bears, my bubbling aquarium and ballerina posters. They were someone else's—a girl whose idea of mischief had been chasing those fish through their tank with her wet arm, touching their slippery tails. For a moment I felt her horror at what I was about to do, and it made me pause. But I had to do something, and this was all I could think of.

Gently but steadily, I sank one corner of the blade into the skin halfway between my elbow and wrist. The pain made tears rush to my eyes, and my nose began to run. I heard an odd humming noise but I continued cutting, determined not to be a baby, determined to be as fierce with myself as I had seen Amanda be. The razor went deeper than the pin had. For a moment the thin cut sat bloodless on my arm—for an instant, and then, like held breath, blood rose from it suddenly and soaked the pillow-case. The white fabric bloomed with red. This happened so fast that at first I was merely astonished, as though I were watching a dazzling science film. Then I grew dizzy and frightened by the mess, this abundance of sticky warmth I could not contain.

I'd done something wrong, that was obvious. In the next room I heard the kettle boil and the creak of Julius's chair as he rose to take it off the stove. I wished my mother were home. I stood up to go to him and ask for help, but my arm seemed huge and heavy to me now, an elephant's arm, and I couldn't carry it.

"Julius," I called. The name sounded unfamiliar, and it struck me that I hadn't said it aloud in nearly a year. The kettle was still whistling, and Julius didn't hear me.

"Dad," I hollered, which sounded even stranger than "Julius" had.

From the next room I heard the stillness of a pause. "Dad," I called again. The wet warmth was soaking through to my legs, and I'd grown lightheaded. As I leaned back

I remembered the Devil's Paint Pots with their wisps of steam, the man beside me on a donkey. Then the door to my room burst open, and Julius ran in.

I was shivering now. My teeth knocked together so hard that I bit my tongue. Julius wrapped me in the fox-fur coat and carried me to the car. I fell asleep before we reached it.

At the hospital they stitched my arm and wrapped it in white gauze. They hung it in a sling of heavy fabric, and despite my shock over what I'd done to myself, I couldn't help predicting the stir my sling would cause in homeroom. Julius spoke to my mother on the phone. From what he said I could tell she was frantic, but Julius stayed calm throughout.

When we were ready to go, he held up the coat. It was squashed and matted, covered with blood. I thought with satisfaction that I had ruined it for good.

"I think we can clean it," said Julius, glancing at me.

He was a big man, with olive skin and hair that shone like plastic. Each mark of the comb was visible on his head. I knew why my mother loved him then—he was the sort of man who stayed warm when it was cold out, who kept important tickets and slips inside his wallet until you needed them. The coat looked small in his hands, like a tiny animal he had shot by mistake. Julius held it a moment, looking at the matted fur. He glanced at me again, and without even meaning to I shook my head. I hated that coat, and it wasn't going to change in a minute.

To my amazement, Julius began to laugh. His wide, wet lips parted in a grin, and a loud chuckle shook him. I smiled back, although I was uneasy.

In a single movement, Julius stuffed the coat into the white cylinder of the hospital garbage can. "What the hell," he said, still laughing, as the silver flap moved back into place. "What the hell." Then he took my hand and walked me back to the parking lot.

Months later, in early summer, Sacred Heart and St. Peter's joined to give a formal dance. I was invited by a boy named Stuart, who had the habit of flicking the hair from his eyes more often than necessary. Stuart's cheeks were smooth and freckled and lifeless, but he seemed as frightened as I was, so I accepted.

I needed white shoes. After school one day in our last week of classes I went to a large store downtown which sold shoes at a discount. Just inside the door I shut my eyes.

Amanda was seated on a small stool, guiding a woman's foot into a green high-heel. There were crumpled tissue papers beside her. I noticed that her hair was longer now, and she was not so thin as before.

I had an urge to duck back out the door before she saw me. Although I hardly thought of Amanda anymore, I still held the vague belief that she had risen from the earth and floated off somewhere. What I felt, seeing her now, was a jolt of disappointment.

"Amanda," I said.

She twisted to face me and squinted a moment. Her confusion amazed me: for all the time I'd devoted to thinking of her, she had barely known who I was.

"Oh yeah," she said, smiling now. "Sacred Heart."

She told me to wait while she finished with her client, and I went to look for my shoes. I picked white satin, with tiny designs of pearl embroidered on top. I brought them to the register, where Amanda was waiting, and she rang them up.

"Where do you go to school?" I asked her.

She named a large public school and said she liked it better there. Her fingers moved rapidly over the keys.

Lowering my voice I said, "Where did you go?"

Amanda flipped the cash drawer open and counted out my change, mouthing the numbers. "Hawaii," she said, handing me the bills.

My mind filled with a vision of grass skirts, flower necklaces, and tropical drinks crowded with umbrellas and canned cherries. Julius had been there, and this was how he described it.

"Hawaii?" I said. It was not what I'd imagined.

"We were there two weeks," Amanda said. "Then my dad came and got us."

She did not sound ashamed of this. As she handed me my box in its plastic bag she said, "He came all the way over, he had to. We would've stayed otherwise."

Amanda closed the register and walked me to the street, where we stood for a moment in silence. The day was warm, and both of us wore short sleeves. Her arms were smooth and lightly tanned. On my own arm, the thin pink scar was nearly invisible now.

Amanda leaned over and kissed me on the cheek. I caught her smell—the warm, bready smell that comes from inside people's clothes. Then she was gone, back at the door to the shoe store, waving. I thought her face looked pink.

I felt a sudden longing not to move from that spot. I could feel where her arms had pressed, where her hands had touched my neck. The smell was still there, warm and rich like the odor a lawn gives off after hours of sunlight. I turned to look back at her, but light hit the window so I couldn't see inside.

Finally I began to walk, swinging my bag of shoes. I breathed deeply, catching the last of her smell, and it was only after several more blocks that I knew what I smelled was not Amanda. It was this day of early summer—the fresh, snarled leaves and piles of sunlit dirt. I was almost fifteen years old.

—Spring/Summer 1991

Louise Erdrich

─────────

The Plunge of the Brave

I never wanted much, and I needed even less, but what happened was that I got everything handed to me on a plate. It came from being a Kashpaw, I used to think. Our family was respected as the last hereditary leaders of this tribe. But Kashpaws died around here, people forgot, and I still keep getting offers.

What kind of offers? Just ask . . .

Jobs for one. I got out of Flandreau with my ears rung from playing football, and the first thing they said was "Nector Kashpaw, go West! Hollywood wants *you*!" They made a lot of westerns in those days. I never talk about this often, but they were hiring for a scene in South Dakota and this talent scout picked me out from the graduating class. His company was pulling in extras for the wagon-train scenes. Because of my height, I got hired on for the biggest Indian part. But they didn't know I was a Kashpaw, because right off I had to die.

"Clutch your chest. Fall off that horse," they directed. That was it. Death was the extent of Indian acting in the movie theater.

So I thought it was quite enough to be killed the once you have to die in this life, and I quit. I hopped a train down the wheat belt and threshed. I got offers there too. Jobs came easy. I worked a year. I was thinking of staying on, but then I got a proposition that discouraged me out of Kansas for good. Down in the city I met this old rich woman. She had her car stopped when she saw me pass by.

"Ask the chief if he'd like to work for me," she said to her man up front. So her man, a buffalo soldier, did.

"Doing what?" I asked.

"I want him to model for my masterpiece. Tell him all he has to do is stand still and let me paint his picture."

"Sounds easy enough." I agreed.

The pay was fifty dollars. I went to her house. They fed me, and later on they sent me over to her barn. I went in. When I saw her dressed in a white coat with a hat like a little black pancake on her head, I felt pity. She was an old wreck of a thing. Snaggle-toothed. She put me on a block of wood and then said to me, "Disrobe."

No one had ever told me to take off my clothes just like that. So I pretended not to understand her. "What robe?" I asked.

"Disrobe," she repeated. I stood there and looked confused. Pitiful! I thought. Then she started to demonstrate by clawing at her buttons. I was just about to go and help her when she said in a near holler, "Take off your clothes!"

She wanted to paint me without a stitch on, of course. There were lots of naked pictures in her barn. I wouldn't do it. She offered money, more money, until she offered me so much that I had to forget my dignity. So I was paid by this woman a round two hundred dollars for standing stock still in a diaper.

I could not believe it, later, when she showed me the picture. *Plunge of the Brave*, was the title of it. Later on, that picture would become famous. It would hang in the Bismarck state capitol. There I was, jumping off a cliff, naked of course, down into a rocky river. Certain death. Remember Custer's saying? The only good Indian is a dead Indian? Well from my dealings with whites I would add to that quote: "The only interesting Indian is dead, or dying by falling backwards off a horse."

When I saw that the greater world was only interested in my doom, I went home on the back of a train. Riding the rails one night the moon was in the boxcar. A nip was in the air. I remembered that picture, and I knew that Nector Kashpaw would fool the pitiful rich woman that painted him and survive the raging water. I'd hold my breath when I hit and let the current pull me toward the surface, around jagged rocks. I wouldn't fight it, and in that way I'd get to shore.

Back home, it seemed like that was happening for a while. Things were quiet. I lived with my mother and Eli in the old place, hunting or roaming or chopping a little wood. I kept thinking about the one book I read in high school. For some reason this priest in Flandreau would teach no other book all four years but *Moby Dick*, the story of the great white whale. I knew that book inside and out. I'd even stolen a copy from school and taken it home in my suitcase.

This led to another famous misunderstanding.

"You're always reading that book," my mother said once. "What's in it?"

"The story of the great white whale."

She could not believe it. After a while, she said, "What do they got to wail about, those whites?"

I told her the whale was a fish as big as the church. She did not believe this either. Who would?

"Call me Ishmael," I said sometimes, only to myself. For he survived the great white monster like I got out of the rich lady's picture. He let the water bounce his coffin to the top. In my life so far I'd gone easy and come out on top, like him. But the river wasn't done with me yet. I floated through the calm sweet spots, but somewhere the river branched.

So far I haven't mentioned the other offers I had been getting. These offers were for candy, sweet candy between the bedcovers. There was girls like new taffy, hardened sourballs of married ladies, rich marshmallow widows, and even a man, rock salt and barley sugar in a jungle of weeds. I never did anything to bring these offers on. They just happened. I never thought twice. Then I fell in love for real.

Lulu Nanapush was the one who made me greedy.

At boarding school, as children, I treated her as my sister and shared out peanut butter-syrup sandwiches on the bus to stop her crying. I let her tag with me to town. At the movies I bought her licorice. Then we grew up apart from each other. I came home, and saw her dancing in the Friday-night crowd. She was doing the butterfly with two other men. For the first time, on seeing her, I knew exactly what I wanted. We sparked each other. We met behind the dance house and kissed. I knew I wanted more of that sweet taste on her mouth. I got selfish. We were flowing easily toward each other's arms.

Then Marie appeared, and here is what I do not understand: how instantly the course of your life can be changed.

I only know that I went up the convent hill intending to sell geese and came down the hill with the geese still on my arm. Beside me walked a young girl with a mouth on her like a flop house, although she was innocent. She grudged me to hold her hand. And yet I would not drop the hand and let her walk alone.

Her taste was bitter. I craved the difference after all those years of easy sweetness. But I still had a taste for candy. I could never have enough of both, and that was my problem and the reason that long past the branch in my life I continued to think of Lulu.

Not that I had much time to think once married years set in. I liked each of our babies, but sometimes I was juggling them from both arms and losing hold. Both Marie and I lost hold. In one year, two died, a boy and a girl baby. There was a long spell of quiet, awful quiet, before the babies showed up everywhere again. They were all over in the house once they started. In the bottoms of cupboards, in the dresser, in trundles. Lift a blanket and a bundle would howl beneath it. I lost track of which were ours and which Marie had taken in. It had helped her to take them in after our two others were gone. This went on. The youngest slept between us, in the bed of our bliss, so I was crawling over them to make more of them. It seemed like there was no end.

Sometimes I escaped. I had to have relief. I went drinking and caught holy hell from Marie. After a few years the babies started walking around, but that only meant they needed shoes for their feet. I gave in. I put my nose against the wheel. I kept it there for many years and barely looked up to realize the world was going by, full of wonders and creatures, while I was getting old baling hay for white farmers.

So much time went by in that flash it surprises me yet. What they call a lot of water under the bridge. Maybe it was rapids, a swirl that carried me so swift that I could not look to either side but had to keep my eyes trained on what was coming. Seventeen years of married life and come-and-go children.

And then it was like the river pooled.

Maybe I took my eyes off the current too quick. Maybe the fast movement of time had made me dizzy. I was shocked. I remember the day it happened. I was sitting on the steps, wiring a pot of Marie's that had broken, when everything went still. The children stopped shouting. Marie stopped scolding. The babies slept. The cows chewed. The dogs stretched full out in the heat. Nothing moved. Not a leaf or a bell or a human. No sound. It was like the air itself had caved in.

In the stillness, I lifted my head and looked around.

What I saw was time passing, each minute collecting behind me before I had squeezed from it any life. It went so fast, is what I'm saying, that I myself sat still in the center of it. Time was rushing around me like water around a big wet rock. The only difference is, I was not so durable as stones. Very quickly I would be smoothed away. It was happening already.

I put my hand to my face. There was less of me. Less muscle, less hair, less of a hard jaw, less of what used to go on below. Fewer offers. It was 1952, and I had done what was expected—fathered babies, served as chairman of the tribe. That was the extent of it. Don't let the last fool you, either. Getting into the big-time local politics was all low pay and no thanks. I never even ran for the office. Someone put my name down on the ballots, and the night I accepted the job I became somebody less, almost instantly. I grew gray hairs in my sleep. The next morning they were hanging in the comb teeth.

Less and less, until I was sitting on my steps in 1952 thinking I should hang on to whatever I still had.

That is the state of mind I was in when I began to think of Lulu. The truth is I had never gotten over her. I thought back to how swiftly we had been moving toward each other's soft embrace before everything got tangled and swept me on past. In my mind's eye I saw her arms stretched out in longing while I shrank into the blue distance of marriage. Although it had happened with no effort on my part, to ever get back I'd have to swim against the movement of time.

I shook my head to clear it. The children started to shout. Marie scolded, the babies blubbered, the cow stamped, and the dogs complained. The moment of stillness was over; it was brief, but the fact is when I got up from the front steps I was changed.

I put the fixed pot on the table, took my hat off the hook, went out and drove my pickup into town. My brain was sending me the kind of low ache that used to signal a lengthy drunk, and yet that was not what I felt like doing.

Anyway, once I got to town and stopped by the tribal offices, a drunk was out of the question. An emergency was happening.

And here is where events loop around and tangle again.

It is July. The sun is a fierce white ball. Two big semis from the Polar Bear Refrigerated Trucking Company are pulled up in the yard of the agency offices, and what do you think they're loaded with? Butter. That's right. Seventeen tons of surplus butter on the hottest day in '52. That is what it takes to get me together with Lulu.

Coincidence. I am standing there wrangling with the drivers, who want to dump the butter, when Lulu drives by. I see her, riding slow and smooth on the luxury springs of her Nash Ambassador Custom.

"Hey Lulu," I shout, waving her into the bare, hot yard. "Could you spare a couple hours?"

She rolls down her window and says perhaps. She is high and distant ever since the days of our youth. I'm not thinking, I swear, of anything but delivering the butter. And yet when she alights I cannot help but notice an interesting feature of her dress. She turns sideways. I see how it is buttoned all the way down the back. The buttons are small, square, plump, like the mints they serve next to the cashbox in a fancy restaurant.

I have been to the nation's capital. I have learned there that spitting tobacco is frowned on. To cure myself of chewing I've took to rolling my own. So I have the makings in my pocket, and I quick roll one up to distract myself from wondering if those buttons hurt her where she sits.

"Your car's air-cooled?" I ask. She says it is. Then I make a request, polite and natural, for her to help me deliver these fifty-pound boxes of surplus butter, which will surely melt and run if they are left off in the heat.

She sighs. She looks annoyed. The hair is frizzled behind her neck. To her, Nector Kashpaw is a nuisance. She sees nothing of their youth. He's gone dull. Stiff. Hard to believe, she thinks, how he once cut the rug! Even his eyebrows have a little gray in them now. Hard to believe the girls once followed him around!

But he is, after all, in need of her air conditioning, so what the heck? I read this in the shrug she gives me.

"Load them in," she says.

So the car is loaded up, I slip in the passenger's side, and we begin delivering the butter. There is no set way we do it, since this is an unexpected shipment. She pulls into a yard and I drag out a box, or two, if they've got a place for it. Between deliveries we do not speak.

Each time we drive into the agency yard to reload, less butter is in the semis. People have heard about it and come to pick up the boxes themselves. It seems surprising, but all of that tonnage is going fast, too fast, because there still hasn't been a word exchanged between Lulu and myself in the car. The afternoon is heated up to its worst, where it will stay several hours. The car is soft inside, deep cushioned and cool. I hate getting out when we drive into the yards. Lulu smiles and talks to the people who come out of their houses. As soon as we are alone, though, she clams up and hums some tune she heard on the radio. I try to get through several times.

"I'm sorry about Henry," I say. Her husband was killed on the railroad tracks. I never had a chance to say I was sorry.

"He was a good man." That is all the answer I get.

"How are your boys?" I ask later. I know she has a lot of them, but you would never guess it. She seems so young.

"Fine."

In desperation, I say she has a border of petunias that is the envy of many far-flung neighbors. Marie has often mentioned it.

"My petunias," she tells me in a flat voice, "are none of your business."

I am shut up for a long time, then. I understand that this is useless. Whatever I am doing it is not what she wants. And the truth is, I do not know what I want from it either. Perhaps just a mention that I, Nector Kashpaw, middle-aged butter mover, was the young hard-muscled man who thrilled and sparked her so long ago.

As it turns out, however, I receive so much more. Not because of anything I do or say. It's more mysterious than that.

We are driving back to the agency after the last load, with just two boxes left in the back seat, my box and hers. Since the petunias, she has not even hummed to herself. So I am more than surprised, when, in a sudden burst, she says how nice it would be to drive up to the lookout and take in the view.

Now I'm the shy one.

"I've got to get home," I say, "with this butter."

But she simply takes the turn up the hill. Her skin is glowing, as if she were brightly golden beneath the brown. Her hair is dry and electric. I heard her tell somebody, where we stopped, that she didn't have time to curl it. The permanent fuzz shorts out here and there above her forehead. On some women this might look strange, but on Lulu it seems stylish, like her tiny crystal earrings and the French rouge on her cheeks.

I do not compare her with Marie. I would not do that. But the way I ache for Lulu, suddenly, is terrible and sad.

"I don't think we should," I say to her when we stop. The shadows are stretching, smooth and blue, out of the trees.

"Should what?"

Turning to me, her mouth a tight gleaming triangle, her cheekbones high and pointed, her chin a little cup, her eyes lit, she watches.

"Sit here," I say, "alone like this."

"For heavensake," she says, "I'm not going to bite. I just wanted to look at the view."

Then she does just that. She settles back. She puts her arm out the window. The air is mild. She looks down on the spread of trees and sloughs. Then she shuts her eyes.

"It's a damn pretty place," she says. Her voice is blurred and contented. She does not seem angry with me anymore, and because of this, I can ask her what I didn't know I wanted to ask all along. It surprises me by falling off my lips.

"Will you forgive me?"

She doesn't answer right away, which is fine, because I have to get used to the fact that I said it.

"Maybe," she says at last, "but I'm not the same girl."

I'm about to say she hasn't changed, and then I realize how much she has changed. She has gotten smarter than I am by a long shot, to understand she is different.

"I'm different now, too," I am able to admit.

She looks at me, and then something wonderful happens to her face. It opens, as if a flower bloomed all at once or the moon rode out from behind a cloud. She is smiling.

"So your butter's going to melt," she says, then she is laughing outright. She reaches into the back seat and grabs a block. It is wrapped in waxed paper, squashed and soft, but still fresh. She smears some on my face. I'm so surprised that I just sit there for a moment, feeling stupid. Then I wipe the butter off my cheek. I take the block from her and I put it on the dash. When we grab each other and kiss there is butter on our hands. It wears off as we touch, then undo, each other's clothes. All those buttons! I make her turn around so I won't rip any off, then I carefully unfasten them.

"You're different," she agrees now; "better."

I do not want her to say anything else. I tell her to lay quiet. Be still. I get the backrest down with levers. I know how to do this because I thought of it, offhand, as we were driving. I did not plan what happened, though. How could I have planned? How could I have known that I would take the butter from the dash? I rub a handful along her collarbone, then circle her breasts, then let it slide down between them and over the rough little tips. I rub the butter in a circle on her stomach.

"You look pretty like that," I say. "All greased up."

She laughs, laying there, and touches the place I should put more. I do. Then she guides me forward into her body with her hands.

Midnight found me in my pickup, that night in July. I was surprised, worn out, more than a little frightened of what we'd done, and I felt so good. I felt loose limbed and strong in the dark breeze, roaring home, the cold air sucking the sweat through my clothes and my veins full of warm, sweet water.

As I turned down our road I saw the lamp, still glowing. That meant Marie was probably sitting up to make sure I slept out in the shack if I was drunk.

I walked in, letting the screen whine softly shut behind me.

"Hello," I whispered, hoping to get on into the next dark room and hide myself in bed. She was sitting at the kitchen table, reading an old catalog. She did not look up from the pictures.

"Hungry?"

"No," I said.

Already she knew, from my walk or the sound of my voice, that I had not been drinking. She flipped some pages.

"Look at this washer," she said. I bent close to study it. She said I smelled like a churn. I told her about the seventeen tons of melting butter and how I'd been hauling it since first thing that afternoon.

"Swam in it too," she said, glancing at my clothes. "Where's ours?"

"What?"

"Our butter."

I'd forgotten it in Lulu's car. My tongue was stuck. I was speechless to realize my sudden guilt.

"You forgot."

She slammed down the catalog and doused the lamp.

I had a job as night watchman at a trailer-hitch plant. Five times a week I went and sat in the janitor's office. Half the night I pushed a broom or meddled with odd repairs. The other half I drowsed, wrote my chairman's reports, made occasional rounds. On the sixth night of the week I left home, as usual, but as soon as I got to the road Lulu Lamartine lived on I turned. I hid the truck in a cove of brush. Then I walked up the road to her house in the dark.

On that sixth night it was as though I left my body at the still wheel of the pickup and inhabited another more youthful one. I moved, witching water. I was full of sinkholes, shot with rapids. Climbing in her bedroom window. I rose. I was a flood that strained bridges. Uncontainable. I rushed into Lulu, and the miracle was she could hold me. She could contain me without giving way. Or she could run with me, unfolding in sheets and snaky waves.

I could twist like a rope. I could disappear beneath the surface. I could run to a halt and Lulu would have been there every moment, just her, and no babies to be careful of tangled somewhere in the covers.

And so this continued five years.

How I managed two lives was a feat of drastic proportions. Most of the time I was moving in a dim fog of pure tiredness. I never got one full morning of sleep those years, because there were babies holed up everywhere set to let loose their squawls at the very moment I started to doze. Oh yes, Marie kept taking in babies right along. Like the butter, there was a surplus of babies on the reservation, and we seemed to get unexpected shipments from time to time.

I got nervous, and no wonder, with demands weighing me down. And as for Lulu, what started off carefree and irregular became a clockwork precision of timing. I had to get there prompt on night number six, leave just before dawn broke, give and take all the pleasure I could muster myself to stand in between. The more I saw of Lulu the more I realized she was not from the secret land of the Nash Ambassador, but real, a woman like Marie, with a long list of things she needed done or said to please her.

I had to run down the lists of both of them, Lulu and Marie. I had much trouble to keep what they each wanted, when, straight.

In that time, one thing that happened was that Lulu gave birth.

It was when she was carrying the child I began to realize this woman was not only earthly, she had a mind like a wedge of iron. For instance, she never did admit that she was carrying.

"I'm putting on the hog." She clocked her tongue, patting her belly, which was high and round while the rest of her stayed slim.

One night, holding Lulu very close, I felt the baby jump. She said nothing, only smiled. Her white teeth glared in the dark. She snapped at me in play like an animal. In that way she frightened me from asking if the baby was mine. I was jealous of Lulu, and she knew this for a fact. I was jealous because I could not control her or count on her whereabouts. I knew what a lively, sweet-fleshed figure she cut.

And yet I couldn't ask her to be true, since I wasn't. I was two-timing Lulu in being married to Marie, and vice versa of course. Lulu held me tight by that string while she spun off on her own. Who she saw, what she did, I have no way to ever know. But I do think the boy looked like a Kashpaw.

Every so often I would try to stop time again by finding a still place and sitting there. But the moment I was getting the feel of quietness, leaning up a tree, parked in the truck, sitting with the cows, or just smoking on a rock, so many details of love and politics would flood me. It would be like I had dried my mind out only to receive the fresh dousing of, say, more tribal news.

Chippewa politics was thorns in my jeans. I never asked for the chairmanship, or for that matter, anything, and yet I was in the thick and boil of policy. I went to Washington about it. I talked to the governor. I had to fight like a weasel, but I was fighting with one paw tied behind my back because of wrangling over buying a washer for Marie.

For a time there, Marie only wanted one thing that I could give her. Not love, not sex, just a wringer washer. I didn't blame her, with all the diapers and the overalls and shirts. But our little stockpile of money kept getting used up before it came anywhere near a down payment on the price.

This wrangling and tearing went on with no let up. It was worse than before I'd stopped or took the butter from the dash. Lulu aged me while at the same time she brought back my youth. I was living fast and furious, swept so rapidly from job to home to work to Lulu's arms, and back again, that I could hardly keep my mind on straight at any time. I could not fight this, either. I had to speed where I was took. I only trusted that I would be tossed up on land when everyone who wanted something from Nector Kashpaw had wrung him dry.

So I was ready for the two things that happened in '57. They were almost a relief, to tell the truth, because they had to change my course.

Number one was a slick, flat-faced Cree salesman out of Minneapolis that came and parked his car in Lulu's yard. He was Henry's brother, Beverly Lamartine, a made-good, shifty type who would hang Lulu for a dollar. I told her that. She just laughed.

"There's no harm in him," she said.

"I'll kill him if he puts a hand on you."

She gave me a look that said she wouldn't call a bluff that stupid or mention the obvious except to say, blasting holes in me, "If it wasn't for Marie. . . ."

"What?" I said.

She bit her lip and eyed me. I went cold. It entered my mind that she was thinking to marry this urban Indian, this grease-haired vet with tattoos up his arms.

"Oh no," I said, "you wouldn't."

I got desperate with the thought, but I was helpless to sway her anvil mind. I laid her down. I pinned her arms back. I pulled her hair so her chin tipped up. Then I tried my best to make her into my own private puppet that I could dance up and down any way I moved her. That's what I did. Her body sweat and twisted. I made her take my pleasure. But when I fell back there was still no way I could have Lulu but one—to leave Marie—which was not possible.

Or so I thought.

That night I left Lulu right after she fell back in the pillows. I got in my truck and drove to the lake. I parked alone. I turned the lights off. And then, because even in the stillest of hours, by the side of the water, I was not still, I took off my clothes and walked naked to the shore.

I swam until I felt a clean tug in my soul to go home and forget about Lulu. I told myself I had seen her for the last time that night. I gave her up and dived down to the bottom of a grave. Perhaps I should have stayed there and never fought. Perhaps

I should have taken a breath. But I didn't. The water bounced me up. I had to get back in the thick of my life.

The next day, I was glad of my conclusion to leave Lulu forever. The area redevelopment went through. I was glad, because if I hadn't betrayed Lulu before, I had to do it now, over the very land she lived on. It was not hers. Even though she planted petunias and put the birdbath beneath her window, she didn't own the land, because the Lamartines had squatted there. That land had always belonged to the tribe, I was sorry to find, for now the tribal council had decided that Lulu's land was the one perfect place to locate a factory.

Oh, I argued. I did as much as I could. But government money was dangling before their noses. In the end, as tribal chairman, I was presented with a typed letter I should sign that would formally give notice that Lulu was kicked off the land.

My hand descended like in a dream. I wrote my name on the dotted line. The secretary licked it in an envelope and then someone delivered it to Lulu's door. I tried to let things go, but I was trapped behind the wheel. Whether I liked it or not I was steering something out of control.

That night, I tried to visit Lulu's window out of turn. It was not the sixth night of the week, but I know she expected me. I know because she turned me away.

And that is where the suffering and burning set in to me with fierceness beyond myself. No sooner had I given her up than I wanted Lulu back.

It is a hot night in August. I am sitting in the pool of lamplight at my kitchen table. It is night six, but I am home with Marie and the children. They are all around me, breathing deep or mumbling in a dream. Aurelia and Zelda are hunched in the roll-cot beside the stove. Zelda moans in the dim light and says "Oh, quick!" Her legs move and twitch like she is chasing something. Her head is full of crossed black pins.

I have my brown cowhide briefcase beside me, open, spilling neat-packed folders and brochures and notes. I take out a blue-lined tablet and a pencil that has never been sharpened. I shave the pencil to a point with my pocketknife. Then I clean the knife and close it up and wonder if I'm really going to write what some part of my mind has decided.

I lick my thumb. The pencil strokes. *August 7, 1957.* My hand moves to the left. *Dear Marie.* I skip down two lines as I was taught in the government school. *I am leaving you.* I press so hard the lead snaps on the pencil.

Zelda sits bolt upright, sniffing the air. She was always a restless sleeper. She would walk through the house as a little girl, to come and visit her parents. Often I would wake to find her standing at the end of our bed, holding the post with both hands as if it was dragging her someplace.

Now, almost full-grown, Zelda frowns at something in her dream and then slowly sinks back beneath her covers and disappears but for one smudge of forehead. I give up. I take the pencil in my hand and begin to write.

Dear Marie,

Can't see going on with this when every day I'm going down even worse. Sure I loved you once, but all this time I am seeing Lulu also. Now she pressured me and the day has come I must get up and go. I apologize. I found true love with her. I don't have a choice. But that doesn't mean Nector Kashpaw will ever forget his own.

After I write this letter, I fold it up very quickly and lay it in the briefcase. Then I tear off a fresh piece of paper and begin another.

Dear Lulu,

You wanted me for so long. Well you've got me now! Here I am for the taking, girl, all one hundred percent yours. This is my official proposal put down in writing.

Yours till hell freezes over,

Nector

And then, because maybe I don't mean it, maybe I just need to get it off my mind, I lock the letters in the briefcase, blow out the lamp, and make my way around sleeping children to Marie. I hang my shirt and pants on the bedpost and slip in next to her. She always sleeps on her side, back toward me, curved around the baby, which is next to the wall so it won't tumble off. She sleeps like this ever since I rolled over on one of them. I fit around her and crook my arm at her waist.

She smells of milk and wood ash and sun-dried cloth. Marie has never used a bottle of perfume. Her hands are big, nicked from sharp knives, roughed by bleach. Her back is hard as a plank. Still she warms me. I feel like pleading with her but I don't know what for. I lay behind her, listening to her breath sigh in and out, and the ache gets worse. It fills my throat like a lump of raw metal. I want to clutch her and never let go, to cry to her and tell her what I've done.

I make a sound between my teeth and she moves, still in her dream. She pulls my arm down tighter, mumbles into her pillow. I take a breath with her breath. I take another. And then my body becomes her body. We are breathing as one, and I am falling gently into sleep still not knowing what will happen.

I sleep like I've been clubbed, all night, very hard. When I wake she has already gone into town with Zelda. They were up early, canning apples. The jars are stacked upside down at one end of the table, reddish gold, pretty with the sun shining through them. I brew my morning coffee and chew the cold galette she has left for me. I am still wondering what I am going to do. It seems as though, all my life up till now, I have not had to make a decision. I just did what came along, went wherever I was taken, accepted when I was called on. I never said no. But now it is one or the other, and my mind can't stretch far enough to understand this.

I go outside and for a long time I occupy myself chopping wood. The children know how to take care of themselves. I pitch and strain at the wood, splitting with a wedge and laying hard into the ax, as if, when the pile gets big enough, it will tell me what to do.

As I am working I suddenly think of Lulu. I get a clear mental picture of her sitting on the lap of her brother-in-law. I see Beverly's big ham reach out and wrap around her shoulder. Lulu's head tips to the side, and her eyes gleam like a bird's. He is nodding at her. Then his mouth is falling onto hers.

I throw the axe. The two lovebirds propel me into the house. I am like a wildman, clutching through my briefcase. I find the letter to Marie and I take it out, read it once, then anchor it on the table with the jar of sugar. I cram the letter to Lulu in my pocket, and then I go.

All I can see, as I gallop down the steps and off into the woods, is Lulu's small red tongue moving across her teeth. My mind quivers, but I cannot stop myself from seeing more. I see his big face nuzzle underneath her chin. I see her hands fly up to clutch his head. She rolls her body expertly beneath his, and then I am crashing through the brush, swatting leaves, almost too blind to see the old deerpath that twists through the woods.

I creep up on her house, as though I will catch them together, even though I have heard he is back in the Cities. I crouch behind some bushes up the hill, expecting her dogs to scent me any moment. I watch. Her house is fresh painted, yellow with black trim, cheerful as a bee. Her petunias are set out front in two old tractor tires painted white. After a time, when the dogs don't find me, I realize they have gone off somewhere. And then I see how foolish I am. The house is quiet. No Beverly. No boys in the yard, either, fixing cars or target practicing. They are gone, leaving Lulu alone.

I put my hands to my forehead. It is burning as if I have a fever. Since the Nash I have never taken off Lulu's clothes in the daylight, and it enters my head, now, that I could do this if I went down to her house. So I make my way out of the dense bush.

For the first time ever, I go up to her front door and knock. This feels so normal. I am almost frightened. Something in me is about to burst. I need Lulu to show me what this fearful thing is. I need her hand to pull me in and lead me back into her bedroom, and her voice to tell me how we were meant for each other by fate. I need her to tell me I am doing right.

But no one comes to the door. There is no sound. It is a hot, still afternoon, and nothing stirs in Lulu's dull grass, though deep in the trees, to all sides, I have the sense now of something moving slowly forward. An animal that is large, dense furred, nameless. These thoughts are crazy, I know, and I try to cast them from my mind. I round the house. The backyard is the one place where Lulu's tidiness has been defeated. The ground is cluttered with car parts, oil pans, pieces of cement block, and other useful junk.

No one answers at the back door either, so I sit down on the porch. I tell myself that no matter how long it takes Lulu to get here, I will wait. I am not good at waiting, like my brother Eli, who can sit without moving a muscle for an hour while deer approach him. I am not good at waiting, but I try. I roll a cigarette and smoke is as slow as possible. I roll another. I try to think of anything but Lulu or Marie or my children. I think back to the mad captain in *Moby Dick* and how his leg was bit off. Perhaps I was wrong, about Ishmael I mean, for now I see signs of the captain in myself. I bend over and pick up a tin can and crush it flat. For no reason! A bit later I bang the side of her house until my fist hurts. I drop my head in my hands. I tell her, out loud, to get back quick. I do not know what I will do if she doesn't.

I am tired. I have started to shake. That is when I take out the letter I have crumpled in my pocket. I decide that I will read it a hundred times, very slow, before I do anything else. So I read it, word by word, until the words make no sense. I go on reading it. I am keeping careful, concentrated count, when suddenly I think of Marie.

I see her finding the other letter now. Sugar spills across the table as she sits, crying out in her shock. A jar of apples explodes. The children shout, frightened. Grease bubbles over on the stove. The dogs howl. She clutches the letter and tears it up.

I lose count. I try reading Lulu's letter once more, but I cannot finish it. I crumple it in a ball, throw it down, then I light up another cigarette and begin to smoke it very quick while I am rolling a second to keep my hands distracted.

This is, in fact, how the terrible thing happens.

I am so eager to smoke the next cigarette that I do not notice I have thrown down my half-smoked one still lit on the end. I throw it right into the ball of Lulu's letter. The letter smokes. I do not notice right off what is happening, and then the paper flares.

Curious and dazed, I watch the letter burn.

I swear that I do nothing to help the fire along.

Weeds scorch in a tiny circle, and then a bundle of greasy rags puffs out in flames. It burns quickly. I leave the steps. An old strip of rug curls and catches onto some hidden oil slick in the grass. The brown blades spurt and crackle until the flame hits a pile of wood chips. Behind that are cans of gasoline that the boys have removed from dead cars. I step back. The sun is setting in the windows, black and red. I duck. The gas cans roar, burst. Blue lights flash on behind my eyelids, and now long oily flames are licking up the side of the house, moving snakelike along the windows of the porch, finding their way into the kitchen where the kerosene is stored and where Lulu keeps her neatly twine-tied bundles of old newspapers.

The fire is unstoppable. The windows are a furnace. They pop out, raining glass, but I merely close my eyes and am untouched.

I have done nothing.

I feel the heat rise up my legs and collect, burning for Lulu, but burning her out of me.

I don't know how long I stand there, moving back inch by inch as fire rolls through the boards, but I have nearly reached the woods before the heat on my face causes me to abandon the sight, finally, and turn.

That is when I see that I have not been alone.

I see Marie standing in the bush. She is fourteen and slim again. I can do nothing but stare, rooted to the ground. She stands tall, straight and stern as an angel. She watches me. Red flames from the burning house glare and flicker in her eyes. Her skin sheds light. We are face to face, and then she begins to lift on waves of heat. Her breast is a glowing shield. Her arm is a white-hot spear. When she raises it the bush behind her spreads, blazing open like wings.

I go down on my knees, a man of rags and tinder. I am ready to be burned in the fire too, but she reaches down and lifts me up.

"Daddy," she says, "Let's get out of here. Let's go."

—Fall 1984

Jessica Neely

Skin Angels

In the beginning of the summer my mother memorized the role of Lady Macbeth four mornings a week and worked the late shift in Geriatrics. She had always wanted to act in a play, a real play, and in the months after my father left home, when it was clear to us that he'd left for good, she would take me to the old converted church, the Bread and Circuses theater. The company players had painted the limestone walls and the windows of the church gray so that no sunlight would interfere with the stage floods. In real life, these people were all students and teachers and housewives. But in the muggy mornings of that summer they would park their cars and walk through the back door of the theater to put on make-up and costumes, to curl their hair and put on large gaudy earrings that only the right shade of blue could make beautiful. Sy was the manager of Bread and Circuses. He told my mother that she could play Lady Macbeth because she had crazy eyes and red hair. So my mother and I went to the theater four mornings each week. She stood just off stage while three witches hunched over a bucket of dry ice and practiced incantations. I sat in the front pew and watched. I was eight years old then.

Before dawn, when my mother came home from work at the hospital, she would double-lock the door. I could smell the cold air and cigarette smoke on her uniform as she lifted me out of bed, carried me into her room. I stood on the bed to take the bobby pins out of her hair. Then I undid the zipper. My mother unclipped her nurse's badge that said "Andrea" in script and laid it on the dresser. When she was nude, she'd stand in front of the mirror with outstretched arms and stare at herself. I'd jump on the bed behind her. I'd bounce high until I could see myself in the mirror above her head. Sometimes she'd laugh so hard she'd have to bend over and hold her stomach. We'd get into bed and pull the covers over our heads to make a tent.

"There's nobody in the world except you and me," my mother would whisper. "No cars, no families, no people, no old people."

"We're in a cave."

"That's right." She'd curl up around my back and pull me close against her warm stomach and breasts.

My sister Serina, who is nine years older than I, had a job dancing at the Brass Monkey. Her boyfriend Ponce usually drove her home around eight. I would hear her key first in one lock, then the other; hear my sister whisper, "Goodbye. Okay, all right. Goodbye," and hold back a giggle, as if she were home late from a date and didn't want to be caught. I'd open my eyes to the windows in my mother's room where the broad sunlight framed Venetian blinds. Serina came into the room and shook me by the shoulders. The fringe on her leotard tickled my face.

"Get ready for school," she said. Then she walked around the bed to our mother, bent down and yelled, "Andy, get up or you'll be late for play practice!"

In the bathroom I turned on the shower, but I could still hear them fighting. My mother screamed, "Does he pay you? How much does that nigger pay you?"

Sy told my mother that she didn't know much about being an actress. She would need to spend afternoons with him going over lines and gestures. He taught her the way actresses dress: purple suede miniskirts, black cigarette holders, berets. On the last day of third grade when I came home, my mother and Sy were in the kitchen smoking pot in their underwear.

"We're going to be beatniks, Carlie," my mother said. "What do you think of that?"

"I don't know."

Sy wore green bikini underpants. He had curly brown hair frosted gray at the temples and a chest and beard furry as a bear's. His fat stomach hung over the edge of his underpants and a little tear split the elastic near his thigh. I turned away and looked at my mother's painted toenails.

"Hey, Carlie, would you like Daddy Sy to get you a new wardrobe?"

"Daddy Sy!" My mother slapped the table. "That's rich. Daddy, Sy in my ear and I'm yours forever."

Sy fell out of his chair, laughing. My mother laughed too. One hand over her mouth, the other hitting her thigh, she looked at me, coaxing. And Sy rolled around on the floor until he bumped into the refrigerator.

I put my report card on the table.

Sy bought me fringed go-go boots like the ones Serina wore to work. He bought me tights in every color, earrings, and he also bought me Conchita, a wooden doll with a black tiara and a red taffeta skirt. Almost every Saturday my mother and Sy took me to the lake. We had a checkered tablecloth that we spread on the deserted part of the beach where Sy's family once had a house. At first we all got sunburns. My mother made me wear a T-shirt so mine wasn't bad, but we had to make Sy a cold bath with tea bags in it.

Sy would lie on my mother's bed and pay me quarters to peel the thin strips of skin off his back. When I'd get a long one he'd say, "Hold it up in front of the window and let the breeze catch it." I'd pinch the top between my fingers and watch it flutter. "Those are skin angels," he said. I'd flick the skin angels out through the window and watch them float away. Sy told me they went straight to heaven.

Some nights while my mother worked, Serina and Ponce stayed home with me. Serina worked on her painting, a mosaic called "Blasted Jesus." She hated water colors and oils were too expensive, so she used to hold crayons over a lit candle and pat the wax drips onto the canvas. Serina used black for Jesus's face, brown for his eyes, white for his teeth. Ponce would stretch out on the sofa while Serina worked. He was a tall, skinny man who wore tight bell bottoms and turtlenecks, and he had an afro that looked perfectly sculpted, like a globe. Serina spent hours on that afro.

One night Ponce said he wanted to take Serina to Greenwich Village to meet gallery owners. "With your legs and my capital. . . . "

Serina said her legs would have nothing to do with it, but Ponce leaned back and laughed. "Lady Cakes, you don't know the score yet, do you?"

"I know what nice legs will get you," Serina said and she pointed over her shoulder to my mother's bedroom.

Ponce laughed. "What about you, Carlie? Do you want to run away to Greenwich Village with us?" he asked. "It's only about five hours south. You could go visit your mommy every second Sunday."

I looked across the room to my mother's doorway. It was open and dark. "Only if you buy me a ten-speed," I said.

"Sweetheart, I'll buy you a Cutlass Supreme. Won't I, Serina?"

"Sure you will."

"We'll sell Serina's mosaics and buy three Supremes in pastel colors. We'll drive down Houston parade-style. You don't want to live with your bird of a mother anymore, do you?"

"She's not a bird," I said. "My mother says your face is dirty."

Ponce arched his back and yawned. "It's her mind that's dirty, honey. Your mommy is a loon."

"Shut up," Serina laughed.

My mother would tell me that she and I were the oddballs in the family; the only ones with red hair. No one was ever allowed to cut my hair except her—a quarter inch off the ends every six months. She put the clippings in a pink shellacked jewelry box and when that was full, she'd put the hair into a paper bag in the closet. When she died, my mother said, I was to make her a pillow out of the clippings. She said that's what God does. He hires swans to fill up pillows with their softest underdown and kick them off the clouds to all of the funeral parlors. But she wanted her pillow to be special, she said; she wanted it filled with my thin red hair.

We sat at the kitchen table. My mother had put an apron over her uniform to keep it clean and her hair was pinned up in a bun. But she had on too much make-up for work. She looked as if she were on her way to perform on the set of a hospital play.

She was telling me that Serina loved Ponce only because she was afraid of him.

"This is something I want you to remember," she said. "A chain is only as strong as its weakest link. Do you know what that means?"

I shook my head.

"I'm trying to teach you about self-respect, Carlie. You don't want to love out of fear. You have to be strong enough to dare everything." She lit a cigarette. "That's the only way we know how to love, you and me, right?"

I said I didn't know and my mother frowned. She watched me move my fork back and forth across my plate. "Answer the question. Do you know what I'm saying?"

"That you aren't afraid."

My mother blew her smoke out in a stream. "Absolutely not. I'm not afraid of Sy and I was not afraid of your father. I loved him completely, until there was nothing left to love him with, but I was never afraid of him. Never. I'm telling you, Carlie, Ponce will leave Serina the way your father left me. He'll leave just like that, in the middle of the night. He won't say anything. He won't slam anything."

She put her hand against her forehead and shut her eyes. The cigarette stuck out between her fingers and the smoke lifted to flat layers above her hair. "He didn't even take his clothes. I kept them in the drawers for so long. I thought he might get cold."

I wanted my doll, Conchita. I wanted to hold her, but I had left her in the bedroom. Slowly I pushed my chair away from the table and stood as quietly as I could. My mother sat still. The only motion around her was the thin twist of smoke in the air.

The next afternoon Sy came over to practice a scene from *Macbeth*. I knocked on my mother's bedroom door because I heard Sy yelling and wanted to know what was going on.

Sy opened the door. "I told you, Carlie, when this door's closed it means no admittance," he said.

My mother snapped her fingers and pointed to the far corner of the room. "Over there. Be quiet."

Sy had put a red light in the sunlamp. He had it pointed up toward the bed where my mother stood with a blanket wrapped around her. A fan on the dresser blew my mother's hair back from her face in tangled strands.

"Okay, I want your voice to build, baby." He walked to my mother and pushed her chin slightly to the right. "You've read the letter and you're enraged. Do you hear? You're begging for evil."

Sy smudged my mother's lipstick across the top of her mouth. "Yeah," he whispered, "evil. Take it from 'Make thick.'" He squatted down by the sunlamp.

My mother lifted her arms so that the blanket slid back. "'Make thick my blood,'" she said. "'Stop up the access and passage to remorse, that no compunctious visitings of nature shake my fell purpose nor—'"

"Stop!" Sy grabbed my mother. "Slow down. Compunctious. Compunctious. Roll your lips around the sound, lick the word. You're Satan's mistress. Okay. Start at 'Stop up the access.'"

"'Stop up the access and passage to remorse that no compunctious visitings of nature shake my fell purpose, nor keep peace between the effect and it!'" My mother ran her hands up along her sides. "'Come to my woman's breasts and take my milk for gall, you murthering ministers, wherever—'"

"Cut!" Sy turned the fan off. "Andy, you're making an ass of yourself. If you're not going to take this seriously. . . ."

My mother went into the kitchen. Conchita and I followed. She poured herself a glass of water then splashed some on her face.

Sy stood in the kitchen doorway. "Look at that," he said. "You're slumped over like some kind of beggar. Hold that glass in front of you. Drink it as if it's the nectar of the gods."

"Knock it off," my mother said.

Sy crossed his arms and stared at my mother and me. "Andy, the only possible way you'll be successful is by listening to me. You've got to be on stage every single minute; breathe and live the tragedy."

"Get out of here."

"Louder."

"Get out of here!"

"Marvelous."

My mother threw the glass on the floor. "Out!"

"Good night, all." Sy bowed slightly and walked out.

Opening night for *Macbeth* was only three weeks away and Sy decided to have a party for the cast. My mother bought four dozen lilies for the party. We went to Sy's condo and taped the lilies to the walls, put them in bud vases, cut the tops off and let them float in coffee cups.

I was supposed to sleep in Sy's bed with Conchita, but that night I was too afraid to sleep. I got out of bed and went to the end of the hallway where I could watch. There were no lights on in the house, only lit candles. Most of the cast members were outside on the pool patio smoking cigarettes and joints. Some wore Batman capes. Others had on dwarf boots, Peter Pan hats. Sy had bought plastic champagne goblets with removable bottoms. A woman in a feathered dress was throwing the plastic bottoms around like tiny frisbees. Sy came in from the patio. Conchita and I crouched in a shadow. He stood beside a thin man who kept peeling lilies off the wall and eating them.

"Banquo, that's no way to treat a lily," Sy said.

"Hey, Sy, how about this?" He offered Sy the top of a lily. "'If you can look into the seeds of time and say which grain will grow and which will not, speak then to me.'"

Sy held the skinny man's wrist and looked at the flower. "'Your children shall be kings.'"

"Beautiful." The man bit off a petal and chewed it up.

I held Conchita and went back to the bedroom. As we fell asleep, I could hear people dancing and jumping on the floor.

Later I awoke because I heard my mother scream. No one was in the living room so I ran out to the patio. I saw Sy and two other men standing naked beside the pool; they were holding my mother above the water, swinging her back and forth. Sy yelled, "One, two, three!" and they threw my mother into the air. Her back arched as she came down.

Under the water I could see her long body sink and her hair fan out like blood against the pool lights. The men dove in, one at a time, and headed for my mother. They took turns swimming between her legs, quick as eels.

I screamed for Sy to let my mother up. She needed air. They had to let her up for air. I ran with Conchita into the kitchen to dial the Brass Monkey where Serina worked.

"I need to talk to my sister, Serina," I said.

"She's busy. She can't come to the phone," the Monkey said.

"It's an emergency. Please," I said. "let me talk to her."

"Who?"

"Serina!" I yelled. "Tell her someone's killing her mother!"

The Monkey screeched into the phone and hung up.

I ran with Conchita out the front door. I was too afraid to look for my mother and I didn't want Sy or the other men to find me. I crouched down beside the house in some trees and bushes. It was raining a little so I made Conchita a lean-to out of leaves and sticks. I put rocks around her bed to make a bumper. There were no sounds from the pool. I could hear only the rain on the leaves around me. I tucked my knees in close to my chest and pulled my nightgown down over them.

After a long while, music began blaring from the house. I heard Sy's voice, then my mother laughing. Her laugh was high and scary. I put my face down on my knees, held my hands over my ears. I didn't want to hear that music; hear Sy's words or the way my mother was laughing. I sat there on the ground until the rain soaked through my nightgown and I began to shiver. And I did not go back inside until the music had stopped and all of the lights in the house were off.

When I opened the door to Sy's room, I could see the bodies of my mother and Sy wrapped up in the blankets. My mother's dress and shoes were on the floor. I took off my wet nightgown and put on my mother's dress. "Mom?" I whispered, but not loud enough to wake her. I walked to the side of the bed and lifted the blanket. Sy's body was curled around my mother's back, his hand flat across her breasts. I bent over and whispered to her again.

A night wind blew the rain in through the screened window. It fell in a mist across my face and neck. I knew it was hours before sunrise, so I pulled the blanket over my mother again and sat down on the end of the bed. It was then I remembered that I had left Conchita outside.

The next morning Sy made breakfast. I sat at the table and watched. He cracked six eggs into a large ceramic bowl.

"I'll bet you love scrambled eggs," he said.

I didn't answer. I watched him cut a square of butter and drop it into the frying pan.

"I'll bet they're your absolute favorite food," he said, but he didn't turn toward me for an answer and again I was quiet.

When my mother came into the kitchen she was still in her bathrobe. Her eye make-up was smeared and her hair was in snarls. She hadn't bothered to brush it.

"Andy, *you'll* eat some of these eggs," Sy said.

"I'm not hungry." My mother looked at me and then she looked down. "Sy, I feel ill." She sat down at the table.

Sy walked to my mother and gently raised her chin. "A star's got to keep her strength up," he said. He took a film container out of his pants pocket, opened it and sprinkled some dope onto a rolling paper. "This will give you an appetite. Because you're a star, Andy. You know that? You're beautiful."

My mother smiled up at him like a child.

"You're my baby, Andy, my little baby." He licked the side of the joint and lit the end.

"Tell me about opening night," my mother said.

Sy inhaled the dope and held the smoke in his mouth. He looked at my mother and tucked a strand of hair behind her ear. With his face up close, he blew the smoke out and said, "Opening night." The words rushed around her cheeks. "Yes, you're standing alone on the stage. You've got the floods on you, and the backdrop is lit up red and purple. There's silence for one, maybe two minutes."

Sy smoked the joint again. "The audience is transfixed. They can't take their eyes off you, Andy, your long red hair flowing around your shoulders. They're amazed. You're a star."

My mother leaned back and laughed softly.

"Then you stretch out your hands. There's a knife in them. The lights reflect off the blade. You don't say a word. You start moving, undulating, waving the knife like you're cutting a big S in the air. And then the lights go down. You're a silhouette against the backdrop. Here." Sy handed her the joint. "Take a hit."

My mother took a drag and started to laugh.

"That's better," Sy said. "I love it when you laugh. Laugh."

My mother began to laugh. She leaned back and laughed straight at the ceiling. Sy started laughing too. Sometimes he giggled and took puffs off the joint. Sometimes he laughed out loud; but my mother just laughed at the ceiling, until it was one long sound, like a yell, which she only broke to catch her breath.

Ponce told Serina that if she didn't go to Greenwich Village he'd burn her with a hot comb. He put the metal teeth on the electric burner until it heated up and the grease smoked a little.

"You're going, Serina, right?" He picked up the wooden handle and waved the teeth at her.

I grabbed my sister's arm, tried to pull her away. But Serina wouldn't move.

Ponce held the hot comb in front of Serina's face. "You pack your bags and be ready by dawn, darling. Got it?"

Serina smiled with the side of her mouth. "Sit down," she said.

Ponce winked at me, but I wouldn't smile back. He sat at the kitchen table and Serina divided his hair into sections. She rubbed grease on his scalp and straightened his hair from the roots upward.

"I just want to make sure when we leave I don't owe nobody nothing," he said.

"You don't," Serina said. She pulled his hair up tall and smooth.

That was the night Serina and Ponce left. I woke up around five. The sun sifted in from the bottom of my mother's blinds, fell in spots on the rug. I moved the flat of my palm along the mattress, but my mother was not home yet and there was no one there. I went down the hall to the lit door of Serina's room. Ponce had gone somewhere.

"Carlie, I'm sorry. I've got to get out of here." She had a big suitcase and she was stuffing it with her dresses, sweaters, and blue jeans.

"Why?"

"You don't realize, but Mom is driving me crazy. I'll be happy in New York. Ponce will get a job and I'll try to sell my paintings. Look, you can have this. You'll grow into it."

"I don't *want* your sweater," I said. "Serina, don't leave."

Serina took a belt from one of her dresses and folded it in quarters.

"You don't have to be afraid of him."

Serina stared at me. Then she began to fold her clothes again. "Carlie, I'm in love with Ponce. Mom doesn't choose to see that. You don't have to—change yourself for a man and you don't have to be a martyr." Serina looked behind me at the door.

My mother was leaning against the wall in her coat. She had her nurse cap in her hand and she was smoking.

"What do you think you're doing?"

"I'm leaving." Serina put the suitcase on the floor and sat down on it to close the latches.

"Mom, tell her not to go."

"I'll do no such thing." My mother raised her chin and spoke in a loud voice as if she were on stage. "Go, Serina, you make no pretense of living here anyway."

Serina pulled her coat out of the closet. "I'll leave a number with the Brass Monkey," she said to me and kissed the top of my head.

My mother walked toward Serina. "You don't give a damn about *me*, do you? Do you? For the first time in my life I'm doing something that's important to me. I'm acting in a play. I've always wanted to act and you know it. But you can't stay home a few afternoons to take care of Carlie." She pointed toward the door. "*You* have to go gallivanting all over East Jesus with that man."

"Just cut the theatrics, Mother."

"Where did you get that? That's your father's suitcase. Put it back in my closet. Now!"

"Mother, move." Serina picked up the suitcase.

"No, Serina, wait a minute. Let's talk for a second," she pleaded. "Okay? Okay?" She stubbed out her cigarette. "There, we'll just talk about this."

Serina put down the suitcase. She looked at me and said, "The only thing I regret is how screwed up Carlie's going to be while you play around with Sy and his sick friends."

My mother stared at her for a second and then she slapped Serina across the face. Serina stared back at her.

"Oh God, honey, I'm sorry. Serina sweetheart, I didn't mean to do that. I love you so much, honey. Wait a second, wait, don't take that suitcase."

Serina pushed my mother away from the door. Then she left.

My mother sat on the floor and hugged her knees. She kept rocking back and forth, calling my sister's name.

Later that day we packed up Serina's room. We put all of her remaining clothes and shoes in shopping bags. My mother stripped Serina's bed and threw the sheets in the trash. Then she took the curtains off the windows and vacuumed the carpet.

My mother asked me to stay in bed with her. She had drawn her shades and unplugged the phone. "Brush my hair," she asked, so I sat on her back, made hairdos with rubber bands and barrettes. I continued to brush my mother's long hair for hours, it seemed, while she slept. Once in a while she would wake up and roll over.

"You love me, don't you Carlie?" she'd ask.

I'd hug her.

"Say it."

"I love you," I'd say and brush the hair back from her face. I lay down on my mother's back and held my cheek against her forehead. I thought about Serina, then I thought of Conchita lying, face down, in the woods behind Sy's house. The rain would twist her wooden body and wash the paint from her lips. It would smooth her arms and fingers flat until they were level and whole with the ground. I felt a loneliness so wide, a loss that would only continue, constant as my mother's breathing and lulled merely by the need for sleep.

—Autumn 1985

Joyce Carol Oates

The Crying Baby

Precisely when the sound was first heard in our household I cannot say, for of course it was not recorded, unless my family without my knowledge or consent has recorded these matters for their own or for medical purposes, but I believe it must have been last autumn, probably mid or late October, when the furnace usually begins to heat the house, so that the familiar sounds of our furnace masked the baby's weaker cries, or were confused with them. And when, frightened, I paused in my kitchen work, or hurriedly shut off the vacuum cleaner, or ran stumbling to find my husband, or one of the children (though the five of them were fully grown, and no longer lived under their parents' roof, the two youngest, my girls, frequently return home to visit—they have come early to the knowledge that the world is a lonely place, not likely to be redeemed by the charity of our hearts), to ask if they too heard the sound, or had they indeed heard any strange startling sound, it was natural that each in turn had the power to convince me that there was no sound other than that of the old furnace with its heaving sighs, its faint whistles and rattles and subterranean quarrels; and if, stubborn woman as I am under duress or doubt, I persisted, begging them to listen, *Don't you hear it?—it sounds like a baby crying,* in turn in all innocence they assured me there was no sound resembling the one I was in terror of hearing. And as the days passed, and the weeks, and the baby's crying returned at odd and never predictable hours of the day and night, now weak and nearly inaudible, now unmistakable, now plaintive, now enraged, in their impatience they chided me out of hearing the very fibrillations of the air I heard, or laughed me out of their possibility, or dismissed the very premise—that there was or even could be a sound new and haunting and foreign to all our ears of a true distinction emanating from the walls, or the floorboards, or pushing through the ducts, vents, and water pipes, as profound in its own element as strands of hair whorled in the wrong direction, or a tremor of wavy glass in an otherwise clear pane, or italic print. They chided me for "hearing things," singly and in a chorus, and when my sons came home for their fond Sunday dinners they too took up the cry as if to beat me into a shamefaced submission: Mother, you must be hearing things!

So I'd date its origin in October of last year, nearly eleven months ago. When our furnace first came on. Which does not explain of course why the mysterious sound (whether mechanical or human) continued to be heard occasionally when the furnace was not in operation: why it *is* heard over and beyond the distracting noises of the furnace; why, in that stark silence when the thermostat shuts off the furnace, and our ears are assailed by a sudden absence of sound, the sound is likely to continue independent of all other sounds—the sound of the crying baby, I mean.

In the beginning, yes, I was so shaky in my own judgment, and so fearful of countryheaded madness, I tried to enlist others to hear what I heard and to substantiate my claims. Father of course, my daughters and my sons, for by instinct we are led to trust what's nearest, or what, in any case, blind touch guides us toward, but also, to my deeper shame, persons outside the family who thereafter carried tales of me about the country like infected individuals spewing contagion at every orifice . . . friends who dropped by to visit and chat, neighbors I may have summoned of my own volition, a cosmetics saleswoman who rang the doorbell, the monkeyish little man employed by the gas company who came one snowy day to repair my stove. And there were others. I would not want to think, how many others. Casting off my pride to ask as if I were hearing the crying baby for the first time, "Do you hear *that*?" or, cocking my head, guessing how the lenses of my glasses caught the light with a stern maternal reprimand, "What on earth *is* that?—it sounds like a crying baby."

Most times they simply frowned, hearing nothing; polite, puzzled, even regretful; though once or twice as if in compliance to my motherly will they seemed, yes, to hear . . . to hear something. But did they hear what I heard, did the very hairs on the nape of their necks stir as mine did? I could not believe it.

And then, that winter day, it was the man who came to repair the stove who cocked his head as I did, and screwed up his face with the effort of concentration, even as the eerie forlorn breathless heart-rending wail could scarcely fail to be heard, rising, as it seemingly did, from the very floor at our feet, "Yes ma'am I think I *do*. I think I do hear something. It follows me around, like, some kind of a sound," he said, giving his repair kit an exasperated shake, "—but I don't know what it *is*, ma'am, I never tried to put a name to it."

This unexpected reply so shocked and stymied me and seemed in a way to have put me in my place, I stood staring down at the little man—he shorter than I by two or three inches, and lighter by thirty pounds—and could think of no proper retort; even as, like water disappearing down a drain, a finite quantity of water down an infinite length of drain, the baby's crying began to subside, and a coarse sort of kitchen silence intervened. At last, fumbling, muddleheaded, I managed to stammer, "But the sound I mean is *here*, in my house, it is a sound to be heard only *here*," following the repair man to the door as if in appeal, and out onto the porch steps, "—I've thought, sometimes, it sounds almost like—a baby's crying." But the wizened little man merely nodded; repair kit under his arm and cloth cap snug on his head; and said, as if the words were a small prayer with which he had learned to comfort himself, "—I never tried to put a name to it."

I should not attempt to deny that, in the beginning, the mysterious sound filled me with a terrible uneasiness, intensifying at times to animal panic; for as the mother of the household, though my childbearing years are long past, I know myself responsible for all life herein, or all human life; and instinct urges me to offer help, yes even to offer suck, to any motherless or apparently abandoned or maltreated infant within my reach. Yet how, given the phantom elusiveness of the crying, *was* an infant within my reach?

The sound seemed to come from the walls much of the time but if I approached and pressed an ear against the plasterboard, it often happened that the sound teasingly retreated, or transformed itself into the rumble of mere plumbing. A telephone's sudden ringing might swallow up the crying and bear it away to nothingness. And there was the interference, on quieter days in particular, of heart- and pulse-beat, the shadowy roaring of the inner ear or the brain's labyrinthine passageways, into which it is a fearsome thing to inquire. Sometimes the sound seemed to be localized in the kitchen, sometimes in another room, upstairs or down, or in the basement, or in the attic, or in the garage adjoining the house; sometimes it began when I switched off the television set; and similarly with faucets, the vacuum cleaner, the washing machine. For a day or so my husband convinced me that it was the wind in the chimney, and on another day he convinced me that it was the wind in the television antenna, and, later, the wind in the telephone wires outside the house, but further investigation proved, to my distress and to his impatience, that, plausible as these explanations were, and, since plausible, seductive, they were simply not true. And indeed as it developed, as I quietly acquiesced, to the arguments of my family and relatives, of course the sound might have been traced to a neighbor's crying baby, or to a neighbor's television set or radio turned up unforgivably high, or to a sick, injured, penned-up or crazed animal in the neighborhood, or to birds, or to sirens, or to train whistles, or to diesel trucks, or to jet planes, or to sonic booms, or even to a malfunctioning of my own hearing, such sources *might* have explained away the baby's crying yet upon thorough investigation, to the annoyance of all, did not: for one by one they were considered.

My hearing, for instance. Of course Father hauled me downtown to the ear doctor who tested me with electrical beeps and whirrs and poked a tiny flashlight into my brain and for good measure, to boost his fee no doubt, ejaculated a syringe of warm throbbing water into both my ears to dislodge the wax, or a pretext of wax. But the unassailable fact was that my hearing was normal for a woman of my age (I am fifty-two years old) and general health. Weeks later, when I persisted in hearing what was there to be heard, and scarcely to be denied, Father hauled me a greater distance to a clinic where enormous humming machines scanned the interior of my skull but failed to detect a brain lesion, or a tumor, or any evidence of a stroke however minute. Anticipating the diagnosis of "schizophrenic"—for this perennial cliché pops effortlessly to even professional lips—I insisted upon the fact, for indeed it was a demonstrable truth, that the mysterious sound could be heard only in the house and only at certain wayward and unpredictable times; never did it sound in *my* head—"Of course I can tell the difference."

And with the passing of time I learned gradually to dissemble out of prudery and caution, assuring my family that, no, I no longer heard the baby's crying, or, if seemingly I heard it, I attributed it to something else, and deftly turned my attention elsewhere, to the impediments of my cooking for instance, or my housewifery, as infinite in its systems as any galaxy of household pipes or electrical wiring bearing away effluvia or erasing along through conductors what is called, simply, "power"— for how otherwise were our lives together to be borne?

Frowning worriedly at me my daughters would sometimes ask was I certain or was I telling them, and Father, only what I believed they wanted to hear, if indeed they *did* want it, for all human motives are ambiguous, and I would reply, curtly, with a derisive little laugh, yes I was certain, yes of course—"For why should *I* lie"?—even as, perhaps, at that very moment, even as I regarded the young women with a face of wounded innocence, the thin forlorn wail of unspeakable heartbreak penetrated the wall at my back, or the ceiling above my head, or the floorboards upon which, so seemingly stolid, and with dominion, my slippered feet rested. For by this time my judgment had shifted; my gravity's center had shifted; there was no algorithm to be shared with the "flesh of my flesh, blood of my blood" from whom I knew myself estranged.

And there was a spell of weeks when, resistant to my apparent fate, I quickly inserted plugs of soft pink warmly malleable wax into my ears when I began to hear the baby's crying, that kept all household sounds at bay but picked up, on some principle of physics far beyond my ken, rhythmic buzzings and hummings and vibrations as of the ether itself, that void of sheer number. And in truth, so armed, or armored, I could not hear the baby's crying . . . and went about my round of household tasks and sipped my afternoon coffee in the delirium of a willed and unnatural silence . . . until, at last, unable to bear it any long, with the helpless violence of the pelvic muscles springing to orgasm, I tore the obscene little clots of wax out of my ears and confronted what it was, the baby's continued crying or, more profound yet, the nullification of that sound, I had tried in my vanity to deny.

Why some are chosen to bear witness while others pass their days in deaf contentedness is, too, beyond my ken, but if I know myself chosen why then I acknowledge my chosenness, and will try to be equal to the task.

Noting the variables of the baby's crying while scrubbing the linoleum-laid floors, polishing the furniture which gleams from the most recent polishing, vacuuming the carpets worn thin and frayed and decent from countless vacuumings, scouring the sinks, and the tubs, and the toilets, removing, with a practiced sweep and twirl of the mop, the gauzy stalactites of cobweb in the corners of the ceiling, washing walls, windows, mirrors in which there floats a face no longer young but fired with the energies of youth, a stubborn grip to the jaws, heavy brows and bone at the brow, bone at the wide bridge of the nose, the steely unflinching light in the eyes, all the while *noting the variables* for instance the high thin wire-like wails that might well be confused by cruder ears, with the mere wind, or winds; and the thicker cries, or murmurings; and a hoarse sound as of gasping for air; and sounds of sheer tremulous emotion—whether fury, hurt, terror, even joy—with the power to stab any mother, perhaps any woman, starkly in the womb, in the pit of the womb, ah! have pity! the mere hearing of it! as if the umbilical cord that binds us all one and another to each has yet to be cut.

The crying is most distinct on days when I am alone in the house, and when the sky is overcast, like a low ceiling; when my family is not only absent but not likely to return for hours; when the telephone or doorbell has not rung for hours; though my capacity for hearing it, my desire alternating with my dread, has no relationship to the sound that I can determine . . . like God's grace conferred upon the heads of the blessed, answering to no human summons, never to any demand. As the baby's crying begins, dissonant, terrifying, of a beauty too austere to be named, my cheeks too bell outward with unvoiced screams and my eyes release a harsh salt mist, Why do you haunt me? Are you the infant of my house?—of the earth beneath the house? *Am I* your mother? *Is* this your womb?—carried now limp and useless as a deflated balloon squeezed inside an aging woman's puffed belly?

And why?

And how long?

But the baby's crying merely continues. Spinning and coiling about my dazed head. And if, in mute appeal, I raise my hand, the sound intensifies, unless indeed it abruptly diminishes, as the sound of a weak-tubed radio intensifies and diminishes when you pass your hand over it. For there is, and can be, no reply; no signal from *that* side to *this*.

Nonetheless! in the space of a brisk no-nonsense housekeeping of the kind I have been doing, and handily, for thirty-odd years, I pass from anticipation to fear to resignation to impatience to panic to a faint-headedness of desire generated, but not contained, by my loins; I pass from sober-lipped silence and eyes on stalks aching to pop from their sockets to the flush-cheeked giddiness of young motherhood, the tipsiness of milk-heavy breasts, and I dare to sing, at last, to sing, to break into song as loud as my lungs and throat will bear, the ancient lullabies once sung to my own babies, how many years ago—

Hush-a-bye little baby!
Hush-a-bye little baby!

—and again, and yet again—

Hush-a-bye little baby!
Hush-a-bye little baby!

until at last the crying fades.

Father and the others, my daughters, my man-grown sons, yes and other busybody kin too, murmur together these days, perhaps it has been these months, worriedly, fearfully, and it's of me—Mother—they murmur, such offensive words as *hearing things, change of life, not herself,* such futile questions as *why?* and I scorn to defend myself against them for the baby's crying is not for their ears seemingly, it is not for them to bear witness to the secret sorrow of the world, and, as I've said, out of prudery and caution, and selfishness too, I have long denied the sound to them, professing innocence, professing ignorance, at times frank annoyance, countering with questions put to them: do *they* hear it now? has it passed from *me* to *them*?

But they spy on me. Shameless persecutors, though flesh of my flesh and blood of my blood, they steal silently into the house to surprise me in the midst of my house-cleaning and singing . . . my lullabies . . . steal upon me in a long droopy-lidded kitchen reverie, or one of those reveries of the cellar steps, always twilight there, and gravity seemingly in abeyance, equidistant between the foot and the head of the old wooden stairs. "Mother, what are you doing? Mother, is something wrong?"—those frightened half-accusatory voices I scorn to answer yet of motherly obligation, though no longer love, must.

"'Wrong'?—what is 'wrong'?—why do you use that word, 'wrong'?"

"But, Mother, you seem so—"

"'Seem'—?"

"—seem so strange—"

"'Strange'? But why? And how? In terms of who? In terms of *you*?"

And whichever one of them it is has dared approach me, one of my daughters, one of my staring sons, grim-faced Father himself, one or another female relative bearing my own features, I banish them: beat them back.

Laughing contemptuously, "Must I be 'normal,' then?—in terms of *you*?"

For my old humor has returned, a scouring pad sort of humor, good for harsh scrubbings, no sentiment and no tears. And I stand foursquare on my ground, beneath my roof, protective of the secret life beneath my roof, all that is newly entrusted to me. All that befits my coarse graying curls, the single hairs that grow stiff and mischievous from my chin, the big-boned skeleton that bears me erect each day, the fleshy bulk of bosom, belly, hips, haunches, and my mica-gleaming eyes.

"Mother," they insist, "we want only what is best for you," they insist, and "Who is the judge of that?" I reply, standing my ground. For I swear I will have to be axed down, and hauled pulpy from the house, before I surrender secrets to enemies or to family alike.

Now it is true, as I have been too preoccupied to note, that, thirty years ago in this house (tall, shingled, steep-roofed, this sparely renovated old farmhouse has been sufficient to bear the freight of my husband's and my issue, as Midwestern as the cornfields and the dull little town adjoining) my first pregnancy ended in what's called "miscarriage"—fancy word for the surprise of bloody clotted tissue. That it was my first pregnancy I could not have confidently foreseen, the first of so many, thus I suppose came tears, and hurt, and a bit of rage, for the young woman that was then was more emotional than the one that is now. But the miscarriage came a mere six weeks into the term and was not truly life, and unnamed, though for a decent while mourned, more as a malady of flesh than a loss of life, still less *identified* life, but I am not a sentimental woman nor do I come from sentimental stock and for the long busy remainder of my motherhood I gave no thought to that loss, I swear—being, should you not know by now, hardly one of your whiney rheumy meek-Christian females, all faints and falls, weak ankles and weak head, a nagger, a snuffler, a weeper-into-Kleenex, quick to bleed and slow to heal, I am another kind of woman altogether, old American stock, standing five feet ten in my stocking feet, carrying my pride in my posture and will I cringe and cower before my own children, or my pot-bellied husband, or old ranting God Himself on His high throne? I will *not*.

So it is a foolish business, and futile, seeing connections where there are none, or may in fact be many, too many for the mind's eye, explaining the fact of Y in terms of X, so tidily, with so parsimonious a spirit, and never Y in terms of Z to follow; and if you had not X but did have Y (and all that precedes Y—yes and shading off into infinity) would you have deduced X from it? Certainly not. With certainty, *not*. Thus with what ignorance compounded by insolence they tried to explain the ghostly music of our household (or is it perhaps in its essence "my" household) in terms of a young woman's miscarriage of thirty years ago—that discharge of mere mute tissue-dappled blood as much embarrassment as grief, and as much simple physical discomfort as either, soaked up in sanitary rags and wrapped in newspaper, bundled off with the trash. For had I remained childless into this, my fifty-third year, would they not say, making their clucking pitying wet noises, that *that* was the explanation?

But the mean grubby things they say, they say, and so long as such things are outside my hearing I do not hear, for I have my secret knowledge, a voiceless cry intimate as the tiny bones of my inner ear or my sharp eye in its socket, regarding them with pity on *my* side, preparing their meals as I have always done, overseeing the household laid out so properly, in order, beneath the Midwestern sky, washing walls, scouring, in season ridding the eaves of hornets' nests and what all else growing like mad embroidery above our heads, amused, bemused, singing the baby to sleep when there is no danger of being overheard, no spies on the premises, all's *mine*.

And when my eldest daughter-in-law, Elsie she's called, my eldest son's wife, bland as a white-meated fish and as slyly fitted out with tiny bones, came in the summer with her infant, my grandson, to nurse him in the kitchen, all the while chatting happily with me, inveigling me to coo and grin and kiss and laugh flush-cheeked as silly grandmothers do, my son, but scarcely, now, *my* son, looking foolishly on, I perceived the stratagem behind it, that the living baby's noises, including, as his diaper was changed, a furious fit of wailing, would erase forever the noises of the other, the invisible baby—I saw, and took in stride, making no comment, knowing what I know.

And overhearing when at last they left, baby adrowse on Elsie's plump shoulder, such murmurings as *There isn't a thing wrong with your mother, Fritz!* and *She doesn't seem at all different to me—how is she different?* and when they were gone I tore open the collar of my dress, and laughed.

And then, in worry and in order, I walked quickly through the rooms of the house, panting up the stairs into the attic, huffing down the stairs into the cellar, brooding that, yes, my infant grandson with his squawling lusty lungs might have banished the other . . . and how pungent the odor of baby shit, which you do well not to forget . . . but early next morning the crying returned, faintly at first, as if teasingly, in the kitchen, then by degrees shifting to the parlor, then to the wallpapered wall be-hind the stairs. For I was alone in the house and the anguished thrumming in the old plasterboard like the beating of invisible wings was not unwelcome. "Who are you?" I cried. "What do you want of me, why have you done this to me?"—but content there would be no answer, now or any morning of my life, for the remainder of my life, and if I descended to the cellar and took up the sledge hammer in my trembling hands, better yet Father's old pick-ax, and if I possessed a demon's power to smash through the very foundation of the house, every haunted fiber and nail, and bring its bulk clattering on my head, there would be no answer, never a whisper of reply. Happiness is this side of oblivion only.

—Winter 1989

Grace Paley

Anxiety

The young fathers are waiting outside the school. What curly heads! Such graceful brown mustaches. They're sitting on their haunches eating pizza and exchanging information. They're waiting for the 3:00 P.M. bell. It's springtime, the season of first looking out the window. I have a window box of greenhouse marigolds. The young fathers can be seen through the ferny leaves.

The bell rings. The children fall out of school tumbling through the open door. One of the fathers sees his child. A small girl. Is she Chinese? A little. Up u u p, he says and hoists her to his shoulders. U u up says the second father and hoists his little boy. The little boy sits on top of his father's head for a couple of seconds before sliding to his shoulders. Very funny, says the father.

They start off down the street, right under and past my window. The two children are still laughing. They try to whisper a secret. The fathers haven't finished their conversation. The frailer father is a little uncomfortable; his little girls wiggles too much.

Stop it this minute, he says.

Oink, oink, says the little girl.

What'd you say?

Oink, oink, she says.

The young father says what! three times. Then he seizes the child, raises her high above his head and sets her hard on her feet.

What'd I do so bad, she says, rubbing her ankle.

Just hold my hand, screams the frail and angry father.

I lean far out the window. Stop! Stop! I cry.

The young father turns, shading his eyes, but sees. What? he says. His friend says, Hey? Who's that? He probably thinks I'm a family friend, a teacher maybe.

Who're you? he says.

I move the pots of marigold aside. Then I'm able to lean on my elbow way out into unshadowed visibility. Once not too long ago the tenements were speckled with women like me in every third window up to the fifth story calling the children from play to receive orders and instruction. This memory enables me to say strictly, Young man I am an older person who feels free because of that to ask questions and give advice.

Oh? he says, laughs with a little embarrassment, says to his friend, Shoot if you will that old gray head. But he's joking I know, because he has established himself, legs apart, hands behind his back, his neck arched to see and hear me out. How old are you, I call. About thirty or so?

Thirty-three.

First I want to say you're about a generation ahead of your father in your attitude and behavior towards your child.

Really? Well? Anything else Ma'am.

Son, I said, leaning another two, three dangerous inches toward him. Son, I must tell you that mad men intend to destroy this beautifully made planet. That the imminent murder of our children by these men has got to become a terror and a sorrow to you and starting now it had better interfere with any daily pleasure.

I waited a minute but he continued to look up. So, I said, I can tell by your general appearance and loping walk that you agree with me.

I do, he said, winking at his friend, but turning a serious face to mine, he said again, Yes, yes, I do.

Well, then, why did you become so angry at that little girl whose future is like a film which suddenly cuts to white, Why did you nearly slam this little doomed person to the ground in your uncontrollable anger.

Let's not go too far, said the young father. We could get depressed. She WAS jumping around on my poor back and hollering Oink, oink.

When were you angriest—when she wiggled and jumped or when she said oink?

He scratched his wonderful head of dark well-cut hair. I guess when she said oink.

Have you ever said oink oink. Think carefully. Years ago perhaps?

No. Well maybe. Maybe.

Whom did you refer to in this way?

He laughed. He called to his friend, Hey Ken, this old person's got something. The cops. In a demonstration. Oink, oink, he said, remembering, laughing.

The little girl smiled and said Oink oink.

Shut up, he said.

What do you deduce from this?

That I was angry at Rosie because she was dealing with me as though I was a figure of authority and it's not my thing, never has been, never will be.

I could see his happiness, his nice grin as he remembered this.

So, I continued, since those children are such lovely examples of what may well be the last generation of humankind, why don't you start all over again, right from the school door as though none of this had ever happened.

Thank you, said the young father. Thank you. It would be nice to be a horse, he said, grabbing little Rosie's hand. Come on Rosie let's go. I don't have all day.

U up says the first father U up says the second.

Giddap shout the children and the fathers yell Neigh Neigh as horses do. The children kick their fathers' horsechests screaming giddap giddap and they gallop wildly westward.

I lean way out to cry once more, Be Careful! Stop! But they've gone to far. Oh anyone would love to be a fierce fast horse carrying a beloved beautiful rider, but they are galloping toward one of the most dangerous street corners in the world. And they may live beyond that trisection across other dangerous avenues.

So I must shut the window after patting the April cooled marigolds with their deep smell of summer. Then I sit in the nice light and wonder how to make sure that they gallop safely home through the airy scary dreams of scientists and the bulky dreams of automakers. I wish I could see just how they sit down at their kitchen tables for a healthy snack (orange juice or milk and cookies) before going out into the new spring afternoon to play.

—Summer 1983

W. D. Wetherell

Nickel a Throw

These are the things Gooden sees from his perch eight feet above the dunking tub at the Dixford Congregational Church's charity bazaar.

The sun touching the ridge on the river's western shore. Orange, underlining of black.

The river itself. A canoe. A boy in a canoe lighting sparklers.

A ferris wheel turning slowly clockwise, dipping into the people massed at its base.

Strings of light. Lights as aural as sounds. Red snap, yellow crackle, blue pop.

Refreshment stands. A tent on the town common. Lobsters held by the belly. Faces disappearing into wads of cotton candy, emerging pink.

Individuals. A girl climbing a slanting rope ladder over an inflated cushion. A baby squatting behind a dusty-looking Golden Retriever, pulling out tufts of the dog's hair. The town band badly tuned. Professorial-looking types from the college, in cardigans, in July. Summer campers down from the mountain, roped together. Stuffed E.T.s dragged by the ears. Farmers, bald. Farmers' wives, shy-looking, toting bags. Ray Stanton in a straw hat manning the goldfish booth. Gooden's wife Angela dispensing change behind the baked goods, smiling with a radiance that pleases and puzzles him at the same time. Angela in the blue gingham dress she had worn on their first date seventeen years ago, as beautiful and desirable as she had been then.

A Frisbee appearing from nowhere. Hovering. Observing. Sailing away.

Space. Starlight. Shadows. And then much closer, in the narrow chute left between the tub and the booth's entrance, a teenager with purple streaks in his hair cocking back his arm to hurl a tennis ball at the saucer-sized target beneath Gooden's stool.

"Missed," Gooden says timidly, in a voice hardly above a whisper.

The boy doesn't pay for another ball. Gooden sees how long the lines are at the other booths, sees how short it is for his, remembers Stanton's advice about banter.

"You throw like a girl," he says, a bit louder.

The boy struts away. Gooden sees the razor blades hanging from his ears, sees the yellow hair mixed in with the purple, hears the music from his huge transistor, tries to remember the right name for it.

"Runts!" he yells, too late. The boy is gone.

Five minutes go by before another customer arrives. Gooden sits on the stool with his head in his hands like Quasimodo above the gargoyles, worried. He sees Angela slicing bread. The sight of her—the wanting to please her—shoots through him in a surge that almost makes him jump into the tub from joy.

A ball whizzes by his head. Down below, a foul-looking man with a size eighteen neck winds up again.

"Shit," he hisses, as the ball curves wide.

He slaps down a nickel, picks up another ball. His throwing is stiff and brutal. Ball mashed between fingers, brought up like a sledge hammer, punched more than thrown.

"Missed!" Gooden yells.

The man's friends begin to ride him. Tubercular-looking with slicked-back hair, "Elvis Lives" buttons, Budweisers stuck in their pants like guns.

"Cretins!" Gooden yells, in a high-pitched voice so different from his usual modulation that it startles even him.

He senses their hostility but for once in his life it doesn't frighten him. Hostility brings in the nickels. Hostility makes the booth a success, enriches the bazaar, supports charities, feeds babies, does good.

"What's the matter, moron? Be a sport and try again."

His loafers. His wire-rimmed glasses and neat sports coat. His superior height there on the stool. Gooden can tell each of these things infuriates the man, but his words anger him not, and the balls fly at him with diminished force. Gooden searches the beefy face for clues.

"Drunkard!" he shouts, slapping the stool's side to gain his attention. "Inebriate!"

He hurls all the insults he can think of, as if they are balls he is firing back at him, aiming for the spot in him that is his trigger. Redneck, hick, bum. But none of them connect, and the man is shaking his head with a laugh, and proudly patting his stomach, and turning away with his friends to the next booth.

The mashed ball. The axe-like chop of the arm. The violent, satisfied grunt as he let it go. Gooden remembers these things and then suddenly he has it, and it is as clear and bright and certain as the lights on the ferris wheel's base.

"Wife beater!" he screams.

The man stops. The man wheels slowly around and comes back to the booth, minus his friends. He takes a nickel out of his pocket, places it on the felt matting beside the bucket of balls. He's a long time in selecting one, but when he does, he closes and re-closes his hand over it, throttling its air. He advances to the line chalked in the grass twenty feet from the tub. He stares toward the target with a grimness and concentration that are totally different from the casual malice he had shown before. In the spotlight, in the tunnel of visibility left between them, it is he and Gooden alone.

"You beat her with your hands," Gooden says softly, almost cooing. "You beat her because it makes you feel good. It makes you feel like a man. You do it until she begs you to stop, and when she begs, you slap her again."

The man brings his hand up to his eyes as if the light is blinding him, but then Gooden realizes it isn't the light, but that he is throwing the ball—that the fuzzy, moon-sized object advancing toward him is the tennis ball released from his hand. "Missed!" he says to himself, with a rush of exhilaration, but the ball strikes the center of the target, tripping the spring that holds him suspended, and the moment he realizes this, he is on the way down.

"I must prepare myself for this," he thinks, but before he decides how, he is at the bottom of the tub in a cloud of bubbles that pop apart on his nose. There is no shock involved. The water feels cool, but yielding. The geyser of spray shooting up from the tub, the man's triumphant yell—he is aware of neither. The tub is soundless. Above him, the surface is dappled with ever-changing shapes and colors, like a kaleidoscope. As he shimmies toward it, the water rides his shirt up his chest with the same gentle, teasing tug Angela would use in slipping off his clothes.

When he emerges gasping at the surface there is a crowd waiting on line for balls. Holding his fist above his head like a victorious prizefighter, Gooden climbs the ladder to his stool.

He goes back to the things he has sensed before, checking his emotions the way another man would check his bones. His booth's line as long as the other lines: envy gone. Angela above a tray of cupcakes: love intact. The view: loftier now, embracing not only the ferris wheel and the ring of lights and the river, but the valley in which the river flowed, the dark mass of hill on either side, the frame in which the fair is mounted.

Damp, his clothes wrapped on him like wet papier-mache, he turns his attention to the balls which fly in more rapid procession past his head.

Teenagers mostly. Petty thieves, masturbators, nickelless liars—he doesn't waste his time on these. It's the next one on line that interests him. A tall, supercilious man with a complexion like cheap corduroy.

"Wimp!" Gooden yells, watching his reaction.

With the man is a girl half his age who strokes the back of his blazer as he throws. He throws studiously, juggling the ball in his hand as if weighing it, squinting, flipping it with a half-hearted gesture that seems to indicate he wants it back.

"Professor!" Gooden shouts.

Almost too easy. The man takes a step forward and smiles, as if he has been called upon to bow.

"Humanist!"

A touch of uncertainty in the smile.

"Sophist!"

A frown. The professor looks around to see if anyone can hear. Bored, the girl tries to pull him away, but he shrugs her off, takes a nickel out of his pocket—takes out three. He cradles the balls in the crook of his arm, like snowballs.

"You sit there in class mumbling inanities," Gooden says as the professor winds up. "You serve up beauty and truth on a tray to morons who will never have any use for either. You prepare dolts to be assistant managers at MacDonalds, and in the depths of your soul you know you're as banal as they are."

Until now, the professor has managed to keep an aloof, mildly amused look on his face. "Second-rater!" Gooden yells, and with that the nap of the corduroy becomes tighter; he grabs the ball as violently as the wife beater and throws it with all his might toward the stool.

"You're superfluous," Gooden whispers. "A relic. A traitor to the truth."

Gooden keeps talking as the ball sails closer, speaking more to it than to the professor, as if his words are a guidance system that automatically corrects variations in its flight. Time-server, dilettante, bore. The words find the ball and draw it with a cymbal-like concussion against the target's metal plate.

A bellywop this time. A gusher of spray breaking apart at its apogee, drenching the people at the next booth. The pain slaps him over in a tight somersault; his head brushes the wooden side of the tub on his way down. He notices things he missed the first time in. How the tub is greasy with vegetation, as if the water hadn't been changed since last year's fair. How dark and oil-like the water is. How by curling his legs under him he can not only cushion his landing against the bottom, but use it as a springboard to shoot back to the surface, emerging as straight and spectacularly as a submarine-launched missile.

The crowd screams with delight.

"Thank you," Gooden yells, mounting the ladder. "Thank you very much!"

A man in his thirties dressed in jeans and a red-checkered shirt separates himself from the mass of bodies waiting on line. One sleeve is empty, and there are lines on his face that belie the youthfulness of his smile. Gooden has seen him around town working at a variety of jobs, all of them menial. He reaches for a name—Bob, Mike, something simple. Whatever it is, he throws with endearing formality. Sideways, peeking over his stub of a shoulder like a pitcher checking the runner on first.

Gooden thinks: "No, not this one." But the power he feels is like a new sense and he feels compelled to test it the way a person without touch, regaining it, would touch everything, even if it means burns.

"Drunk driver," Gooden says, probing. "You were drunk, you killed a kid, and your missing arm can't make up for the guilt I see on your face."

The young man looks at him uncomprehendingly—he stops in mid-stride, balking. Gooden tries again.

"Dealer in drugs. Pothead. Junkie."

Gooden tries to look harder, not at the man himself, but the larger frame surrounding the man, the frame he had only become conscious of when he first mounted the stool. He sees the man and the other innocent, foolish, armless men his age of which he is representative, and then he has it, and it comes out sadly and reluctantly, nothing personal, with no wish to blame only him.

"Nam," he says simply. "Nam."

Bob or Mike or Bill takes out a dollar, and with one hand scoops up balls from the table on which they are arranged. He no longer throws like Whitey Ford. He lobs them overhand like grenades, as reluctantly as Gooden says the word, but with the same kind of compulsion.

The two of them in spotlight. Balls in a rainbow arc. Closer, closer. . . .

"Nam!" Gooden yells, and the ball embeds itself in the target, ejecting him into the air. Feet kicking, arms flailing, mouth open, he falls against the metal rim of the tub and backflips over, his arm scratching open on a nail someone has forgotten to remove from the side. As he floats to the surface, a watery spiral of blood climbs with him. He fights down a panicky urge to inhale.

It takes longer to mount the ladder. Climbing, he thinks of Stanton asking him to volunteer.

Stanton (smiling): "It's a funny job."

Gooden (curious): "Funny how?"

Stanton (mysterious): "It changes a man being up there."

Gooden (worried): "Changes how?"

Stanton (laughing): "You'll see."

He can pick Stanton out now, grounded among the goldfish and the ping-pong balls, twirling a cane. Gooden wants to call out to him, tell him that he is right. He does feel changed, feels like he does when he's finished his monthly bottle of wine and the trivialities that beset him have fled. The stool seems much higher than before, as if there is a handle on its bottom and someone is cranking him up. Not only does he see the frame of mountains ringing the fair, but the plains forming the inverted wall on which the frame hangs, plains sparkled with lights and mysterious undulations.

A ball heads toward his face. He bats it away with a contemptuous, paw-like gesture—a boy brushing aside flies.

Higher. The varicolored lights of the midway become streamers radiating out of the Maypole on top of which he sits. He shivers, hugs himself in the thrill of it. It's much harder now to pick out faces at the other booths, and the only person besides Stanton he can identify for sure is Angela, looking up at him from the baked goods, her expression shorn of everything except question. Seeing her, he has the urge to show off—he quickly estimates his chances of doing a handstand on the stool—and he is about to call out to her to watch when he makes the mistake of looking down.

The tub is a thimble. A shot glass. A target through a bomb-sight. He stares at it in a kind of vertigo—he has to grab the stool with both hands to keep from falling off.

"Steady, Gooden," he says, closing his eyes.

Below him, a mass of swirling shapes.

"Fornicators!" Gooden shouts, deepening his voice like a king calling to his subjects from a throne. "Vainglorious egotists!"

A nickel a throw. Spake Rollins, president of Dixford's hospital, clothed in flannel as soft and fine as a girl's hair. Smiler, shaker of hands, a born politician throwing out the first pitch.

"You feed on other people's suffering," Gooden shouts. "You have taken pain and turned it into a raw material to enrich a handful of doctors and administrators, doing it so smoothly and secretly that people call you humanitarians and you bask in that glow."

The ball striking home, Gooden instantaneously dumped, spreading his arms out like a sky-diver, steering himself for the thimble. . . .

A nickel a throw. Sylvia Thorpe, architect, her current lover dropping balls into her hand as delicately as grapes.

"Builder of malls!" Gooden shouts, like a town crier warning of plague. "Designer of prisons, destroyer of grace!"

The head-first entry. The concussion on his face; the water tumbling him over and over, drowning him, not permitting him to drown. . . .

Nickel a throw. Helmut Konner, owner of the mill, Gooden's boss. Taut, handsome, pulling his wife through the obsequious faces waiting on lines as if she is a prize he has won at an earlier booth. On his head, every hair stays obediently in place; on his face, each wrinkle lies dormant. He picks up the ball like a belonging—an expensive paperweight, precious china, a deed.

"Konner!" Gooden yells, as if the name is accusation enough. "Poisoner of the river, poisoner of the air! You fired Henry Waite because he suggested putting in pollution controls on stack number five. You bribed the state inspector so he wouldn't report what comes out of that discharge pipe near the elementary school. You lay off the mill hands after nineteen weeks so they'll never be eligible for unemployment and call it their 'vacation'—give them the minimum wage and moan about how they're cheating you. You make your furniture out of the cheapest wood and charge the highest prices, your ethics being the only thing shoddier than your product."

On the bottom now, gathering his legs under him for the thrust back to the surface. But the power of his legs is gone, the water presses the buoyancy out of him like a piston, and he begins to gag. Urine! he wants to shout. Sewage! Filth! He sees bits of fabric stuck on the tub's sides, senses other people who have been dunked in previous fairs, tries to summon strength from them as he endures the slow, exhausting rise to the top.

"Thank you." he yells weakly, draping himself on the ladder. "Thank you very much."

He climbs wearily back to his stool. The line has grown since Konner. It stretches back beyond the goldfish booth, past the canning exhibit, past the ferris wheel, past the church, up Main Street toward the interstate highway where it forms a black strip on the lighter gray. Seeing it, a chill clutches at Gooden's middle, and he almost climbs down voluntarily from his perch. Just in time he spots Angela, leaving her baked goods, edging her way towards him through the crowd.

His dizziness is worse. The long hours alone beneath the sun when no one came, the booth's sudden popularity, the series of falls—it's adding up. Down below people are fanning themselves with their programs, but the stool is so high that he's exposed to the buffets of a different air stream. Smells blow past. Familiar, carnival smells first: dough being fried, maple syrup, cheap perfume. They act as a stimulant to fainter, more distant smells: the stone-hard smell of—what? Appalachia? The gagging sweet smell of refineries around Pittsburgh; the smothered smell of mashed and cooking wheat further west. Bits of jetsam float by. A stalk of corn from—where? Iowa? It could be Iowa. It could be orange blossoms from California, sticky pine needles from the Pacific Northwest. They deposit themselves on his wet shirt as if it is a fly tape attracting the detritus of the entire continent—the soot and the ashes and the flowers.

He shivers so feverishly that his seeing becomes caught up with it, too, and his vision blurs and jumps frames and brings in not only the here and now, but the past as well. There is a stir in the line, and to the head steps his father, not as he had been when he had died, but as he would be now, nearly a hundred, shrunken and lame.

He examines the balls like they are eggs, holding them to the light, shaking them inquisitively by his ear. His father who from the day Gooden was born never stopped worrying that his boy might turn out to be smarter than he was and leave him behind. He rolls his sleeves up, brings his thick farmer's arms above his head so Gooden can see the knots and scars.

"This is truth," Gooden says, talking for him. "The truth is in my fingers and hands, the misery in my back, the stiffness in my knees. Truth is suffering and pain."

"Lies!" Gooden shouts, but his father has selected a ball now, and is throwing it at the target with surprising force. It sails wide, but another person joins him at the head of the line, and it is his mother, grown old now, too, in the soft gray dress they had buried her in fourteen years before. His mother who dreamed large dreams for him, and—making him share them—condemned him to failure. She picks up a ball, smiles her sweetest smile, closes her eyes.

"Truth is soft," Gooden says, reading her thoughts. "Things will get better. What will be will be. Everything works out for the best. Truth is something prettied up, a spoiled daughter dressed in fine clothes."

"Truth is neither hard nor soft!" Gooden shouts. "Truth is the trajectory between hearts! Truth is this stool, this target, this tub."

They shake their heads in the regretful, indulgent way of loving parents. His father puts his arms around his mother, guides her in the proper motion for throwing the ball, and Gooden is so busy trying to form the mingled exhilaration and despair he feels into words that he doesn't see that the ball is making directly for the target.

"Truth is love!" he wants to shout, but he is already plummeting stone-like into the tub. He knows what to expect now—the core-piercing coldness, the turgidness, the stench—but even so, it is worse than before, and he claws his way in panic back to the top.

The ladder sways. His feet and hands tremble. He fights down the urge to bite the rung.

His mother and father are still there, but before he can call out to them that he is okay, they are pushed away by frowning, officious-looking women in blue pants. After a pause, a squarish man in a general's uniform steps forward. Gooden is still wondering what a general could be doing in Dixford, when he begins to throw balls rapid-fire, not just at the target, but everywhere, forcing everyone to duck. A second later he is joined by a man Gooden recognizes as president of one of the television networks—a bald, folksy man he's seen in commercials promoting the shows that will appear in the fall. He throws balls with as much gusto as the general, turning to say something to a functionary at his shoulder with a pad, the functionary nodding, laughing, as if they have stumbled upon a new game show that promises to be a hit.

Their balls come closer and closer to the target—the general's are illuminated by neon into tracers—when they both suddenly stop and stand respectfully aside, making way for President Reagan in a cardigan sweater and white bucks. He looks at the ball, looks at the crowd, points to himself, shrugs a question mark, laughs at their applause, picks the ball up, kisses it, poses, kisses it again, cocks it back over his ear like a football, poses, kisses it one last time, lets it go. As he follows through, his lips, visible only to Gooden, form the words "Screw you."

"Old man!" Gooden yells hoarsely. "Old man, old man, old man!"

There is no glory left in it anymore. If he manages to climb out of the tub a final time and mount the ladder, it is only from a kind of half-demented persistence so hopeless and irrational that it mocks itself. He just barely makes it back to the stool, but when he does, he stands on the seat and spreads his arms apart like someone preparing to swan dive. Miraculously, his shivering stops. He stares down at the crowd waiting to throw at him with something approaching calm.

Angela steps to the head of the line, the breeze teasing back the curls off her forehead, the light showing off her figure. Gooden waves to her, points to the nickels piled on the felt matting, indicates the crowd. He can't be sure, but she seems impressed. In the dark, in the flickering yellow beams, it could be admiration that is caught on her face. There is something definitely new there—not new, but something he hasn't seen in years. A radiance, a concentration and dreaminess combined, the look of a woman examining herself in a mirror and thinking of someone else at the same time. I love, I am loved, it seems to say. He waits for her to lift her eyes to the stool so he can acknowledge her love and reflect it back, but she just stands there, and when he calls to her, she drops her eyes and holds them on the ground.

Gooden tries to force his vision away from her, but she stands in the beam where his compulsion must have her.

"Your love is not for me," he says softly, without malice. "I am an embarrassment to you, a spectacle. Those curls, that dress. Ornaments for a lover I don't know."

He teeters, and for a moment it seems that he will fall off the stool of his own volition. Catching himself, he stands erect on the stool again and leans his head back as far as it will go, a raven screaming to the sky.

"Cheater!" he yells, joyfully.

Her eyes meet his. He waits to see if she will pay for a ball, then sees one in her hand, realizes that she had already taken one before stepping out of line. She brings it over her head with the graceful, feminine gesture she would use in the shower, stretching up on tiptoes as he soaped her back. Turning towards him, she lets it go, as delicately and wistfully as a girl boosting a butterfly back into flight.

Gooden sees the ball leave her hand, sees her follow-through as a lingering wave, then the ball hides her face and comes toward him in slow motion.

One part of him falls fast. The other half—the half that still sits on the stool, watching the clown in him fall—drops slower, giving him time to see himself in all his shame: the fattest man in Dixford splashing into a tub of water as his neighbors cheer.

He hits bottom and starts toward the surface, but just as his head begins to break free, a hand comes down on it and forces him back under. He wiggles, tries to slip away and emerge more to the side, but another hand reaches in and holds him there, then another, then a third. In the blurred refraction of the lights he can see the wife beater and the professor and Sylvia Thorpe and Mr. Konner and then Angela, too, looking down at him with the stern, grotesque expressions of spectators at an aquarium, their arms the spokes of a wheel at the hub of which is his skull.

Finished, he thinks calmly. He closes his eyes and waits for the darkness to take him, but a moment before it does, the pressure on his head suddenly relaxes and he is permitted to bob belly-up to the top. Alive, gasping, whimpering, warned.

—Fall 1983

Jorge Luis Borges

Things that Might Have Been

I think of the things that might have been and were not.
The treatise on Saxon mythology that Bede did not write.
The unimaginable work that Dante glimpsed fleetingly
when the last verse of the Commedia was corrected.
History without the afternoon of the Cross and the afternoon of the hemlock.

History without the face of Helen.
Man without the eyes which have shown the moon to us.
In the three labored days of Gettysburg, the victory of the South.
The love we do not share.
The vast empire which the Vikings did not wish to found.
The world without the wheel or without the rose.
The judgment of John Donne on Shakespeare.
The other horn of the unicorn.
The fabled bird of Ireland, in two places at once.
The son I did not have.

Translated from the Spanish by Alastair Reid

—Summer 1979

Lucie Brock-Broido

Elective Mutes

Nobody suffers the way I do. Not with a sister. . . . But this sister of mine, a dark shadow robbing me of sunlight, is my one and only torment.
                                                        —June Gibbons

TUESDAY AFTERNOON, BROADMOOR

I.

In summertime, when we were little, I remember we
walking with synchronized steps, a four-armed girl,
we've got everything
the same. We were eleven, a shadow & a shadow
of her shadow. I am born
first & I teach my sister to be quiet.
Here's the secret:
One day we will burn buildings together.
One day we will set fire to great things.
It sends shudders down my spine.
In the heat of swing park, we will take boys
down & mingle with them in the brushes.
In a basket, we will float down rivers, Venus
rising infrared, you've no idea
what it's like to have this other
half. We floating like hot house
fuchsia, two Chinese lanterns
through the water edge, a bulrush, shooting
stars. I will teach you to be perfect, more
quiet. I will teach you to be hard high self
mutilating. We will talk patois, speeded
up 78 on the record player, so no one else
can understand. We do, we know
the languages of hemlock, jimson weed.
Sometimes, my hands smell like sex.
That summer if anyone looked at one of us
we froze, like girls made of bloodstone,
crackleware. We kiln things.
We love each other like we grew

from the same set of pelvic bone,
as if we were attached like clethra
flowers to their stems.
We're budding now.

    II.

We were sixteen & took to our room.
J & I are two colored girls of history.
We do dolls, most are twinnies like we are.
I am the vicar here, the dolls marry
on the floor, kneeling on a red patch
of my mother's velvet dress.
We sing hymns we illuminate the hymnsheets
in the colors of medieval manuscript,
the color of Mars, some nights bloodred,
the blue of Mercury, azury
like the sky lit up all over America,
a clear suburban summer
night & the lawnmower's stopped
& the swimming pools are filled up
with the bice of night
water, a town in mid-America gone
mad, deserted. Someday we'll live there
when everyone's gone to the drive-in
& blonde twins are on the roofs of cars
or lounging on their sunchairs in the dark, soaking
up their moon, all the convertible tops
are down & the speakerbox hangs
on the rear view mirror like a locust,
slow & distorted like that,
& you climb in back to have a boy
inside you, that's what I want, on the backseat
sprawling in the noises like an animal
he makes, but you're shy, you're bourgeois, you talk
American which I sort of like but it's kind of sleazy, you know?
But me & Jennifer are up here in our room, broadcasting
Radio Gibbons in the gloom of an English outpost of the RAF.
These are my children now.

From the Register of Deaths of Dolls:

    Jane Gibbons, Aged 9. Died of leg injury.
    George Gibbons, Aged 4. Died of eczema.
    Bluey Gibbons. Aged 2 1/2. Died of appendix.

Peter Gibbons. Aged 5. Adopted. Presumed dead.
Polly Morgan-Gibbons. Age 4. Died of a slit face.
Susie Pope-Gibbons died the same time of a cracked skull.

We forecast the weather from our room.

III.

Dear Lord, you have no idea
what it was like. *11 June, 1981.*
I want a baby of my own, caged wren, tiny
trapped inside me like a blow of laurel
growing in a field, high & taking
from my own blood like an other only smaller,
someone I can call my own.
We to Welsh Hook & down into the barn.
J's lover, Carl, is there he broke
my virginity tonight. She
watched us, there was we
& blackeyed broken glass fallen
from the windows & a wild bird caught up
in the rafters, couldn't find his way back out.
Shrike: hangs its prey on wire fences, thorns.
This is what it felt like: for the first time
now I am alive. We did it
to the Stylistics, J watching
then we lay down heavy in the hay, heat
sticking stalks up under my blouse,
strawflowers, a resurrection weed inside of me.
Smoke: indicates confusion.
Fire: desire for escape.
Shoes off, summer night, whole world
smells of fennel, all romance
from the Book of Red Dreams:
Arson: indicates a twining.
Bitch: flammable, a lover.
Nakedness: perfection, fire inside thing consumed.
Sometimes we even dream the same, get that.

I burned it down today.

IV

Without my shadow, would I die?
At school once, in a tuberculosis scare
when we uncurled our limbs for vaccination
ours were the only colored arms.
Pink pink pink pink black. I love
flowers. When we grow wild we are.
No one can hear us talk, we mute we shy.
The other girls are none of we.

From *The Little Books for Little Angels:*

> It is Christmas Day. The TV's on all afternoon. Lassie, Bonanza, imports from
> America. It is ten years ago, I have this dream. There are five children, blue-
> eyed little angels. There's a bird on top our tree. The TV's gone blue, all the
> stars of the show are Twinnies. My father in his big old resting chair. Everyone's
> dressed in Victorian clothes, as if there's been a wedding. White gloves & some-
> thing catches fire. J is on her knees. We've come home from putting flowers on
> our mother's grave. She isn't really dead yet, she feeds us bloodpudding for
> supper. Everyone talking with no vowels. It's snowing hard & our house is
> getting more & more muffled. I've blue eyes, covered with lace. J & I are brides.
> We both have this disease of the lung. We are inseparable.

We'll die early & be stars.

V.

By the next summer, we'd bandaged our breasts
down so hard we could barely breathe.
High on vodka & glue, we both fuck the same
boy. Lupine, hawthorne, love-lies-bleeding
small violence of scent.
Something like magic is happening.
You've no idea how much I am
she. I am she. *Dear Lord,*
I am scared of her. She is not normal.
Someone is driving her insane. It is me.
Tonight she wound a cord around my neck
to strangle me, *6 November, Furzy Park.*
She broke our ritual, she goes too far.
We take brandy from beneath our bed,
go to Gipsy Lane to walk.
Wolfbane, daphne, trillium.

Really it's more of debris
there than anything else, the river's drying up.
But tonight, everything is full.
It has been raining for days.
Everything is dripping
like pen & ink drawings, long & lean
as the blackened Modigliani faces of my sister's art.
We entice each other constantly
in these beautiful nights
after neverending rain—

First of all, I wept to God

—when world is wet & shy, under the bridge, I hold her
head down under
water & I feel her thrash
against me, just this once, I murder her,
it's a once in a lifetime thing you know?
You have no idea
how much I love her, I am she.
Sweet alyssum, larkspur, yew.
We kiss. Monkshood, nasturtium,
forget me not.

—Fall 1987

Hayden Carruth

Eternity Blues

I just had the old Dodge in the shop
With that same damn front-end problem,
And I was out, so to speak, for a test run,

Loafing along, maybe 35 MPH,
Down the old Corvallis road,
Holding her out of the ruts and potholes.

That's out in Montana, the Bitteroot Valley.
Long ways from home is how they say it.
Long ways from home, boys, long long ways from home.

Might as well not put this clunker in the shop
And keep my hard-earned in my pocket,
She wobbles and humps like a scared rabbit.

But it's a real fine summer day in Corvallis,
And I'm loafing along watching the sprayers
Do their slow drag on the fields of alfalfa,

And I come to a side road with a little green sign
Says "Kurtz Lane" and I said to myself out loud,
"Mistah Kurtz—he alive. Him doing just fine,"

Because of the sign, you see, and because I'm lonesome
And maybe kind of bitter in spite of the sunshine.
It's still a goddamn long ways from home.

That's one thing, though, that *Heart of Darkness,*
I read that story every year, I never forget
That crazy old son-of-a-bitch, that Kurtz.

And the next thing I see about a quarter-mile
Down the road is somebody small on the shoulder.
A kid looking for a ride home, I figure.

And he's a kid all right, maybe ten or eleven,
But no Montana boy, he's an Oriental,
One of those Laotians that got resettled.

Can't figure why they brought them to Montana.
He's got those big eyes and caved-in cheeks
Like the pictures on the TV during Vietnam,

And his mouth is open a little, I say to myself,
I'll give him a ride if he wants, and I even
Begin to slow down, but he didn't

Put up his thumb. Just when I went by, he waved,
Real quick and shy, but like he was still trying
To reach me. I drove on. I damn near bust out crying.

—Spring 1984

Raymond Carver

Alcohol

That painting next to the brocaded drapery
is a Delacroix. This is called a divan
not a davenport; this item is a settee.
Notice the ornate legs.
Put on your tarboosh. Smell the burnt cork
under your eyes. Adjust your tunic, so.
Now the red cumberbund and Paris; April 1934.
A black Citröen waits at the curb.
The street lamps are lit.
Give the driver the address, but tell him
not to hurry, that you have all night.
When you get there, drink, make love,
do the shimmy and the beguine.
And when the sun comes up over the Quarter
next morning and that pretty woman
you've had and had all night
now wants to go home with you,
be tender with her, don't do anything
you'll be sorry for later. Bring her home
with you in the Citröen, let her sleep
in a proper bed. Let her
fall in love with you and you
with her and then . . . something: alcohol,
a problem with alcohol, always alcohol—
what you've really done
and to someone else, the one
you meant to love from the start.

It's afternoon, August, sun striking
the hood of a dusty Ford
parked on your driveway in San Jose.
In the front seat a woman

who is covering her eyes and listening
to an old song on the radio.

You stand in the doorway and watch.
You hear the song.
        But you don't remember.
You honestly don't remember.

                              —Summer 1982

Amy Clampitt

Keats at Chichester

There would have been the obligatory tour
of the cathedral. Stone under boot heels,
the great, numbed ribcage chilled-to-the-bone
cold. The aisles of sculptured effigies stone
dead. Tom dead at the beginning of December.
It was January now. Buried at St. Stephen's
Coleman Street. The bare spire, the leafless
trees. The church bells' interminable reminder.
One Sunday evening, hearing them, he'd dashed
off—with Tom there in the room, timing him—
a sonnet "In Disgust of Vulgar Superstition."
Here, the recurrent chatter of those great
metal tongues would have brought it back,
setting his memory on edge again. *Poor Tom.*
The scene out on the heath forever lurking
in his mind. Back in October he'd underlined
the words: Poor Tom. Poor Tom's a-cold.

His friends meant well, had kept him occupied.
Visits. A play. Dragged him down to Sussex
for a prizefight. Mrs. Isabella Jones, with
new notions for him to write about. Miss
Brawne: beautiful, elegant, graceful, silly,
fashionable and strange. He'd set down the
words with care. It was important to keep
things accurate. A minx—he'd called her
that, and also ignorant, monstrous in her
behavior, flying out in all directions, call-
ing people such names. Hair nicely arranged.
Loved clothes. Eighteen years old. Down here,
best not to think very much about her. Brown
playing the fool, putting on an old lady's

bonnet. At night, old dowager card parties.
As always, the anxiety about getting down to
work. No progress with the epic since Tom
died. Isabella Jones urging him to try an-
other romance. Why not, she'd said, the legend
of St. Agnes' Eve? A girl going to bed. . . .

He must have whistled at the notion that struck
him now. And then blushed. Or vice versa. A
girl going to bed on St. Agnes' Eve—that very
night, or near it—without supper, so as to
dream of the man she was to marry. Imagine
her. Imagine. . . . He blushed now at the
audacity. But the thing had taken hold:
St. Agnes' Eve. A girl going to bed. . . .
On the twenty-third of January, they walked
thirteen miles, to a little town called (of
all things) Bedhampton. The house they stayed
in there still stands. Out of the frozen
countryside they'd passed through, once his
numb hands had thawed, he had what he needed
to begin: the owl, the limping hare, the
woolly huddle inside the sheepfold. Even
the owl a-cold. *Poor Tom.* The cold stone
underfoot, the sculptured effigies. How
they must ache. His own numb fingers. How
the Beadsman's hands must ache. Paid to hold
a rosary for the souls of others richer and
more vicious. The stones he knelt on cold.
The girl's bedchamber cold, the bed itself
too, until the girl—blushing, he saw her
kneel—had warmed it. He saw it all.

He saw it: saw the candle in the icy draft
gone out, the little smoke, the moonlight,
the diamond panes, the stained-glass colors
on her as she knelt to say her silly prayers.
Saw her, smelled her, felt the warmth of the
unfastened necklace, the brooch, the earrings,
heard the rustle as the dress slid down;
backed off, became the voyeur of a mermaid.
Discovered, while she slept, that the sheets
gave off a sachet of lavender. Admired but
did not taste the banquet his senses had

invented, and whose true name was Samarkand.
He was in fact too excited to eat. What is
a poet to do when the stumbles onto such
excitement? He was not sure. He was also
somewhat embarrassed. Later he'd declare,
hotly, that he wrote for men, not ladies
(who are the ones who dream such things),
that he'd despise any man who was such a
eunuch as not to avail himself. . . . It was
the flaw, as he must have known. He'd
imagined it all. He'd imagined it all.

For ten days that lush, decorated stanza,
with its shut casements and dying fall,
had been the room he lived in. He'd
imagined it all; his senses had seduced
an entire posterity into imagining what
had never happened. His own virgin vision,
of a solitude that needed no wife, had been
seduced by that imaginary place, that stanza,
where nothing at all happened. The minx
who was eighteen, beautiful, silly, strange
and fond of clothes, and who had never lived
there, was real. The cold outside was real.
Dying was real, and the twitch of the old
woman's palsy. The effigies were real,
and the stones in the churchyard at St.
Stephen's Coleman Street. *Poor Tom.*

—Winter 1983

Stephen Dobyns

Cemetery Nights II

Because the moon burns a bright orange,
because their memories beat them like flails,
because even in death it is possible
to take only so much, because the night-
watchman has slipped out for a drink,
the dead decide to have a party. Helter skelter,
they hurry to the center of the graveyard,
clasp hands and attack the possibility
of pleasure. How brave to play the clarinet
when your fingers fall off. How persevering to dance
when your feet keep fleeing into the tall grass.
How courageous to sing when your tongue flops dow
on the stage and you must stop to stick it back.
And what does she sing, this chanteuse of the night,
Melancholy Baby? I Got Plenty of Nothing?

Where we have come from we'll soon forget.
Where we are going is the dust at our feet.
Where we are now is the best we can expect.

Slim pickings, says a crow to his buddy.
Just wait 'til the world flips over, says the other,
then we'll eat until our stomachs burst.
In a nearby bar the nightwatchman says, They can't
keep me down, I'm going places, I got plans.
The bartender yawns and glances from the window.
Some great bird is flapping across the face of the moon.
He thinks, Whatever happened to Jenny Whatshername?
Car crash, cancer, killer in the night? He remembers
once watching her pee in the woods, how she just
squatted down and pulled up her pink dress.
For fifteen cents she let him see her crack.

So white it looked, the wound that would never heal;
then how pink when she had delicately
spread it apart with two fingers. Excitedly,
he had galloped through the woods waving a stick,
hitting trees, clumps of earth; seeking marauders,
Indians, pirates to kill just to protect her.

—Summer 1986

Rita Dove

The Oriental Ballerina

twirls on the tips of a carnation
while the radio scratches out a morning hymn.
Daylight has not ventured as far

as the windows—the walls are still dark,
shadowed with the ghosts
of oversized gardenias. The ballerina

pirouettes to the wheeze of the old
rugged cross, she lifts
her shoulders past the edge

of the jewelbox lid. Two pink slippers
touch the ragged petals, no one
should have feet that tiny! In China

they do everything upside down:
this ballerina has not risen but drilled
a tunnel straight to America

where the bedrooms of the poor
are papered in vulgar flowers
on a background the color of grease, of

teabags, of cracked imitation walnut veneer.
On the other side of the world
they are shedding robes sprigged with

roses, roses drifting with a hiss
to the floor by the bed
as, here, the sun finally strikes the windows

suddenly opaque,
noncommital as shields. In this room
is a bed where the sun has gone

walking. Where a straw nods over
the lip of its glass and a hand
reaches for a tissue, crumpling it to a flower.

The ballerina has been drilling all night!
She flouts her skirts like sails
whirling in a disk so bright,

so rapidly she is standing still.
The sun walks the bed to the pillow
and pauses for breath (in the Orient,

breath floats like mist
in the fields), hesitating
at a knotted handkerchief that has slid

on its string and has lodged beneath
the right ear which discerns
the most fragile music

where there is none. The ballerina dances
at the end of a tunnel of light,
she spins on her impossible toes—

the rest is shadow.
The head on the pillow sees nothing
else, though it feels the sun warming

its cheeks. *There is no China*;
no cross, just the papery kiss
of a kleenex above the stink of camphor,

the walls exploding with shabby tutus. . . .

Georgianna Magdalena Hord, 1896–1979

—Fall 1984

Norman Dubie

A Dream of Three Sisters

From night rocks, above an ocean alive with yellow kelp,
The ghost of Samuel Taylor Coleridge tossed
Raw chunks of a disquieting muse
To three ragged mermaids . . . each
Had a long tooth the white of gruel.
Coleridge knelt in his velvet coat
With a prune-dark dog
That barked at the sagging breasts of the women.
When the sisters stopped tearing at their meat
To scowl back at the benefactor, the dog
Would whimper under the silks of a tent
In which he and Coleridge slept
Like evangelists of a new forebearance.
Two old philosophers not troubled by death
Like the moon Phobus which rises and sets
Twice each day above this martian landscape.
Here, the ghost of Coleridge sat, fully disconsolate,
With little more than thought for the fatal opiate. . . .
But how, you must ask, exactly did that dog
Become spirit? It was a winter day
On a small farm in Massachusetts.
White winged horses were feeding like geese
From the very bottom of a pond placed among trees.
The dog was to be shot that morning by the farmer Smith
Who shot himself instead. His wife
Drowned the mongrel the next day
In a sack half filled with nails for weight.
The dog was not sick. It was rumored
He had killed the cat. It was in this manner
That a mongrel entered the esteemed company
Of the addict Coleridge.
The afterlives of the gentle farmer and cat

Are an open subject. Perhaps
They live on the happy side of the same ocean
That is a torment to the dog and poet.
They were the first to burst upon this lonely sea.
They often wonder what it must be like being wholly ordinary.

                          —Winter 1989

Stephen Dunn

––––––––

Kansas

I've imagined a heaven
of replications, dull, pacific
a place where you're sent
for having been a gentleman
in the face of great passion.
In short, I've imagined and lived
lesser moments than this,
fixed as it is
in its quiet passing, a house
full of plants, animals, windows,
and the faint ticking of the dishwasher
in its cycle of drying.
The spirit is asleep
in its sac of comfort.
The blood that rushes to the penis
has no reason to move.
                              Truth is
everyone knows comfort
is wonderful, even dullness
is wonderful if the heart's right,
the mind at ease with it. Truth is
there's always another person
concealed in a poem
or down the street or across the country,
but in this case she's upstairs
in her vague purgatory, that Kansas
of affections.
I didn't know I was concealing her
until this moment, which changes nothing,
the dishwasher finished now,
the windows offering a view
I've often known from the other side—
unspectacular, blameless.

—Spring 1982

Richard Eberhart

A Dream

A loon's cry is a chortle from another world.
Gluts of silver, the dawn conclamant,
The ruffian band appears at our house.
Cinematographic, they move in,
Each face set in a rigid throat,
Their unity impressive and ominous.
The owners hover in an upper room.
Two knock, say they have come,
They need not say it, to destroy our house.
They break plates all over the place.
Their youthfulness and zest are mastery,
Without qualitative argument.

We do not have to argue either,
But touch relatives with quick glances.

In a room chock with swarming braggarts,
One is perhaps startled as two abreast
A column forces in with long guns vertical.
Our sin is putting rouge on our faces.
They march with marionette absolutism,
When they get in they dissolve in the ground.
The leaders are arguing at the pedestal.

I am waking in a university city,
The halls crowded with brutal faces.
Hundreds force into the large lecture,
Dr. Faction is lecturing on culture.
He cannot be seen, cannot be heard
Behind the solid mass of twisting flesh.
In an anteroom women gossip and knit.
It is said he is being transferred to Harvard,
To the greatest university on the continent.

The loons are savage and absolute,
Their cries annihilate the relative.
Our house is being destroyed, the crowd
Is dancing and mounting in a high glee.
We are ashamed of an old order
Of sanity for which it is useless to contend.

I have fled to a new adjacent city.
Two men are struggling with polar bears,
Each has his polar bear in his arms
As big as a dog: each is wrestling
And wrestling his away from the other.

One denounces the other, "You know
You stole my polar bear," he accuses
With righteous anger. The other fades out.
They dissolve in an intrusive symmetry.

By me
Is a jewelled reindeer bright and tangy,
The flesh of another world inviolate,
Attached to a sledge of violent colors,
It is a reindeer taxicab. I ask,
Shall I take the reindeer taxicab
Back to the consequential city?

The past of abandoned truth fades,
The new dawn appears.

—Spring 1981

John Engels

Autumn Poem

One cannot ask loneliness how or where it starts.
—Priest Jakuren

Under the pines are the first rusty needles
scattered about the sand like the tracks
of large and fragile birds. Already
the star moss carpeting the birch grove
has drawn back into itself, begun the withering
into its tiny straw: how have we learned

to live in this place in which the flaming outward
is the flaming back? From deep in the woods
we smell the souring of oak leaves,
from deeper yet the rankness of hickory.
We give way to the changes: everything turning
from the minor hues, ourselves as well,

bearers of an unseasonable color
which blooms inward upon the nakedness of limb
from which there is no turning. In autumn
night comes on with a silky darkness
deeper than that in the lily's throat.
It is the lightlessness that in the youth of autumn

displays itself as light
in the trees and grasses.
And though we cannot often ask loneliness
how or where it starts, how else
shall we understand and celebrate these changes?
In this season we may ask.

—Fall 1982

Tess Gallagher

Black Pudding

Even then I knew it was the old unanswerable form of beauty
as pain, like coming onto a pair of herons
near the river mouth at dawn. Beauty as when the body
is a dumb stick before the moment—yet goes on,
gazes until memory prepares a quick untidy room
with unpredictable visiting hours.
So I brought you there, you who didn't belong, thinking to outsave
memory by tearing the sacred from

its alcove. I let you see us, arms helplessly tender,
holding each other all night on that awkward couch
because our life was ending. Again and again
retelling our love between gusts of weeping.
Did I let you overhear those gray-blue dyings?
Or as I think now, like a Mongol tribesman, did I stop the horse
on its desert march, take the meal of blood

from its bowed neck to be heated. This then is my black pudding
only the stalwart know how to eat. How I climbed
like a damp child waking from nightmare to find
the parents intimate and still awake.
And with natural animal gladness, rubbed my face
into the scald of their cheeks, tasting salt
of the unsayable—but, like a rescuer who comes too late, too
fervently marked with duty, was unable to fathom

what their danger and passage had been for. Except
as you know now, to glimpse its intrusion enough,
and when there is nothing else to sustain, blood will be thickened
with fire. Not a pretty dish.
But something taken from the good and cherished beast on loan to us,
muscled over in spirit and strong enough to carry us

as far as it can, there being advantage
to this meagerness, unsavoriness that rations itself
and reminds us to respect even its bitter portion.
Don't ask me now why I'm walking my horse.

—Fall 1991

Ebony

I need these dark waves pulsing in my sleep.
How else make up for the pungency
of that carnation's breath freshened over us,
night on night? Just to lie next to love
was to have the garden in all its seasons.
I see that now. Gently, and without
the false lustre of pain meant to tempt
memory into crushed fragrance.
In the pull and toss of stones below the house
a soothing spirit sifts and laves its weights,
and those that were tears in some oriental legend
are strongly effaced in the wearing. You,
who were only a stone, taught stone to me in aftermath.
Which is to mock containment at its rich periphery.
The gray, the green in my black.

—Fall 1991

Albert Goldbarth

Donald Duck in Danish

ONE

This woman's tongue is being torn out. Yes. And I'm not being
sensational merely to clench your attention. It is, if anything, horribly
matter-of-fact: one Guard-of-Honor grips her hair and the other
saws, two strokes, then pulls. Tomorrow they'll hurt her
sexslit so it grows closed over itself and will never be operable
for pleasure again, will dump her on her doorstep
with their fist-sign burnt to her breast. This poem
can't do a thing about it, can't do one small sprig or whisper
of rescue about it, this or any poem, it hasn't the words. This
poem can say the pizzicati spring rain plays a shingle roof
all day, but it won't help. The deckled edges of antique maps
won't help, the whole ennobled halcyon-to-maggotass wordmastery
this poem can possibly lug to its surface can't heal, although
its empathy is great, although it will not flinch and swears
it won't forget, no, not in its leastmost inky valence,
although it parallels the dark world of that torture room,
touches it, nuzzles, but never penetrates it, like. . . . That woman.
Her husband. Years later, in bed. Two bodies so cell-known and
soul-known by each other! Though he can't enter. So known, so
much one—as we say about lovers—they share a common knowledge.

*

Pizzicati spring rain plays a shingle roof. The Ducks look
out. It clears. They'll soon be whisked from this domestic setting:
Bank Bank Bank is Knock Knock Knock and a door opens
into another adventure. This one, on the High Seas. Oncle Anders
(Uncle Donald) and his nephews, over the dignified deep-blue breves
of waves in comicbook art that must be, on the Ducks' level,
terrible lunges of oceanic pique, or crooks of watery fingers
beckoning islandward. They're following an antique map,
its deckled edges trembling in their tufted glovey hands.

Den naeste morgen, "Land I Sigte!" (*Next morning,* "Land ahoy!")
From then on: pirates, lost doubloons, portcullis-jawed sharks, and
avian Good in battle with rodent Evil until the final panel's SLUT
(THE END). Then more adventures: Tibet, The North Pole. Here,
in Egypt (most exotic *ancient* Egypt, too, through plot-twist trickery)
the plucky Ducks are puzzling at a sphinx's hieroglyphics, which
would "SWOOSH" them magically back in sandy swirls to home, if only
they could read these jackals and ibises. And above them: real
gulls in real sky. And above that: strangely UFO-ish things,
the real eyes of a real Danish reader, who closes her
comicbook slowly then looks up: ducks in high migration, squawking.

✳

It rains, in ancient Egypt. Some. The rest of the sun-drummed
time it's heat that, bad days, makes the greasy edging
of fat along pigmeat froth like a rabid animal. And a man?
Could drag home empty in his spirit, empty-handed,
from the river nets. And a woman. This heat. This shitty little meal
of salt-dried marsh reeds, and this heat. His name is Yuti.
Hers, Taheret. Now, for me, this broken (and mended) red breccia
jar in the shape of a dumb plump duck is something
curatorially attended—labeled, in its cased air. But it isn't
hard to see how it held grain once, or cosmetics, or once, and only
a rage-red moment, was the focus of two people's one day of
absolute ire, was flung, and cracked (and found exactly
with that fracture up its wingline 5 millennia later)—jar
in a world of cobra-hooded hippo-headed deities I'll never read
anything comprehensible into. But I understand that jar.
It isn't hard. The living hands it filled. It isn't hard
because the grief or orgasm-pleasure that make a human face
a dreamy prototype and sweep it to a place above
indigeny, are timeless speech—are everyone's
fatherland's mother tongue. Now Taheret stomps out, mad, muttering.

✳

When I first met Claudia, "Pepe's mom" was "dying"—whoever
Pepe was. At 4 AM his *bank!bank!bank!* exploded the sugary
loaf of sleep and sex-exhaustion over the bed, and I was left
in darkness while she murmured him calm in her livingroom, in
their language, from an ongoing story I'd entered mid-plot
and illiterate. —How it always is. —How I must seem, to others.
When I first met Morgan, her sister I couldn't picture was in

a Dallas hospital coughing the mucousy ropes of cystic fibrosis
out of bunched lungs. When I first met Judy, she already owned
that ticket to Japan. Rice paper, green tea, *kanji,* futons. What
we always are is new vocabulary strangers need to learn, to be
less strange, and fluency is a sign of some love or another. That
first morning driving home blur-eyed from Claudia's, I saw
clearly enough, in the pearly unreeling early light and car exhaust,
the carcass of an alleycat was folded as neat as a waiter's linen
over the interstate's guardrail, with a crate of potatoes beside it—one
quick undubbed scene from the foreignest movie imaginable,
though "real life." When Judy left, I read this: "Sweet, my
heart is a maimed dove fluttering." —from the ancient
Egyptian, though true and now and native on my lips.

cockscream heyhelpme YOWYUMYUM allclawmarks pisssss
the fur-thing fin-and-mane-my-lovely oh wings oh breathing
—Dreaming. Something like Egyptian gods now: the animal
in us risen into, and becoming, the head. Baboon. Hawk. So, in
balance, what's human can rise to the head of an animal: Lucy,
"fastidious, toilet-trained chimpanzee princess," raised her first
11 years in an affluent human family (Oklahoma), learning "about
130 words" in American Sign Language, even compounding her
own: a radish signed as "cry hurt food." On an island
in the blood-warm sluggish Gambia River in Africa (now
that she's large and willful) she's fitfully learning her birthright: how
to be a wild chimp, trap ants, fool snakes, and over time has been
uneducated down to around 20 remnant words I see her
sadly scoring on the shoreline air to no one: "food" . . . "drink"
. . . "Lucy hurt." I think of this de-articulating one morning when
its opposite pulls up: a schoolbus of thirty or more
deaf 5-year-olds, their banter and excited flock of hands,
and someone doing the consuming work of teaching them further
word-stores. Who could live with such labor? I know; and I'll
tell, if only you'll read part 2 of this. My poem. My language.

TWO

And I know where we've left the Ducks: perplexed, pith-helmeted,
frustrated—facing a faint inscription, all its persea trees
and cows and asps. . . . They have some serum ailing Duckburg
needs; but also have the camel corps of the Rats of Evil
lolloping ever nearer over the dunes and, in the way of menace on this

level, cursing in comicbook esperanto (!**!#!) and spitting *(ptooey!)*
daylong. . . . Oh untangle the magic formula, Donald, get your uphackled
feathers out of this jam or pickle or stew or whatever colloquial
Danish calls trouble! . . . In preparation, over years, to decipher
the mystery-glyphed Rosetta Stone, Champollion studied Arabic,
Syrian, Chaldean, Sanskrit, Persian—and a little Chinese grammar text
"for amusement." Donald and company have their Disney Studio
script to rely on, solely, and the very sand seems closing in. She's
followed them, my comics-scanning Danish reader, over those
exotic miles as surely as his "thirteen cheeping mallard ducklings"
followed Konrad Lorenz, that implausibly "imprinted" parent, their own
far waddling way. Again, she closes the book. Again, she goes
to the bedroom. They've had a bad fight. He's sleeping now—her man.
Posed on the sheets, Enigma. Hieroglyph figure. Conversant in worlds,
like all of us, to which, when we wake, we're the deaf and the dumb.

*

Toes unrinded of bandage for better display, and face the same, so
now her grayish grimace and carrot-red henna coiftop jut
like an ancient surgical blade and its balled-up bloody rag, this
part-ecdysiast mummy lathers us up, as any stripper ought,
for more, and leaves us wanting. "Who *was* she?" There's no real
explanation on her label, and of course the sarcophagus's luscious
wraparound script of knees and waves and lotuses only stymies.
A few cases over, the bones of Jews death's long dismantled are still
awaiting resurrection in their steamer-trunk-sized ossuary boxes
with the writing of my people neatly incised, black pods, black flames.
I'm sorry: I think time won't reflesh that devotional clutter.
I think the closest we may ever come to second life is someone
else's fancy reading the shards of us back to a wholeness. When
I do, I see it's night: the Nile moon's a dazzling platter, and she
brings some of its silver filigree in on her skin, and stands there
staring at her sleeping man—who's on no Danish silks but
on a knuckley hempen pallet, and yet who serves as a translation
for the Danish scene. He wakes and sees her, "I mended it,"
Taheret says. The duck jar in her palms. The moon on fire in her
oranged hair. The glue they make out of their kisses.

*

Everything's normally peachy in Duckburg. (Even so, they need that
serum). Once, in Chicago, I listened hard as Gus's oldest girl who was
retarded spoke, her tongue a treadle embellishing out such fine and

faulty lace! But that's here . . . Over there . . . the problem of being
alike or separate also plagues their sages, in the terms of
over there. Just now, the Darwin of Duckburg might be writing: "We
all come from the primordial ink, and a trace of its composition still
informs our bodies. After that, the how and why of who
we are is garbled. Horace Horsecollar is
a bipedal sentient horse who, in his wingtip shoes,
tweed gadabout slacks and tuxfront-likened horsecollar, can,
when out West tracking ne'er-do-wells with Mickey, ride
pellmell across the sagebrush, on domesticated beasts.
The question of *sapiens*: vexes. The theory of common ancestor stock
survival-of-the-fittest or cosmic rays divided: vexes. Daisy
has Donald over for duck hollandaise; licked fingers. Clarabelle
Cow visits Horace in fieldmouse-gray chichi high heels like gravy boats.
And now his trousers on the floor, and the collar, and now
from the bedroom a pleased and compassionate eloquence of whinnies."

✳

O that you would come to me swiftly, like a horse
of the king's, that cannot be restrained by any chief of grooms
is ancient Egyptian for what I've heard in the buzzed-up wee-hours
mumble between parked Caddies at The Deuces Wild's lot: *oooh*
baby I gon' spread on th' grass fow you, though any lawn was neighborhoods
away from that spot and its jargon. Male porcupines in heat
may spurt their female sweeties with urine from up to 7 feet
as indication of wooing. If I'm confounding love most *haute*
with lust or even simple, instinctual mating, or speech
with sign . . . well, still, it's true the universe is little more than layer
on layer of language, often without elucidating
phrasebooks in between. That summer after Morgan's sister died,
she'd call out during sleep, in words the alphabet for which was
crisscrossed hummingbird bones, stone snowflakes, sunspots, DNA. And
Wart the slops-boy, who would one day be King Arthur, you know
was turned by Merlin's wand to a snake, a badger, a kestrel,
a moss-mouthed gar, and later when he needed them their spirits
surrounded his shoulders like smoke that spoke—and each its own
patois and wisdom. Maybe they're around the Ducks now, who this last
split-second succeed in their task, and sandy whirlwinds lift them:

✳

"SWOOSH!" and they're dumped, on their ornithologically-nonexistent
rumps, in real Duckburg, safe, and the serum really delivered

into the Mayor's canine hands. Parades. A sticky kiss from Daisy.
In their better world the best's occurred, and sun sets
down these peaceful streets in maraschino splendor. While
in ours. . . ? In times when "necessary counterproductive numbers" is
a village burnt, a village with its blistered dead
hauled wholesale into the trash wagons, good is never
absolute. Today it's simply this woman, in front of this class.
She can't talk, with her tongue torn from its root, but she can
"talk." That is, can sign. That is, a garnet fist is branded
in her breast-flesh, but her real hands can really open,
splay, twine, buck and fly. It feels good. Her thirty
charges look agog and learn "Vocabulary Drill" without a single fuss
or pee-drenched pair of shorts today, and everything feels good.
The lousy cafeteria tuna lunch is good, the kids do "shoreline birds"
impeccably, and the sky out the window is smooth blue like a square
of drying laundry. There really are days like this. Her husband
picks her up at 5. "So whaddidyou teach the half-pints today?"
The *duck* sign. Then a kiss. SLUT. (THE END.)

—Summer 1987

Jorie Graham

An Artichoke for Montesquieu

Its petals do not open of their own accord. That is our part,
as the whisper is the hand we tender
to the wish, though each
would rather rule the field. What remains
is the heart, its choke a small reminder to be mindful
lest we go too far
for flavor. These are the questions
its petals part in answer to: where
is God? how deep is space? is it inhabited? The artichoke
is here that we imagine
what universe once needed to create it,
penetrable jewel;
what mathematics.
And then, now,

when the earth is no longer the world, it offers
a small believable cosmology:
each tiny leaf an oar
in the battle where each pulled his own; and the whole,
the king himself, tiered, like his crown or the multitude
laughing. The mind meets the heart
on such terrain as this, where each
can give in to the other
calling it victory,
calling it loss—
a no man's land where each of us
opens, is opened, and where
what we could have done locks to the very core
with what we have.

—Summer 1979

Robert Hass

Calm

1.

September sun, a little fog in the mornings. No sanctified terror. At night Luke says, "How do you connect a b to an a in cursive?" He is bent to the task with such absorption that he doesn't notice the Scarlatti on the stereo which he would, in other circumstances, turn off. He says chamber music sounds worried. I go out and look at the early stars. They glow faintly; faintly the mountain is washed in the color of sunset, at this season a faded scarlet like petals of the bouganvillea which is also fading. A power saw, somewhere in the neighborhood, is enacting someone's idea of more pleasure, an extra room or a redwood tub. It hums and stops, hums and stops.

2.

In the dream there was a face saying no. Not with words. Brow furrow, crow's feet, lip curl: no, it is forbidden to you, no. But it was featureless, you could put your hand through it and feel cold on the other side. It was not the father-face saying no among chalk torsos and the pillars of aluminum nor the mother-face weeping at the gate that guards rage; it was not even the idiot face of the obedient brother tacking his list of a hundred and seventy-five reasons why not on the greenhouse door. This face spits on archetypes, spits on caves, rainbows, the little human luxury of historical explanation. The meadow, you remember the meadow? And the air in June which held the scent of it as the woman in religious iconography holds the broken son? You can go into that meadow, the light routed by a brilliant tenderness of green, a cool v carved by a muskrat in the blue-gray distance of the pond, black-eyed susans everywhere. You can go there.

—Winter 1979

Shunga

I've been thinking about the ordinariness of life.
A woman I know, almost forty, sees a man
three times a week who pounds her rigid spine.
She does this to be rid of everything her parents,
long dead, wanted of her. Last night I studied shunga.
Male and female swirls of silk: apple blossoms
white on salmon-colored ground, pale moons rising
on a field of purple fringed with red. In the center
were genitals, flowers returning to the worm's gut,
the worm's gut flowering, a blind otter entering the mouth
of a very sleepy turtle. There were faces,
teeth clenched, lines tight about the eyes. In the picture
they want this more than anything.

                                        —Winter 1979

Seamus Heaney

Field Work

Where the yellowhammer flared out of the bushes,
Where the perfect eye of the nesting blackbird watched,
Where one fern was always green

I watched you through the mossed shins of the hedge
Take the pad from the gate-house at the crossing
And lean to pluck a white wash off the whins.

I could see the vaccination mark
Stretched on your upper arm and smell the coal smell
Of the train that comes between us, a slow goods,

Waggon after waggon of big-eyed cattle.

—Fall 1978

The Birthplace

1.

The deal table where he wrote, so small and plain,
the single bed a dream of discipline.
And a flagged kitchen downstairs, its mote-slants
of thick light: the unperturbed, reliable
ghost-life he carried, with no need to invent.
And high trees around the house, breathed upon
day and night by winds as slow as a cart
coming late from market or the stir
a fiddle could make in his reluctant heart.

2.

That day, we were like one
of his troubled pairs, speechless
until he spoke for them,

haunters of silence at noon
in a deep lane that was sexual
with ferns and butterflies,

scared at our hurt,
throat-sick, heart-struck, driven
into the damp-floored wood

where we made an episode
of ourselves, unforgettable,
unmentionable,

and broke out again like cattle
through bushes, wet and raised,
only yards from the house.

3.

Everywhere being nowhere,
who can prove
one place more than another?

We come back emptied
to nourish and resist
the words of coming to rest:

birthplace, roofbeam, whitewash,
flagstone, hearth,
like unstacked iron weights

afloat among galaxies.
Still, was it thirty years ago
I read until first light

for the first time, to finish
The Return of the Native?
The corncrake in the aftergrass

verified himself, and I heard
roosters and dogs, the very same
as if he had written them.

—Fall 1978

Juan Felipe Herrera

———

Iowa Blues Bar Spiritual

Little Tokyo bar—

ladies' night, smoky gauze balcony, whispering. Tommy Becker,
makes up words to La Bamba—request by "Hard Jackson,"

mechanic on the left side of Paulie, Oldies dancer, glowing
with everything inside of her, shattered remembrances, healed

in lavender nail polish, the jagged fingernail tapping. So
play it hard above this floor, this velvet desert. I want

the Titian ochre yeast of winter, keyboard man, fix your eyes
on my eyes and tell me handsome, how long will I live?

How many double-fisted desires, crushed letters, will I lift
in this terrain? And this rumbling sleeve, this ironed flint

of inquisitions and imaginary executors, where shall I strike,
what proud stones? Will this fauna open for me, ever, this fuzz

anointed beak inside the bartender's mirrors, etched doves,
a cautious spiral Harley tank, hissing, this Indian bead choker

on Rita's neck? How long shall we remain as wavy reflections,
imitators of our own jacket's frown? Who shall awaken first?

Margo Fitzer, the waitress? I will say, Queen Margo, sing to me
stoic priestess of slavering hearts, three faint lines creased

on your satin belly, toss our planet onto your umber lacquer tray,
too empty now; make the earth spin its dog rhapsody, erotic

through this silvery offramp and flake, unfurl. We tumble across
this raceway in honey-glazed traces, our arms ahead, the hands

flying to Ricky's Ice Cream Parlour, outside. I want to own one
someday, maybe on Thirty-Second Street. You will see me

in my gelled waved hair, my busy wrists—so fast, a clown's
resolute gloves, dipping faster than finger painting—except

I'd be stirring milk and the light chocolate foam of love, churning,
burning this sweet spirit, more uncertain, than the celestial

sheaths above the prairie frost. See the boy coming, they chide,
leaning, how he crosses his legs, his eyes dreaming, sideburns

just shaved clean. He weighs the sour slate on his father's breath;
perfume, fortune, cards left on the bleeding table. Milo Wilkens, drummer

at the curve, strokes his nipples with his arms as he hits the high hat.
Somewhere in the back rooms, I know, a shrine, orange sponge cushions,

two toilets and a wire wound wicker box, to leave flowers, occasional
offerings by the Johnson County dudes, detasslers in jersey ties.

Talk no more, enjoy. Darling singer, let your starry blouse sway me,
steal this fresh peach half from its amber juice; I want the moon

in this nectar, too. The flashing cymbals, feverish. Who can strike
a votive candle, love, or sleep in this electronic night? Just listen

to the two-part harmony, laughter, peeling beyond the cemetery, beyond
the Iowa river—where the spike hat rooster bristles his tiny ears,

bows his head and sips from the dark cannister under the carved pearlstone.
And then, returns. Let us drink, salute the bright spokes of meal, the dying

wands of river blossoms, grandmother's sacred hair; listen, her soprano
owl, her bluish melody, so thin. Another glass please, we shall dance

once again, our eyebrows smearing against each other's cheekbones, loud
with a Midwest sweat, a cantata from the cross-hatch amp, click it.

Click it, for wild kind rain, forgiving seasons, for the blushed bread
of our shoulders and thighs, this night, everyone is here. Even Jeff Yoder

came all the way from Illinois, to fill a bucket with passion, ruffled,
thick. O Sax player with a jail needle tattoo, leap onto this wet pavement,

call my lonesome tempest heart, its buried mother's kiss, bless us
in staccato, with quivers of Oak branch greenness and sparrow longings

riff over this brutal sky, give us your bell filled, conjure your tropic,
our lover's breath. Blues bar dancers, jangling gold popcorn, chord makers,

opal-eyed Suzie in a flannel shirt; we beckon the spark, the flaring,
this lost body to live.

—Spring/Summer 1991

Edward Hirsch

My Father's Back

There is an early memory that I carry around
in my mind
        like an old photograph in my wallet,
a little graying and faded, a picture
that I don't much like
            but nonetheless keep,
fingering it now and then like a sore tooth,
knowing it's there,
          not needing to see it anymore. . . .

The sun slants down on the shingled roof.
The wind breathes in the needled pines.
And I am lying in the grass on my third birthday,
red-faced and watchful
           but not squalling yet,
not yet rashed or hived up
           from eating the wrong food
or touching the wrong plant,
          my father's leaving.

A moment before he was holding me up
like a new trophy, and I was a toddler
with my face in the clouds,
           spinning around
with a head full of stars,
           getting so dizzy.
A moment before I was squalling with joy
in the tilt-a-whirl of his arms,
drifting asleep in the cavern of his chest. . . .

I remember waking up to the twin peaks
of his shoulders moving away, a shirt clinging
to his massive body,
                        a mountain receding.
I remember the giant distance between us:
a drop or two of rain, a sheen on the lawn,
and then I was sitting up
                        in the grainy half-light
of a man walking away from his family.

I don't know why we go over the old hurts
again and again in our minds, the false starts
and true beginnings
                        of a world we call the past,
as if it could tell us who we are now,
or were, or might have been. . . .

                        It's drizzling.
A car door slams, just once, and he's gone.
Tiny pools of water glisten on the street.

                        —Winter 1989

Garrett Kaoru Hongo

Village: Kahuku-Mura

I'm back near the plantation lands of cane and mule trails
and narrow-gauge track rusting in the rainbow distance
against the green cliffs and bridal veils of the *pali*.

I know the mill is just beyond my sight,
around the sand point, past old caneland
cleared now for prawn farms and melon patches,
and that the village is beyond them, quonset huts
and barracks in clusters arranged without pattern.

I remember someone—Iiyama-*san*—kept a carp pond,
and someone else made bean curd, fresh,
every day, and my chore was to fetch it,
in a bucket or a shallow pail or a lunchbox,
and I'd rush through the dusty, unpaved streets
winding past the rows of tiny shotguns,
thrilled with my job, anxious to get to
the low, barn-like building all in shadow
and cool as a cave in the middle of the tropical day.

I'd knock or call—*Tadaima!*—as I was taught,
in Japanese for this Japanese man (other words
for the Portuguese or Chinese or Hawaiian),
and he'd slide the gray door back, *shōji*-like,
on its runner, opening up, and I'd see,
under dim lab-lights, long sinks like flumes
in three rows all brimming with a still water
lustrous and faintly green in a weak light.

There was an odor too, stark as dawnlight,
of fermentation I'd guess now, the cool paste
curdling in the damp, cold dark, silting

clear water milky under the coarse wire screens,
the air gaseous and fragrant and sharp.

It must have been a dime or a nickel—
I remember its shine and the coin's neat fit
in my hand—and he'd take it, drop it in
a slotted coffee can, then reach a slick palm,
small spade of flesh, into the supple water,
draw the raw, white cube, delicate and new,
drenched in its own strange juice, and place it,
without words or ceremony, into the blank pail
I held before me like a page to be written on.

How did I know it would all recede into nothing,
derelict shacks unpainted and overgrown
with morning glories, by canefields fringed
with *ekoa* and castor beans swinging
their dark, brittle censers over the road?
How did I know my own joy's beginning
would be relic in my own lifetime?

I turn up the dirt road that took me in,
the green cane all around me, flush by the roadside,
a parted sea of masts and small sails scissoring the air,
whispering their sullen history on a tuneless wind.

—Spring 1987

Richard Hugo

Piping to You on Skye from Lewis

—for Iain MacLain

Pipe the Gaelic back for one last dance.
One long war over, you took a private vow:
say goodbye to islands only once.

Honor them daily with music, those dead attendants
of the fate of living Gaels: to lose.
Pipe the dead Gaels back for one more dance.

In war you might die English, might get buried in Provence.
Best concentrate on what the Skye dead did and do—
say goodbye to islands only once.

Goodbye home you said to Bragar, there's a bony chance
bones stay whole in cairns. From Stornoway, your radio
pipes the dead Gaels back for one more dance

and you bend close to the static, convinced
you'll find in bagpipe overtones the drumming reason to
say goodbye to islands only once.

War's tough on personal reconnaissance.
Spy from this green distance on your life and pray you
say goodbye to islands only once.
Gaels who die at home show up for every dance.

—Summer 1979

David Ignatow

———

Sleepy

Now where can I move to get peace,
I already live in the Bronx
near the Yonkers line? I suppose
I could turn off the TV showing
how the bombs fall and explode;
my bed shakes at each impact,
but then there is that funny commercial
following, a fat man astride a balloon
to test its strength, and up it takes him
too late to slip off without falling far,
his eyes wide as balloons, his mouth open
and round, forming his fear, his paunch
pressing up against the sphere, embraced
by his pudgy arms, legs dangling. I hear
a squeaky, comical Help, reminding me
of what I can't say exactly—the stupidity
of the fat man who knows enough to gorge himself?—
the point being that rubber is stronger than ever.

It drifts out of his hands in the force
of the upper currents, and he goes trailing
head over heels in one direction, the balloon
in another; his stomach becomes the whole of him
spinning in the wind as he drifts off
and vanishes into space—
the second commercial message being
that whoever tries to make his weight felt
is going to get a reaction.

—Summer 1983

Mark Jarman

Lost in a Dream

When I drove the L.A. canyon with a dead cat
in three Chinese boxes in a garbage bag,
the eucalyptus hedges like rows of embassies
and the sun diplomatic and the radio on for its voice,
its cool, odorless voice counseling love—to a beat—
up ahead, bees pranced obsessed with a queen,
drunk on the formic in their stingers.
I heard the rock at Madame Ling's the night we dressed
as if ties knotted right would annex us a home.
The singer wore triangular sunglasses, had starred as a child
in ads for kiddie medicine. He bounced up and down.
And his mom matched him spasm for spasm; dad, too.
It was the music of home and we had come back,
planning to do more than dance, but we couldn't stay.
Late, as we left, a bald giant appeared
with a life-sized doll in a box under his good arm.
With his teeth, he ripped the cellophane window open
and called for Madame Ling, to give her his gift.

As the bees descended, I saw the pet shelter
and the quivering air above its incinerator
and rolled up my window, thinking the cat's death
would not sweeten the teeth of these fat bees.
We had lain in bed that morning, our baby 10 days old,
and tried to bless our leaving like our home.
When Persian jasmine mingled with gasoline
and the sun, like a piece of bait, stained the ocean
and the canyon crows blew past as if cut
from cathedrals of black paper, and faint tremors
sailed our bed at dawn toward the horizon,
we had no explanation for what we felt.
Outside our window, the cat returned

and stretched out with its right hip laid open.
Its fur had been the color of hearth-fire.
Its dog-faithful gait had followed from room to room.
We lay in bed, talking, sensing only
the satisfying taste of our native salt.

First, the cat's cold body shocked us, then
the pale gash that kindled black ants
out of the damp clay-and-sand soil,
then, it was the tongue clenched as always—
kittenish—at the tip between his front teeth.
We had imagined it would redden the baby's cheek.
Who would tear us out of this box of a day?
But we had to leave. We had a year and a child.
Circumstance like instinct pointed away.
I drove slowly, the pelting rain of bees
glanced off the windshield, the beat thumped
the dashboard grid over the radio speaker,
and rising from the shelter chimney, the column of mirage,
the sort of air that paradise must rest on,
straightened the bent eucalyptus—those trees
so delicious in honey, so tart in the blood
that natives carry their blue-green fruit into exile.
We had to leave. This death would see us off.

That day is nailed in place by that chimney.
After the bees cleared, after I dumped
the odd coffin into white-coated arms,
I wanted to flow back down to the beach,
collect you and the baby and head out to sea
or cling like sand to the agate-webbed rocks
where we had walked every evening throughout the pregnancy.
The banked houses would catch the sunset
in wide, complacent windows as we climbed
up from the beach every evening as if toward
a room we knew with our eyes closed,
the simple need to find another home.
At night, the cat would listen at your belly,
hearing a purr as deep as his own. Deeper.
And when he returned outside our bedroom window,
having dragged a surprise of blood through the garden,
he heard the baby snuffling and sputtering
and heard us saying, "What a year this has been."

—Fall 1984

Rodney Jones

The First Birth

I had not been there before where the vagina opens,
the petals of liver, each vein a delicate bush,
and where something clutches its way into the light
like a mummy tearing and fumbling from his shroud.
The heifer was too small, too young in the hips,
short-bodied with outriggers distending her sides,
and back in the house, in the blue *Giants of Science*
still open on my bed, Ptolemy was hurtling toward Einstein.
Marconi was inventing the wireless without me.
Da Vinci was secretly etching the forbidden anatomy
of the dark ages. I was trying to remember
Galen, his pen drawing, his inscrutable genius,
not the milk in the refrigerator, sour with bitterweed.
It came, cream-capped and hay-flecked, in silver pails.
At nights we licked onions to sweeten the taste.
All my life I had been around cows named after friends
and fated for slaughterhouses. I wanted to bring
Mendel and Rutherford into that pasture,
and bulb-headed Hippocrates, who would know what to do.
The green branch nearby reeked of crawfish.
The heavy horseflies orbited. A compass, telescope,
and protractor darted behind my eyes. When the sac
broke, the water soaked one thigh. The heifer lowed.
Enrico Fermi, how much time it takes, the spotted legs,
the wet black head and white blaze. The shoulders
lodged. The heifer walked with the calf wedged
in her pelvis, the head swaying behind her like a cut blossom.
Did I ever go back to science, or eat a hamburger
without that paralysis, that hour of the stuck calf
and the unconscionable bawling that must have been a prayer?
Now that I know a little, it helps, except for birth
or dying, those slow pains, like the rigorous observation

of Darwin. Anyway, I had to take the thing, any way
I could, as my hands kept slipping, wherever it was,
under the chin, by tendony, china-delicate knees,
my foot against the hindquarters of the muley heifer,
to bring into this world, black
and enormous, wobbling to his feet, the dumb bull, Copernicus.

—Winter 1984

Donald Justice

In the Attic

There's a half hour towards dusk when flies,
Trapped by the summer screen, expire
Musically in the dust of sills;
And ceilings slope towards remembrance.

The same crimson afternoons expire
Over the same few rooftops repeatedly;
Only, being stored up for remembrance,
They somehow escape the ordinary.

Childhood was like that, repeatedly
Lost in the very longueurs it redeemed.
One forgets how small and ordinary
The world looked once by dusklight from above. . . .

But not the moment which redeemed
The little arias of the flies—
And the chin sank then onto palms above
Numbed elbows propped on rotting sills.

—Fall 1978

Thinking About the Past

Certain moments will never change, nor stop being—
My mother's face all smiles, all wrinkles soon;
The rock wall building, built, collapsed then, fallen;
Our upright loosening downward slowly out of tune—
All fixed into place now, all rhyming with each other.
The red-haired girl with wide mouth—Eleanor—
Forgotten thirty years—her freckled shoulders, hands.
The breast of Mary Something, freed from a white swimsuit,
Damp, sandy, warm; or Margery's, a small, caught bird—
Darkness they rise from, darkness they sink back toward.
O marvelous early cigarettes! O bitter smoke, Benton. . . .
And Kenny in wartime whites, crisp, cocky,
Time a bow bent with his certain failure.
Dusks, dawns; waves; the ends of songs. . . .

—Fall 1978

Brigit Pegeen Kelly

Imagining Their Own Hymns

What fools they are to believe the angels
in this window are in ecstasy. They
do not smile. Their eyes are rolled back in annoyance
not in bliss, as my mother's eyes roll back
when she finds us in the dirt with the cider—
flies and juice blackening our faces and hands.
When the sun comes up behind the angels
then even in their dun robes they are beautiful,
with their girlish hair, and their mean lit faces,
but they do not love the light. As I
do not love it when I am made clean
for the ladies who bring my family money.
They stroke my face and smooth my hair. So sweet,
they say, so good, but I am not sweet or good.
I would take one of the possums we kill
in the dump by the woods where the rats slide
like dark boats into the dark stream and leave it
on the heavy woman's porch just to think
of her on her knees scrubbing and scrubbing
at a stain that will never come out.
And these angels that the women turn to
are not good either. They are sick of Jesus,
who never stops dying, hanging there white
and large, his shadow blue as pitch, and blue
the bruise on his chest, with spread petals,
like the hydrangea blooms I tear from
Mrs. Macht's bush and smash on the sidewalk.
One night they will get out of here. One night
when the weather is turning cold and a few
candles burn, they will leave St. Blase standing
under his canopy of glass lettuce
and together, as in a wedding march,

their pockets full of money from the boxes
for the sick poor, they will walk down the aisle,
imagining their own hymns, past the pews
and the water fonts in which small things float,
down the streets of our narrow town, while
the bells ring and the birds lift in the fields
beyond—and they will never come back.

—Fall 1986

Richard Kenney

The Evolution of the Flightless Bird

1. THE FIRST POEM IN FIVE MONTHS

awkward as evolution of flight itself taxis
for airspeed, paddles twitching, recalling carrion
from a thousand feet, but oh, the eyes, cobalt
ice and flashing in a field of green—
Lips back, legs drive, bald flippers flap the grabbled
air—He tries to lift, to leave his tracks—
too heavy, except the eyes. . . . Say *genus Icarus,*
feathering hope as a green point describes an arc
on an oscilloscope: symmetrical, motif
reversed, the first stray subatomic particle in months
now crawls the stale cloud chamber, look! O faint desire!
The arms snap and leap like frayed cables. Locomotive,
cannonballing past his green foolscap and mincing
scribe, barbed lines thick with downy wool and *cire*

2. PERDUE—

Downcast a sour glosseur goes cluck and tsk:
"calligraphers and gamekeepers hold merchandise
alike, behind fencewire. How could a Circe's grotesque
ilk of *this*—," (he gestures) "—cross the courtly margins
of illuminated sheets, or ever mongrel
in among the white thighs of the Ninefold
Muse?" "What, ho! Fresh spoor," the grounds man growls:
"I glimpsed his grand trajectory—he rifled
through here five and six feet at a bound,
a boar let off a bowstring, burst these fencerails smack
down howling off in the bushveldt, shoot, leaves ribboned
out behind, crushed alders, sumac, cinquefoil. . . ." Mark
now: so distraught, a pastoral poet kneels by tender
shoots and ferns and coos. He keeps indoors

3. THIS POET

Glosseur, Grounds Man at the old Botanical
Gardens and Arboretum. He cups bird calls
in hand during the dog-watch, patiently waits
for new and strange wingbeats he cannot claim
or ape; he hides, and rolls out fruit to eat
in case there are flying foxes, South American
fruit-eating bats, caught in his green cloud chamber.
He loves all birds, spends hours on aerodynamic
theory, and keeps his hand in with the pterosaurs.
Half blind, this poet half believes the Orphic
epic of his age. . . . He lies back now, lies passive
in a dream of tall grass, great savannahs: *Phororhacos,*
seven-foot flightless Miocene carnivore
with curly feathers and unbridled rapacity.

—Fall 1978

Galway Kinnell

In the Bamboo Hut

There would come to me the voices
of the washerwomen at the stream
where they threw dresses, shirts, pants,
into the green water, beat them,
wrung them out, arranged them empty
in our shapes on stones, murmuring,
laughing, sometimes one more forlorn
singing, a sound like the aftersinging
of her who lay with me those nights
when we sang and cried to one another
our last breathing, under the sign
of the salamander, who still clings,
motionless, erect, attentive,
skeleton of desire inside the brain.

—Spring 1980

Edward Kleinschmidt

To Remain

November sixteenth, nineteen eighty-nine,
In San Salvador, the unsaved city,
The soldiers rephrase *Genesis*: Let there be

Light, so we can see those we're killing,
The right bodies or the wrong bodies.
The death squad posters say, *Be A Patriot,*

Kill a Priest. And on this night the Atlacatl
Battalion, accents of training drills at Fort
Benning, Georgia, still in their ears, *Made*

In the U.S.A. bullets in their belts, circle
The University of Central America. Inside the gates,
They drag five Jesuits from their cots, men who

Yesterday said masses for the massacred, their
Minds now reminded of no new future testament.
They are now face down, fatherly eyes in the dust

Of the courtyard. And according to the official
Report, the bodies are lined from north to south,
With their heads toward the west, and their feet

Stretched toward the east. And after the killing,
After the commander's simple words, "Let's proceed,"
There remains Amando López, 55, theology professor,

Found in the following position: head to the west,
Feet pointed to the east, mouth down, left arm bent
Toward the west, right arm bent to the east, dressed

In striped shorts, green poncho, green jeans. And easily
Found next to him, there remains Ignacio Martín Baró, 46,
Psychology professor and Vice-Rector, found in

The following position: head to the west, feet
To the east, left arm to the west, right arm bent
To the north, right foot on the left foot, mouth

Down, wearing a blue shirt, black leather belt, gray
Pants, black shoes and socks. And Segundo Montes, 56,
Sociology professor and Director of Human Rights, who

Had said, "I want to live with the people who suffer
And deserve more," found in the following position:
Mouth down, feet extended to the northeast, head

To the southwest, left arm and right arm bent
Below the head with direction to the south,
Wearing beige shorts, beige shirt, and green jeans.

And next to him, Ignacio Ellacuría, 59,
University Rector, mouth down, head to the north,
Feet to the south, left arm to the north, right

Arm bent toward the face, wearing a brown bathrobe,
Beige shorts with vertical stripes, blue shoes. And
Next to him Juan Ramón Moreno, 55, theology professor,

Found in the following position: mouth down, head
To the east, feet to the west, arms extended toward
The southwest, dressed in black corduroy pants, black

Belt, long-sleeved blue shirt, purple shorts, brown
Leather shoe on the right foot. And inside
The residence, one remaining priest, called Lolo,

Joaquin López y López, 71, Director of Fé y Alegría,
The quiet one, who was chased through the corridors,
Found in the following position: mouth up, head

To the east, feet to the west, arms bent over
The chest, hands semi-closed, wearing a white sleeveless
Undershirt, brown pants, black belt, shorts with vertical

Stripes. And in the room off the kitchen, where they asked
To spend the night to escape the night of city violence,
Of quiet killings done quickly, the new siege, civilians

Beholding that one brightest star exploding, as their
Roofs are torn off by bombs, children watching
Fire fights after curfew through cracks in the walls,

In this room, Elba Julia Ramos, 40, Jesuit Community cook,
Mouth up, head to the north, left foot to the south and right
Foot to the southwest, right arm to the northwest, left arm

To the southeast, both extended, wearing a blue dress, beige
Slip, black leather shoes, white bra; and her daughter,
Celina Ramos, 15, high school student, mouth up, head to the north,

Feet to the south, right arm over the chest, left arm
Perpendicular to the left side with direction to the north,
Wearing blue shorts, black, orange, red, and beige vertically

Striped blouse, white leather shoes with laces. Elba and Celina,
Who were "rekilled" when heard moaning from wounds, were
Found embracing before the M-16 fired ten more bullets

Into their bodies. And Elba was discovered that morning
By her husband at the same moment that Celina was discovered
That morning by her father, a *campesino* who can not

Write this down, but instead weeks later planted two white rose
Bushes in the courtyard, one for Elba, one for Celina,
And surrounded them with six red rose bushes, one to the north,

One to the south, one to the east, one to the west, cardinal
Points, and two to directions that haven't been invented yet,
A compass of roses that searches for where we are going,

That can tell us where we have been. The white bushes
Are like the needle in the compass that rises to point
Beyond compassion. Or to tell us who the third person left

Standing is, the one who sees all, the witness, the one
Who has testimony, who has lamentation, who stands in
For the 70,000 Salvadoreans killed in one decade.

—Winter 1990

Yusef Komunyakaa

―――――

Starlight Scope Myopia

Gray-blue shadows lift
shadows onto an ox cart.

Making night work for us,
the starlight scope brings
men into killing range.

The river under Vi Bridge
takes the heart away

like the Water God
riding his dragon.
Smoke-colored

Viet Cong
move under our eyelids,

lords over loneliness
winding like coralvine through
sandalwood & lotus,

inside our skulls years
after this scene ends.

The brain closes down
to get the job done. What
looks like one step into the trees,

they're lifting crates of ammo
& sacks of rice, swaying

under their shared weight.
Caught in the infrared,
what are they saying?

Are they talking about women
or calling the Americans

beaucoup dien cai dau?
One of them is laughing.
You want to place a finger

to his lips & say "shhhh."
You try reading ghost-talk

on their lips. They say
"up-up we go," lifting as one.
This one, old, bowlegged,

you feel you could reach out
& take him into your arms. You

peer down the sights of your M-16,
seeing the full moon
loaded on an ox cart.

—Summer 1984

Maxine Kumin

Shelling Jacobs Cattle Beans

All summer
they grew unseen
in the corn patch
planted to climb on Silver Queen
Butter and Sugar
compete with witch
grass and lamb's-quarters
only to stand naked, old crones,
Mayan, Macedonian
sticks of antiquity
drying alone
after the corn is taken.

I, whose ancestors
put on sackcloth and ashes
for the destruction of the Temple
sit winnowing the beans
on Rosh Hashonah
in the September sun
of New Hampshire.
Each its own example:
a rare bird's egg
cranberry- or blood-flecked
as cool in the hand
as a beach stone
no two exactly alike
yet close as snowflakes.
Each pops out of the dry
husk, the oblong shaft
that held it,
every compartment a tight fit.

I sit on the front stoop
a romantic, thinking
what a centerpiece!
not, what a soup!
layering beans into
their storage jars.
At Pompeii the food
ossified on the table
under strata of ash.
Before that, the Hebrews
stacked bricks
under the Egyptian lash.

Today in the slums of Lebanon
Semite is set against Semite
with Old Testament fervor.
Bombs go off in Paris,
Damascus, New York,
a network of retaliations.
Where is the God of
my fathers, that I
may pluck Him out of the lineup?
That I may hand back my ticket?

In case we outlast
the winter, in case
when the end comes
ending all matter,
the least gravel
of Jacobs Cattle remain,
let me shell out the lot.
Let me put my faith in the bean.

—Summer 1983

Stanley Kunitz

Route Six

The city squats on my back.
I am heart-sore, stiff-necked,
exasperated. That's why
I slammed the door,
that's why I tell you now,
in every house of marriage
there's room for an interpreter.
Let's jump into the car, honey,
and head straight for the Cape,
where the cock on our rooftree crows
that the weather's fair,
and my garden waits for me
to coax it into bloom.
As for those passions left
that flare past understanding,
like bundles of dead letters
out of our previous lives
that amaze us with their fevers,
we can stow them in the rear
along with ziggurats of luggage
and Celia, our transcendental cat,
past-mistress of all languages,
including Hottentot and silence.
We'll drive non-stop till dawn,
and if I grow sleepy at the wheel,
you'll keep me awake by singing
in your bravura Chicago style
Ruth Etting's smoky song,
"Love Me or Leave Me,"
belting out the choices.

Light glazes the eastern sky
over Buzzards Bay.
Celia gyrates upward
like a performing seal,
her glistening nostrils aquiver
to sniff the brine-spiked air.
The last stretch toward home!
Twenty summers roll by.

—Spring 1979

Sydney Lea

Wedding Anniversary

—for MRB

Even past sunrise, frog-legions peeped in spring
where—as if for him—the creek jagged near.
And yet from dawn, from spring, something was missing.
There were quartzes and pyrites and schists and mica plates
on the opposite scarp. They'd crackle. He would stir
the backpool's gathered algae with a stick
till the world spun in a vortex that contained
lights, quicksilver minnows, verdigris newts.
And after, reflected, riverside trees would shiver,
their birds odd lapidary fruit that *sang*.
His awkward schoolroom recitations seemed
an age away. And yet there was something missing.

The stars above the pastures of adolescence
were profligate, scattered; and all the whispered words
he traded with his friends, though banal, thrilled him.
It was as if rich adulthood would take
the form of speech, as if to talk enough
to companions would be to lisp his way to treasure,
various as those stars, or the sighs and chippings
of amorous insects, nightbirds, rodents, cattle,
or summer timothy stalks, or breezes panting
warmly. He recalls how their radio crooned
"Shangri-La," "Rags to Riches," whatever.
Rifeness was all. But there was an absence too.

Later he learned the words, the syntax, moods
of another language. Still later he found himself
high in the Pyrrenees, unsponsored, free.
He had no cash, but could speak and charm no less
than *Monsieur le maire*, who accepted his draft and poured
coin from the hamlet's coffers and poured him wine.

They leaned out over a rail to see September's
shatter of water on rocks in the gorge below.
Then mayor and manchild stumbled house to house—
he remembers the musical speeches of introduction,
as if the boy himself were somehow a treasure.
Copious tears at parting, then something missing

All through the long, olfactory ramble north:
meadow-scent, soft coal, diesels' perfumes,
sawdust-and-urine whiff in the tiny *relais,*
Gauloises, cheroots, and, once in Paris, *cassis.*
Liquor-courageous, he nodded to the lady.
And then, upstairs, the spirits fading, he bellowed,
to mask his shyness, "I have had enough!"
"J'en ai marre!" To which she replied, *"De quoi?"*
Mute, he handed over what money was left
from the Mayor's store, and mortified waited outside
on the balcony, its grillwork broken by light.
He thought, *"De quoi?"* Exactly. Enough of what?

Trout, platooned and hungry in western Montana,
the gilded Browns, the Rainbows more than rainbows,
the Cutthroats' cheek-plates crimson as any wound:
breaking the flawless surface, flawless themselves,
they arched their backs and sipped his little fly
with its tinsel and feather, never so lovely as they were.
Coyotes sang the sun to splendid disaster.
It fell on the rim of the mesa, imploding in flame,
across which flew the tuneful, crop-full geese
while blackhawks wheeled, while great bull elk came forth
to bugle challenge, courtship down the buttes,
which shone like mercury now. And something missing.

Something that failed as well to show from ice
outside his house, New Hampshire. Within, soft groans
from his ancient timbers. His clothing snapped with static.
One songless nuthatch lit to taste his feeder.
It seemed that nature vanished into mind,
that pool and pasture, mountain and minnow, frogs,
odors, effects of touch and sound and light
had each become mere object of recall.
The newest New Year passed and seemed not new,

but raced to retrospection, as would spring
and summer and autumn, so he though, like winter
missing something. How could he know *you*
would come, and come the day of which he sings?
Has gone on singing. Will go on to sing.

—Spring/Summer 1991

Philip Levine

Belief

No one believes in the calm
of the North Wind after a time
of rage and depression.
No one believes the sea cares nothing
for the shore or that
the long black volcanic reefs
that rise and fall from sight
each day are the hands
of some forgotten creature
trying to touch the unknowable
heart of water. No one believes
that the lost breath of a man
who died in 1821 is my breath
and that I will live until
I no longer want to, and then
I will write my name
in water, as he did, and pass
this breath to anyone who can
believe that life comes back
again and again without end
and always with the same face—
the face that broke in daylight
before the waves at Depot Bay
curling shoreward over and over
just after dawn as the sky cracked
into long slender fingers of light
and I heard your breath beside me
calm and sweet as you returned
to the dark crowded harbor of sleep.
That man will never return. He ate
the earth and the creatures of the sea
and the air, and so it is time he fed

the small tough patches of grass
that fight for water and air
between the blocks on the long walk
to and from school, it is time
that whatever he said began
first to echo and then fade
in the mind of no one
who listened, and that the bed
that moaned under his weight
be released, and that his shoes curl
upward at last and die, for they too
were only the skins of other animals,
not the bear or tiger he prayed to be
before he knew he too was animal,
but the slow ox that sheds his flesh
so that we might grow to our full height—
the beasts no one yearns to become
as young men dream of the sudden fox
threading his way up the thick hillside
and the old of the full-bellied seal,
whiskered and wisely playful. At the beach
at Castelldefels in 1965 a stout man
in his bare socks stood
above two young women stretched out
and dressed in almost nothing.
In one hand he held his vest,
his shoes, and his suit jacket
and with the other he pointed to those
portions of them he most admired,
and he named them in the formal,
guttural Spanish of the Catalan gentleman.
He went away with specks of fine sand
caught on his socks to remind him
that to enter the fire is to be burned
and that the finger he pointed would
blacken in time and probe the still earth,
root-like, stubborn, and find its life
in darkness. No one believes he
knew all this and dared the sea
to rise that moment and take him
away on a journey without end
or that the bodies of the drowned collect
light from the farthest stars and rise
at night to glow without song.

No one believes that to die
is beautiful, that after the hard pain
of the last unsaid word I am swept
in a calm out from shore
and hang in the silence of millions
for the first time among all my family
and that the magic of water
which has filled me becomes me
and I flow into every crack and crevice
where light can enter. Even my oak
takes me to heart. I shadow the yard
where you come in the evening
to talk while the light rises slowly
skyward, and you shiver a moment
before you go in, not believing
my voice in your ear and that the tall trees
blowing in the wind are sea sounds.
No one believes that tonight is the journey
across dark water to the lost continent
no one named. Do you hear the wind
rising all around you? That comes
only after this certain joy. Do you hear
the waves breaking, even in the darkness,
radiant and full? Close your eyes, close
them and follow us toward the first light.

—Spring 1981

Above Jazz

A friend tells me he has risen above jazz. I leave him there. . . .
—Michael Harper

There is that music that the hammer
makes when it hits the nail squarely
and the wood opens with a sigh. There is
the music of the bones growing, of
teeth biting into bread, of the baker
making bread, slapping the dusted loaf
as though it were a breathing stone.
There has always been the music
of the stars, soundless and glittering
in the winter air, and the moon's
full song, loon-like and heard only
by someone far from home who glances
up to the southern sky for help and finds
the unfamiliar cross and for a moment
wonders if he or the heavens
have lost their way. Most perfect
is the music heard in sleep—the breath
suspends itself above the body, the soul
returns to the room having gone in dreams
to some far shore and entered water
only to rise and fall again and rise
a final time dressed in the rags of time
and made the long trip home to the body,
cast-off and senseless, because it is
the only instrument it has. Listen, stop
talking, stop breathing, do you hear
the song of the circle and the center,
do you hear it? That is music
whatever you hear, even if it's
only the simple pulse, the tides
of blood tugging toward the heart
and back on the long voyage that must
always take them home. Even if you

hear nothing, the breathless earth
asleep, the oceans at last at rest,
the sun frozen before dawn and the peaks
of the eastern mountains upright, cold,
and silent. All that you do not hear
and never can is music, and in the dark
creation dances around the single center
that would be listening if it could.

—Spring 1981

Linda McCarriston

Second Marriage

The sense of fifteen years of almost
anything shared is what she sometimes misses
with him, even the awful, silent suppers,
when, with everything already said,
she had longed for words, all over again.
In bed at night, his chest is not
the chest she wept on, learning,
where breast-hair inscribed her cheek,
of onset and ceremony, those whole and open places
that one may fully occupy, like the future.

How happy, even sadly, to have been
young together, to have held off loneliness
with the shiny locket of *we,* as if
whatever could not be found, must, nonetheless,
turn up inside that circle.
Now, neither memory nor need sustains.
She sees the land take shape beneath her,
as birds must, on the first migration,
trusting their bodies as they veer away.
This second love is possible, and chosen.

She wants him. Every broken edge of her
abuts the world, of which he is a portion.

—Fall 1981

William Matthews

Bmp Bmp

Lugubriously enough they're playing
Yes We Have No Bananas, at deadpan
half-tempo, and Bechet's beginning
to climb like a fakir's snake,
as if that boulevard-broad vibrato
of his could claim space in the air,
out of the low register. Here comes
a spurious growl from the trombone,
and here comes a flutter of tourist
barrelhouse from the pianist's left hand.
Life is fun when you're good at something
good. Soon they'll do the *Tin Roof Blues*
and use their 246 years
of habit and convention hard.
Now they're headed out and everyone
stops to let Bechet inveigle his way
through eight bars unaccompanied
and then they'll doo dah doo dah doo
bmp bmp. Bechet's in mid-surge as usual
by his first note, which he holds, wobbles
and then pinches off to a staccato spat
with the melody. For a moment this stupid,
lumpy and cynically composed little money-
magnet of a song is played poor and bare
as it is, then he beings to urge it out
from itself. First a shimmering gulp
from the tubular waters of the soprano sax,
in Bechet's mouth the most metallic
woodwind and most fluid, and then
with that dank air and airborne tone
he punches three quarter-notes
that don't appear in the song but should.

From the last of them he seems to droop,
the way in World War II movies
planes leaving the decks of aircraft carriers
would dip off the lip, then catch the right
resistance from wet air and strain up,
except he's playing against the regular disasters
of the melody his love for flight and flight's
need for gravity. And then he's up, loop
and slur and spiral, and a long, drifting note
at the top, from which, like a child decided
to come home before he's called, he begins to drift
back down, insouciant and exact, and ambles
in the door of the joyous and tacky chorus
just on time for the band to leave together,
headed for the *Tin Roof Blues*.

—Fall 1981

John Montague

Foreign Field

Paddy's whole place was a clearing house:
A public phone in the hallway,
People huddled around a tiled fireplace.

But we were given tea in the front parlor,
Chill as the grave, a good place to talk,
Among brass trinkets, Long Kesh harps.

A patrol catwalks through the garden.
"You can see how we are being protected"
Paddy jokes, with a well rehearsed laugh.

A single shot. "Jesus, that was close!"
The whole patrol crouches to the grass,
Though one slumps. "Your man's hurt.

You don't take cover with your rifle
Between your legs, like starting to dive.
Let's lay out and see if he's alive."

All the soldiers barked was "Freeze!"
But Paddy led us to where he lay,
A chubby lad, only about eighteen,

That hangdog look, hair close cropped,
Surplus of a crowding England, now
Dying in a puddle of wet and blood.

And still the soldiers: "Don't move!"
Paddy ran back in to fetch some linen.
"Don't touch him!" He kneels down

To cover his skull gently, a broken egg.
"When a man's got, he's a non-combatant"
Paddy apologized, shepherding us inside.

An hour later, an army ambulance raced up,
An army doctor leaps down. Out again, play-
Ing, the children chant: "Die, you bastard!"

Next morning, they checked out the area.
Someone had pruned an old tree in a garden,
Opening a new line of fire, instead.

—Fall/Winter 1982

Sharon Olds

———

Parts of the Body

—*Berlin airport, 1932*

Seeing the wind at the airport blowing on his hair,
lifting it up where it was slicked down, you
want to say to the wind Stop, that's
Hitler's hair, but the wind keeps lifting it
gently and separating the fine strands and
fanning it out like a delicate weed-head in the air.
His brows look blond in the airport light, his
eyes are crinkled up against the sun, you
want to say to his eyes Stop, you are
Hitler's eyes, close yourselves, but they are
on his side, no part of his body
can turn against him. His thumb-nail is long and
curved, it will not slit his throat for the
sake of the Jewish children, his feet in their
black shoes won't walk him into the
propeller and end the war. His heart won't
cease to beat, even if you tell it
it's Hitler's heart—it has no loyalty to
other hearts, it sees no future outside his body.
And you can't suddenly tell his mind
it's Hitler's mind, get out while it can,
it already knows it's Hitler's mind, its
whole space is taken up with the
gold memorial statue they'll erect when he
dies of old age in 1984. They'll
place a copy in every major
German capitol around the world,
Berlin, Paris, London, New York,
Tokyo, a giant statue of him, *Hitler,*
Friend to German Children—
which will mean all children, then,
all those living.

—Fall/Winter 1982

Mary Oliver

_____

A Poem for the Blue Heron

1

Now the blue heron
wades the cold ponds
of November.

In the gray light his hunched shoulders
are also gray.

He finds scant food—a few
numbed breathers under
a rind of mud.

When the water he walks in begins
turning to fire, clutching itself to itself
like dark flames, hardening,
he remembers.

Winter.

2

I do not remember who first said to me, if anyone did:
Not everything is possible;
some things are impossible,

and took my hand, kindly,
and led me back
from wherever I was.

3

Toward evening
the heron lifts his long wings
leisurely and rows forward

into flight. He
has made his decision: the south
is swirling with clouds, but somewhere,
fibrous with leaves and swamplands,
is a cave he can hide in
and live.

4

Now the woods are empty,
the ponds shine like blind eyes,
the wind is shouldering against
the black, wet
bones of the trees.

In a house down the road,
as though I had never seen these things—
leaves, the loose tons of water,
a bird with an eye like a full moon
deciding not to die, after all—
I sit out the long afternoons
drinking and talking;
I gather wood, kindling, paper; I make fire
after fire after fire.

—Spring 1982

Robert Pinsky

Flowers

The little bright yellow ones
In the January rain covering the earth
Of the whole bare orchard
Billions waving above the dense clumps
Of their foliage, wild linoleum of silly
Green and yellow. Gray bark dripping.

Or the formal white cones tree-shaped
Against the fans of dark leaf
Balanced as prettily in state
As the wife of the king of the underground
Come with palms on her hips to claim the golden apple of the sun.

Sexual parts; presents. Stylized to a central
O ringed by radiant lobes or to the wrapped
Secret of the rose. Even potatoes have them.
In his dead eyeholes
The clownish boy who drowned
In the tenth grade—Carl Reiman!—wears them
Lear wears them and my dead cousins
Stems tucked under the armpit
Button of orange in the mouth,

In a vernal jig they are propelled by them:
Dead bobbing in floral chains and crowns
Knee lifted by the pink and fuchsia
Half-weightless resurrection of heel and toe
A spaceman rhumba. Furled white cup
Handfuls of violet on limp stems
The brittle green stalk held between arm and side
Of one certain dead poet—

And they push us away: when with aprons
Of petals cupped at our chin
We try to join the dance they put
Their cold hands on our chest
And push us away saying No
We don't want you here yet—No, you are not
Beautiful and finished like us.

—Fall/Winter 1982

Stanley Plumly

Waders and Swimmers

The first morning it flew out of the fog
I thought it lived there.
It floated into shore all shoulders,
all water and air. It was cold that summer.
In the white dark the sun coming up was the moon.
And then this beautiful bird,
its wings as large as a man, drawing the line
of itself out of the light behind it.
A month or more it flew out of the fog,
fished, fed, gone in a moment.

There are no blue herons in Ohio.
But one October in a park I saw a swan
lift itself from the water in singular, vertical strokes.
It got high enough to come back down wild.
It ate bread from the hand
and swallowed in long, irregular gestures.
It seemed, to a child, almost angry.
I remember what I hated
when someone tied it wing-wide to a tree.
The note nailed to its neck said this is nothing.

The air is nothing, though it rise
and fall. Another year
a bird the size of a whooping crane
flew up the Hocking—
people had never seen a bird that close
so large and white at once.
They called it their ghost and went back to their bibles.
It stood on houses for days, lost,
smoke from the river.
In the wing-light of the dawn it must have passed

its shadow coming and going. I wish I knew.
I still worry a swan alive
through an early Ohio winter, still worry
its stuttering, clipped wings.
It rises in snow, white on white, the way
in memory one thing is confused with another.
From here to a bird that flies
with its neck folded back to its shoulders
is nothing but air, nothing but first light and summer
and water rising in a smoke of waters.

Merriman's Cove, Maine

—Fall/Winter 1982

Charles Simic

Navigator

I summoned Columbus
At four in the morning
He came out of the gloom
Looking a little like my father

In this particular voyage
He discovered nothing
The ocean I gave him was endless
And the ship an open suitcase

He was already lost
I had forgotten to provide the stars
Sitting with a bottle of wine in his hand
He sung a song from his childhood

In the song the day was breaking
A barefoot girl
Stepped over the wet grass
To pick a sprig of mint

And then nothing for him and me
But the wind rushing off with a high screech
As if it knew
Where it's going where it's been.

—Fall 1978

Dave Smith

Crab

Like other crabs Callinectes sapidus probably evolved from the ocean. But it is now an estuarine organism, having found its best place in life where river and ocean waters blend. What primal drive, then, impels females to die in their evolutionary cradle? Why are they not accompanied by males, who are believed to seek out the deepest Bay channels when their moment comes? And what can we say of the sea runs who return, befouled and spent, to sample briefly once more the estuarine gardens of their youth?
—William W. Warner, *Beautiful Swimmers: Watermen, Crabs, and the Chesapeake Bay*

I read once that when he had opened Thomas Wolfe's head,
the surgeon did not even look up,
his fingers needling and cradling

                     back the deep-hidden meat.

The book said postules or nodules, I forget exactly,
and more than once I have caught myself
in the Lazyboy, fingertips testing

                     the uneven round of my skull,

and again, then again.
              They must have been something
gray as bubbles I dream
in the chittering crab-teeth
at the bottom of my historical place.

    *

Late summer finds us ready to leave ancient Lake Bonneville
where the Salt Lake laps the jet runway.

My son thinks of the Little League, my wife
comforts our infant daughter with a vision
of the family waiting, preparing
her for arms that will reach
among many voices
whose talk is, well,
            funny!

    *

I am seated separately with the middle child who is just
six, a stern dreamer like me. She takes time
to walk to the edge of our yard,
singing, remembering,

though she has nothing to remember yet, being six.

She will sit beside me, at the porthole, serene as a clam
while I describe our country's true geography,
those wiggling rivers that come out in the end
where you always knew they would, her
unfathomable love storing it all,
each fact, guess, bald lie, and jittery joke.

                                    I like to think about that,
things sinking in, the hand she'll hold
when my knots have finally come to something,

as we sail South.

        ✶

The story starts in the DC-10's roar, recurrent, a dream
where a boy ratty-tatty as Huck Finn floats
as if on a tide to a secret spot.
He knows the big crab is there,
on dancing, hardly touching feet.

Yesterday one swipe with the dipnet and it was out,
caught, but he turned his back, and crabs
move quicker than jets. Now he'll try again.

        ✶

I'm prepared to explain how this beauty is hard come by, and do.
The bigger a crab grows the harder to survive
that necessary shuck of the self's house.
He gets tired, sometimes gives up,
but tries to ride the current
home like a familiar dream. The sun calls him.

        ✶

                                        I dream
a white string dangling in the marshgrass,
my chicken neck ripe.

I've come from the butcher, kind as a man can be,
who shook my small hand. I'm on my way
with a bag full.

My grandmother's sleeping in the dark house
always crackling with fried chicken.
I go in and go out, and do not see her

for the tide is turning. A kid I remember waves from shadows
of the Sisters of Mercy Hospital, his uniform
spanking white, glove slung on his bat.

I don't stop for him. I don't have time.

I seek out the mooring of boats and run when I see the masts
sway gently as feelers, run dizzied as bait,
string, bucket, dipnet chafe like armor.

Magnolia is white, mulberry red in this fine, soft hour.

In the garage, under the dried droppings of the mud-dauber's
generations, we seek string wound on a stick.
It waits where the walls join,
the skin of moss long hardened black flecks.
We cut away the rotted part.
We stretch whatever has some life left
toward the old house where the family chatters gravely.

Look, make the picture in your memory of me, him, who I was,
learn how doing it right means the climb out
until your face is in the water, knees hooked
at the borrowed transom, the secret
place.
        See how I bend my neck,
letting sunburn cut deeply in, and clean salt?
We must hear no thing in the world,

breathing inch by inch, paying out the string,
passionately becoming, for all a crab can tell, beautiful swimmers.

＊

Rehearsing in flight the haul of crabs, I talk her through
ways to manage the claws of fear.
                              At six, the mystery's
heart-tugging and true. Already she can see
what's felt along the taut string,
even those festering bubbles, and the place

              deep in my head. It now will be
                    remembered right. Loved.

＊

When we come home to the family house, there will be gifts.
There will be painfully drawn, too small faces.
We will wear the sun's stitches and blisters,
the oxide smell of childhood.

She will not divulge where we have been all day crawling
loyal as the tide, then the boy, slumping and homesick,
will lash at her.
              Slowly she will retreat

into the story, her rehearsal of each deep color, touch and claw
I've planted all these long hours. Remembering
she will inch them all through
everything again and again.

                    Flying home

she will draw on the dream's power,
on the dark junked corner of the garage
where crabs bubble in thickets of old string,
the one who will pay me out all the years just as I was
when she and I were six,
                    burned,

at grandmother's.

                              —Summer 1981

Gerald Stern

———

All I Have Are the Tracks

All I have are the tracks, there were a dog's
going down the powdered steps, there was a woman
going one way, a man going the other, a squirrel
on top of the man; sometimes his paws were firm,
the claws were showing—in fear, in caution—sometimes
they sort of scurried, then sort of leaped; the prints
go east and west; there is a boot; there is
a checkerboard style, a hexagram style; my own
I study now, my Georgia Loggers, the heel
a kind of target, the sole a kind of sponge;
the tiny feet are hopping, four little paws,
the distance between them is fifteen inches, they end
in the grass, in the leaves, there are four toes and a palm,
the nose isn't there, the tail isn't there, the teeth
that held the acorn, the eyes that thought; and the hands
that held the books, and the face that froze, and the shoulders
that fought the wind, and the mouth that struggled for air,
and love and hate, and all their shameless rages.

—Fall 1986

My First Kinglet

I saw my first kinglet in Iowa City
on Sunday, April twenty-second, 1984,
flying from tree to tree, and bush to bush.
She had a small yellow patch on her stomach,
a little white around her eyes. I reached
for a kiss, still dumb and silent as always. I put
a finger out for a branch and opened my hand
for a kind of clearing in the woods, a wrinkled
nest you'd call it, half inviting, half
disgusting maybe, or terrifying, a pink
and living nest. The kinglet stood there singing
"A Mighty Fortress Is Our God." She was
a pure Protestant, warbling in the woods,
confessing everything. I said goodbye,
a friend of all the Anabaptists, a friend
of all the Lutherans. I cleared my throat
and off she went for some other pink finger
and some other wrinkled palm. I started to whistle,
but only to the trees; my kinglet was gone
and her pipe was gone and her yellow crown was gone,
and I was left with only a spiral notebook
and the end of a pencil. I was good and careful
for all I had left of the soul was in that stub,
a wobbling hunk of lead embedded in wood,
pine probably—pencils are strange—I sang
another Protestant hymn; the lead was loose
and after a minute I knew I'd just be holding
the blunt and slippery end. That was enough
for one Sunday. I thanked the trees, I thanked
the tulips with their six red tongues. I lay
another hour, another hour; I either
slept a little or thought a little. Life—
it could have been a horror, it could have been
gory and full of pain. I ate my sandwich
and waited for a signal, then I began
my own confession; I walked on the stones, I sighed

under a hemlock, I whistled under a pine,
and reached my own house almost out of breath
from walking too fast—from talking too loud—
from waving my arms and beating my palms; I was,
for five or ten minutes, one of those madmen you see
forcing their way down Broadway, reasoning with themselves
the way a squirrel does, the way a woodpecker does,
half dressed in leaf, half dressed in light, my dear face
appearing and disappearing, my heavy legs
with their shortened hamstrings tripping a little, a yard
away from my wooden steps and my rusty rail,
the thicket I lived in for two years, more or less,
Dutch on one side, American Sioux on the other,
Puerto Rican and Bronx Hasidic inside,
a thicket fit for a king or a wandering kinglet.

—Fall 1986

Leon Stokesbury

———

Unsent Message to My Brother in His Pain

Please do not die now. Listen.
Yesterday, storm clouds rolled
out of the west like thick muscles.
Lightning bloomed. Such a sideshow
of colors. You should have seen it.
A woman watched with me, then we slept.
Then, when I woke first, I saw
in her face that rest is possible.
The sky, it suddenly seems
important to tell you, the sky
was pink as a shell. Listen
to me. People orbit the moon now.
They must look like flies around
Fatty Arbuckle's head, that new
and that strange. My fellow American,
I bought a French cookbook. In it
are hundreds and hundreds of recipes.
If you come to see me, I shit you not,
we will cook with wine. Listen
to me. Listen to me, my brother,
please don't go. Take a later flight,
a later train. Another look around.

—Spring 1981

Robert Penn Warren

Weather Report

In its deep little chasm my brook swells big,
The color of iron rust, and boulders bang—
Ah, where is the sun that yesterday made my heart glad?

Rain taps on the roof of my air-swung workhouse,
On one side in pine tops above the chasm.
The only code being tapped is this: *Today is today.*

Where are the warblers that yesterday
Fluttered outside my screen walls, or ignoring
My presence poured out their ignorant joy to my ignorant heart?

Where are the warblers? Why, yes—there's one,
Rain-colored now like gunmetal, rain-slick like old oil.
It is motionless in the old stoicism of Nature.

Yes, under a single, useless maple leaf,
The tail with a fringe of drops, like old Tiffany crystal,
And one drop, motionless, hung at the beak-tip.

I see that beak, unmoving as death—today
No note of ignorant joy to instruct
My ignorant heart, no promise of joy tomorrow.

But yet the code taps on the tar-paper roof.
Have I read it aright? *Today is today.*
Yes, earth grinds on its axis,

With a creak just this side of silence.
It lurches, perhaps.

—Spring 1979

Snowshoeing Back to Camp in Gloaming

Scraggle and brush broken through, snow-shower jarred loose
To drape shoulders, dead boughs, snow-sly and trap-laid,
Snatching for thongs of my snowshoes, I
Stopped. At the edge of the high mountain mowing, I
Stood, westward stared
At the half-mile of white alabaster unblemished
To the blackness of spruce forest lifting
In a long scree-climb to the cliff-thrust,
Where snow, in level striations of ledges, stretched, and the sun,
With spectral spectrum belted, pale in its ghost-nimb,
Unmoving, hung
Clear yet of the peak-snagged horizon.
The shadow of spruces, magenta,
Bled at me in motionlessness
Across unmarred white of the mowing.

And Time seemed to die in my heart.

So I stood on that knife-edge frontier
Of timelessness, knowing that yonder
Ahead was the life I might yet live
Could I but move
Into the terror of unmarred whiteness under
The be-nimbed and frozen sun.

While behind, I knew,
With the garrotte of perfect knowledge, that
The past flowed backward: trees bare
As though of all deeds unleafed, and
Dead leaves lost are only
Old words forgotten in snowdrifts.

But the crow, in distance, called, and I knew
He spoke truth, for
Higher a wash of pale pink had suddenly tinted the mowing,
And from the spruce-blackness, magenta

Leaped closer, and that instant
The sun-nimb made contact
With jag-heave of mountain,
And magenta lapped gray at my feet, with pink, farther up,
Going gray.

Hillward and sky-thrust, behind me,
Leafless and distanced to eastward, a huge
Beech clung to its last and lone twinge
Of pink on bole elephant-gray—far under
One star.

The track, pale in tree-night,
Floated downward before me, to darkness.

So starward, I stared
To the unnamed void where Space and God
Flinch to come, and where
Un-Time roars like a wind that only
The dead, unweeping, hear.

Oh, Pascal!
What does a man need to forget?

But moved on, however, remembering
That somewhere—somewhere, it seemed—
Beautiful faces above a hearthstone bent
Their inward to an outward glow.

Remembering, too, that when a door upon dark
Opens, and I, fur-pricked with frost,
Against that dark stand, one gaze
Will lift and smile with sudden sheen
Of a source far other than firelight—or even

Imagined star-glint.

—Spring 1979

Timeless, Twinned

Angelic, lonely autochthonous, one white
Cloud lolls, unmoving on azure which
Is called the sky, and in gold drench of light
No leaf, however gold, will stir, nor twitch

A single blade, now autumn-honed, of cat-tail by the pond. No voice
Speaks, since no voice knows
The language in which a tongue might here rejoice.
So silence, like a transparent flood, thus overflows.

In it I drown, and from my depth my gaze
Yearns, faithful, toward that cloud's integrity,
As though I've now forgot all other nights and days,
Anxiety of the future's snare, or nag of history.

What if, to my back, thin-shirted, brown grasses yet bring
The heat of summer, or beyond the northern rim, wind,
Snow-bellied, lurks. I stare at the cloud, white and motionless I cling
To our one existence, timeless, twinned.

—Spring 1979

Rosanna Warren

Antietam Creek

22,000 dead September 17, 1862

The lovers cross the bridge, and the brown stream
slides along rusting fields. The lovers hear
papyrus shush of cornstalks as they climb
the hill, and a crow calling. October air

burns gold, auburn. High, a hawk
laces the sky in loops. The slow blood crawls
up pokeweed, bright pink in the stalk
to blurt black in the berry. The couple strolls

the hillcrest now, hand held in hand, as though
Sumner has never slashed through Bloody Lane
nor Hill's mistaken "About face" split his ranks

while Burnside fumbled. The lovers read no
bronze plaques bolted to granite. They will drink wine,
make love in the fluvial field by crumbling banks

till evening drains the landscape, and they go
hand gripping hand, coats buttoned, heads held low.

—Winter 1981

C. K. Williams

Artemis

The lesbian couple's lovely toddler daughter has one pierced ear with
    a thin gold ring in it
and the same abundant, flaming, almost movie-starlet hair as the
    chunkier of the women.
For an entire hour she has been busily harrying the hapless pigeons
    of the Parc Montholon
while the other two sit spooning on a bench, caressing, cradling one
    another in their arms
then striking up acquaintance with a younger girl who at last gets up
    to leave with them.
They call the child, but she doesn't want to go just yet; she's still in
    the game she's made.
It's where you creep up softly on a pigeon, and, shrieking, stamp and
    run and wave your arms,
then watch as it goes waddle, waddle, and heaves itself, to your
    great glee, into the air.

—Winter 1985

The Dirty Talker, Boston

Shabby, tweedy, academic, he was old enough to be her father and I
     thought he was her father,
then realized he was standing closer than a father would so I
     thought he was her older lover.
And I thought at first that she was laughing, then saw it was more
     serious, more strenuous:
her shoulders spasmed back and forth; he was leaning close, his
     mouth almost against her ear.
He's terminating the affair, I thought: wife will, the kids . . . the girl
     won't let him go.
We were in a station now, he pulled back half a head from her the
     better to behold her,
then was out the hissing doors, her sobbing wholly now so that
     finally I had to understand—
her tears, his grinning broadly in—at *me* now though, as though I
     were a portion of the story.

                        —Winter 1985

Shame

A girl who, in 1971, when I was living by myself, painfully lonely,
     bereft, depressed,
offhandedly mentioned to me in a conversation with some friends
     that although at first she'd found me—
I can't remember the term, some dated colloquialism signifying odd,
     unacceptable, out of things—

she'd decided that I was after all all right . . . twelve years later she
    comes back to me from nowhere
and I realize that it wasn't my then irrepressible, unselective,
    incessant sexual want she meant,
which, when we'd been introduced I'd naturally aimed at her and
    which she'd easily deflected,
but that she'd thought I really was, in myself, the way I looked and
    spoke and acted,
what she was saying, creepy, weird, whatever, and I am taken with a
    terrible humiliation.

                       —Winter 1985

Charles Wright

Self-Portrait

In Murray, Kentucky I lay once
On my side, the ghost-weight of a past life in my arms,
A life not mine. I know she was there,
Asking for nothing, heavy as bad luck, still waiting to rise.
I know now and I lift her.

Evening becomes us.
I see myself in a tight dissolve, and answer to no one.
Self-traitor, I smuggle in
The spider love, undoer and rearranger of all things.
Angel of Mercy, strip me down.

This world is a little place,
Just red in the sky before the sun rises.
Hold hands, hold hands
That when the birds start, none of us is missing.
Hold hands, hold hands.

—Fall 1978

Robert Cantwell

He Shall Overcome: Pete Seeger

In their romance with folk song, revivalists often thrust upon brilliantly gifted but sometimes sheltered and unworldly people, or upon tough, ill-used, implacable people, the unaccustomed, occult, and often capricious role of "folksinger." Some have flourished in that role; some have not. Better, perhaps, in the end, as Joseph Conrad put it, "in the romantic element to immerse oneself"—even if the signs are not entirely auspicious. That is what Pete Seeger did—and he did it voluntarily, penitentially, in a redemptive career of self-effacement born of a uniquely inventive reconciliation of gifts and opportunities. His has been a peculiar bravery which, while signifying profound and inarticulable injury, at the same time emboldened him to jettison the fears and prejudices which normally prevent us from negotiating an agreement between personality and society which is uniquely our own.

From a welter of influences and occasions Seeger fashioned a character and a career frugal but imaginative in its economy, rugged but genteel in its texture, and simple and consistent in motive—one which spun the fibers of diverse cultural traditions into a continuous thread that led him out of, but has remained steadfastly anchored in, his basic sadness. Though he allied himself with ideologues, his ideas were not complicated. His convictions, deeper than ideas, sprang from basic drives and consequently were unassailably pure—and, from the ideological viewpoint, deeply contradictory. Had Seeger turned out differently, had he become a casualty of idleness, depression, or failure, causes enough might have been unearthed from the record; but he outdistanced the record. Though Seeger's unique personal document has been anathema to some, many have been signatories to it, and it has become a permanent part of the literature of the American identity.

Once I asked a friend, a cloistered monk, if I might meet the abbot of his monastery, said to be a holy man. "There wouldn't be much point in that," was the answer. "There's nothing to meet." Seeger is notorious for his inaccessibility, his general withdrawal from the field of personal or intimate relations. "Only Pete knows Pete," Moe Asch once told folklorist Gene Bluestein. "I don't think even Toshi"—Pete's wife— "knows Pete" (Bluestein 291). In Seeger the person as such, that which emerges through engagement with others in a series of social masks, is wholly sublimated, a larval stage lingering only in vestiges, its forces marshaled on behalf of an achieved self that appears not through engagement, but in affiliation, commitment, and, most of all, in performance.

Seeger's performances have changed lives: that is because unlike the great mass of performers who have secured their personal privacy behind a facade of public roles and masks, Seeger makes in performance, I believe innocently and unconsciously, a most intimate and personal revelation. All of him is there: the elegantly disciplined unworthiness; the fundamental embarrassment put temporarily at bay by energetic, liberal, and scrupulously amateur musicianship; the refinement politely disguised, the delicacy waived, the theme of social injustice persistently, compulsively sounded with beseeching gestures from within a private sorrow. Revealing himself, he remakes us.

A doctor's son from Passaic, Ralph Rinzler, and a lawyer's from Philadelphia, Roger Abrahams, heard Pete Seeger together at Swarthmore in 1953. "We realized that this was what we wanted to do for the rest of our lives"—that's how Abrahams remembers the occasion. For him, Seeger was a man with "clarity of spirit and vision," who gave no evidence in his presentation of any particular ideological associations—with the Communist Party or the Popular Front—through whom in any case life flowed purely, without subtle ideological nuances or convolutions. For Rinzler, "everything fit together" in Seeger; "he seemed absolutely coherent." Immediately the two young men went out to buy banjos; in a few years both were well established as revivalist musicians; in the fullness of their careers Abrahams has become one of the most respected of folklore scholars and theorists, and maintains his close association with Rinzler, who after his work with Doc Watson, Bill Monroe, and the Newport Folk Foundation, went on to become the founder and director of the Smithsonian's Festival of American Folklife and a leading figure in the federal public folklife establishment.

There is a peculiar kind of authenticity in what Rinzler calls "the coming together of ideology and musicianship." But, whether creed or ideology, philosophy or faith, it offers to the literate and secular young person in a complex plural society—who has not yet learned to live with ambiguity, whose identity in the moment of its annealing demands a certain definiteness and rigidity—a way of achieving, or of seeming to achieve, the apparent unity and singularity of mind, not hobbled by self-consciousness, nor folded by guile, nor sickened with irony, which is the apparent blessing of folk culture. "In folk societies," revivalist John Cohen writes, "the limitations are often clear and strong."

The influence of tradition is heavily respected and goes unquestioned. In the city, each individual is constantly in search of values . . . This search for values is becoming the tradition of the city. If we from the city are attracted to folk music, it is because we appreciate the clarity of the limitations within which folk music developed. But ultimately we appreciate the *order* that comes of these limitations. (32–33)

In folk song, that order is the order of culture; in urban, secular, literate society it is the order of ideas and arrangement of them that we call ideology, and the declaration of commitment to them that we call belief. Somewhere between these poles lay the folk revival and all the youth movements that followed it, whose commitment was to an order of signs, not words. The authenticity of that commitment is that of the directed will, like that of wedding vows, which, rooted in love—the source of love's own strength lying in the unperceived cultural forces working in it—secures its truth in and by "forsaking all others."

It is not immaterial, of course, that both Rinzler and Abrahams were young men of German-Jewish background, with its assimilationist ethos, both powerfully influenced in boyhood by admired elder men, an uncle and a father respectively, with socialist leanings; Seeger touched them, clearly, on a level deeper than ideas, though in retrospect ideas provide a useful way of explaining the force of Seeger's presence. Nevertheless, as the boys' first impulse, to go out and buy a banjo, indicates, it was in his musicianship, and in the banjo particularly, that the meaning of him seemed to be concentrated.

As Alan Lomax and many others have observed, Pete Seeger looks like, and in a sense *is*, his banjo—the anomaly of anomalies in his anomalous personality. Seeger's own banjo is an oddly elongated variant of its nineteenth-century original, with a tuning peg fixed halfway up a neck to which three extra frets have been added—an innovation of Seeger's in 1944. While it permitted him to play in more keys, it also exposed the conspiracy of elongation—of legs, arms, and banjo neck—in which man and instrument were passionately involved. Culturally, the banjo was a complete enigma, having been thrust out of a series of social niches by virtue of associations which had themselves become vague and indefinable: abandoned by black culture, which had reconstructed it from an African progenitor, forsaken by the Gilded Age parlor society in which it had had a brief vogue, repudiated by jazz as jazz moved uptown—it was the instrument that history had left behind. To take it up, as Seeger did, was a gesture at once disarmingly candid and hauntingly emblematic, a fundamentally comic piece of cultural scavengery which like a clown's broken umbrella solicits ordinary good will in conventional terms at the same time that it legislates independence of norms and conventions.

That independence was, symbolically, economic—like the independence represented by the jazzman's horn or "axe." But it was moral as well: with his banjo on his back like a soldier's carbine, the solitary Seeger seemed but a foot soldier in a vast invisible banjo army, at once a crusader and apostate. As minstrelsy's signature instrument the banjo embodied not only the victimization and marginality of the plantation slave but the spartan and adventurous spirit of the itinerant theatrical player or circus roustabout, uncompromised by ties to family, community, or society; to play it was a simple and honest, even a homely occupation, a kind of trade, like carpentry—hence Seeger's rolled shirt cuffs. In short, it was the perfect icon of Seeger's achieved self— and to the young imagination of the folk song revival he would help to inspire, which looked across the landscape of postwar society and found not a single opportunity to its liking, the banjo was a door, and Seeger was knocking on it.

I first encountered Pete Seeger, though I didn't realize it, in the early nineteen-fifties, at summer camp. Seeger did not visit us as he did so many other summer camps during the period, no doubt because we were in Wisconsin, not upstate New York; but our camp director, a Rabbi's son from New Orleans who spoke transcendentally of nature and filled our hearts with holy dread when he donned a great ceremonial headdress of eagle feathers and carried his giant frame like a brimming cup around our Council Ring to the beat of an Indian drum, liked to play Weavers' songs on our public address system—especially, at summer's end, when we were all packing our trunks, Woody Guthrie's "So Long, It's Been Good To Know Ya." I loved that song—maybe because I associated it with going home; but even then I could hear in that gang of voices—Hays, Hellerman, Gilbert, Seeger—a kind of neighborliness, and I never forgot it.

Of folk song, then, perhaps I knew a little: my mother's brother Bernie, who worked for a phonograph company, had given me a little plastic record in which the folksinger Tom Glazer told the story, with some catchy Irish work songs, of the completion of the transcontinental railroad. But I was innocent of politics. I knew nothing of socialism, or the Spanish Civil War, and still less of blacklisting, though I'd seen the Army-McCarthy hearings on our brand new Emerson television—without, of course, understanding anything about them. Of communists I knew only that they were sinister men with eyeglasses and neckties whom I was supposed to fear. My mother's father had emigrated from St. Petersburg in 1898, peddled fish, and lost a hard-won real-estate fortune in the Depression: she voted, with the rest of her family, for Stevenson. But my father had voted for Eisenhower. He was a Missourian, son of an old-time Methodist preacher, and he reminded everyone, me included, of Gene Autry.

Some years later a young man I admired—a bit ahead of me, with an Ivy-League haircut I could not, with my cowlick, imitate, already in his first year at the University of Michigan, the son of an old-world Jewish patriarch who owned a furniture store and an affectionate, bookish, chain-smoking, goggle-eyed woman, thin and small as a dancer, who had been one of my mother's childhood playmates—introduced me to two artifacts of his world: Peter Gunn, the hip television detective, and a Vanguard record album called "The Weavers at Carnegie Hall." There were those voices; and on the cover was a tall man with a big nose, a tuxedo, and a banjo, whose name was Pete Seeger.

Soon all my friends had guitars or banjos, and were singing everything from "Lemon Tree" to "Havah Nagiela." I had a beautiful long-necked banjo, the "Pete Seeger" model, with a smiling face white as table linen, a whiskery surface and a set of shining steel strings that crossed it like the Golden Gate Bridge. I played it constantly. I had a sweetheart, too, who gave me a Pete Seeger record album for my birthday, and on summer evenings we let his lonesome banjo tunes carry us out over the yellow hinterlands. At last Pete Seeger came to Orchestra Hall, and spread wide his elegant arms as we sang to him, and it changed me. It was thirty years ago, and I have not changed back.

It is commonplace of course to look back in middle age to the formative experiences of youth and to understand them in a new light. I've been studying what we now call the folk revival, and with David King Dunaway's sensitive biography of Pete Seeger, and Joe Klein's dashing and learned account of probably the most important life to have intersected Pete's, Woody Guthrie's, and other bits and pieces, I've begun to read in my own memory the image of Pete Seeger. Like a verse in an old text, though it will never finally give up its secret, it never exhausts the passion to discover it. Peter Seeger was born, as his biographer David King Dunaway tells us, in 1919, on his grandparents' fifty-acre estate near the Taconic Mountains, of unhappy young parents already estranged who sent him away to boarding school at the age of four and divorced when he was eight. His grandfather, having made a fortune in sugar-refining and rubber, expected his boys to follow him in business; but Charles, Pete's father, perhaps because of the elder Seeger's enthusiasm for Wagner, studied music at Harvard, and aspired to become an avant-garde composer—aims entirely consistent with a family that traced its ancestry to German aristocracy. But by the time of Pete's birth he had lost a teaching position at Berkeley on account of his uncompromising opposition to America's entry into the first World War.

Charles had his family's "probity, self-control, and strict table manners," one of Pete's brothers recalled, and expected perfection in everything. Pete's mother, Constance de Clyver Edson, raised in Tunisia and Paris, was, it seems, a humorless and self-conscious girl persistently anxious, apparently, about matters of money and respectability, devoted to her violin and inflexibly conservative in her musical tastes. She never convinced Peter to play the classical violin, for he had absorbed his father's contempt for "fine"—that is, ruling class—music; but she infused in him a sense of what is "classical" in music even more exacting, perhaps, than her own.

Until he was seventeen, Peter saw his family only on school holidays, boarding in what was the only home he knew as a child, the barn at the family estate in New York; family life itself was strict, coolly formal, tightly controlled emotionally, with, as family friend George Draper noted, "no tears allowed at family separations." Not, perhaps, the childhood we might want for our own children—but thoroughly compatible with the Seegers' Puritan ancestry and the Calvinist tradition to which they belonged, with its watchful asceticism, its self-reproving moral rigor, its all-pervading conviction of sin which it is a principal business of life to nurture—not only in oneself, but in others.

Here, it seems, must be the real spiritual foundation and fountainhead of Seeger's politics: a repressed and repressive personality, often competent, dependable, and proud, given to detachment and reasonableness, often compulsively self-sacrificing but capable of intimacy only with great difficulty, the habitual and unconscious suppression of anxiety, anger, loneliness, and hurt, the tendency to place the needs of others always before one's own, acquired of necessity from the emotional frustrations of childhood. "Toshi reminds me of something we've been through that's very unpleasant," Peter told Dunaway, "but I haven't the faintest memory of the occasion. It's as if I have some protective device inside my brain; instead of causing grief by remembering it, I simply erase it."

Old wealth cannot guarantee that parents will bestow the unequivocal love from which spiritual freedom flows, or earn the trust upon which worldly confidence is based. But it does confer a certain habitual sense of immunity, whether actually warranted or not, from the specters of disgrace and indigence, and hence a certain independence of social convention—and this may better equip a child to compensate early emotional deprivations. Certainly such a sense of immunity helped Charles Seeger to resist the enormous tide of anti-German political opinion in 1917. The true child of privilege need not think or do as others do; on the widened field upon which he will squander, repudiate, or sublimate his advantages he enjoys a sense of indomitability which others do not. Hence the phenomenon of the young gentleman adventurer, like Peter's uncle Alan Seeger: Harvard man, friend of John Reed and Mike Gold, Greenwich Village bohemian, volunteer to the French Foreign Legion in which he was shot to death leading a charge—and the poet who wrote the now familiar line "I have a rendezvous with death."

The Calvinist personality was a formula designed to issue precisely in the efficiency, indefatigability, and moral ardor which brought it to prominence in the industrious mercantile society which began its cultural ascent in the seventeenth century. But spiritual growth in every tradition entails the transcendence of personality, which in Calvinism, as indeed in other religious traditions, discovers the long-sought infantile lost love in a transcendent divine love abroad impersonally in nature or in humanity. With a precision that robs all his actual and potential biographers of their thunder, Pete Seeger compared himself, in his regular column in *Sing Out!,* the folk song magazine, to John Chapman, the Swedenborgian mendicant from Massachusetts called "Johnny Appleseed" who in the early nineteenth century prepared the wilderness for the westward expansion by planting seedling apple nurseries through the Alleghenies into central Ohio. Chapman believed that the innermost human soul was divine, and that with resistance to temptation, and disciplined obedience to the word of God, human nature itself could be glorified by its indwelling influence. In folklore Chapman was remembered for his kindness to animals, his feats of strength, his ability to live in the wild, and for the stewpot he wore for a cap.

Pete Seeger's longing for the "morally consistent life," then, was a venerable Yankee tradition—but it found its fulfillment in an original structure of influences from the experiences of his own family, class, culture, and times. Seeger was only one of many young boys who read the works of Canadian naturalist Ernest Thompson Seton, a founder of the Boy Scouts, who challenged his young readers to "survive in the woods with just yourself and an axe"; through woodcraft and Indian lore Seton promulgated a juvenile version of "muscular Christianity" with its basic analogy of physical fitness and cleanliness to moral rigor and purity, bodily hardiness being essentially a hedge against sexual temptation—particularly that sexual bugaboo of the period, masturbation—and a corrective for the feminizing influences of bourgeois society.

New Russia's Primer, the Bolshevik children's book Seeger discovered as a boy in the Spring Hill School library at Litchfield, inculcated a similar message: to remain watchful for decadent tendencies in parents and teachers, and to help those nostalgic for pre-revolutionary Russia, or who clung to their superstitious religions, to see the error of their ways. Seton's Little Savage and Lenin's Young Pioneer expressed, in different ways, the idealism and discipline which were Seeger's both by temperament and by tradition, and the young man's embrace of them may perhaps be taken as the original union which produced the synthesis of politics and folk song that became his vocation and identity.

Though isolated and exquisitely shy, Seeger had already found his favorite social mode at Spring Hill, where he and a roommate, accompanied by Peter's ukulele and in the end by an entire auditorium of voices, had led a program of sea chanties. At sixteen he had not yet come into his full height—he was just over five feet—and with his girlish complexion and long curls found himself in the theatricals at Avon Old Farms preparatory school, citadel of "the elite of the well-ordered mind," in female roles. He was subscribing to *New Masses,* memorializing his uncle Alan by reading John Reed and Mike Gold, and for spare change shining his classmate's shoes. At Avon, attracted by Gershwin songs, he put aside his uke, bought a disused tenor banjo from a faculty member, and joined the Hot Jazz Club.

But he could not reproduce on his four-string tenor banjo, a ragtime and jazz instrument, the sounds of the five-string southern mountain banjo, which he heard on the Library of Congress recordings his mother Ruth Crawford was in the summer of 1936 transcribing for John and Alan Lomax. Bascom Lamar Lunsford was there, along with Pete Steele, Buell Kazee, Wade Ward, Lily May Ledford—names which would become household words to folk revivalists of the sixties—and Uncle Dave Macon, whom Seeger considered the best banjo player in the world. That the folk banjo had *five* strings, not four, Pete did not discover until, later that summer, his father took him to Bascom Lamar Lunford's Mountain Folk Song and Dance Festival of 1936, in Asheville.

Discovering the five-string, however, and playing it, were different matters. Seeger's career as a folksinger began inauspiciously in New York, where, having dropped out of Harvard and taken up residence with his brothers on the Lower East Side, unable to find work in his chosen career as a newspaper reporter, he was forced back upon his banjo. His sister-in-law had dared him to perform on the street: so he stood on Park Avenue and sang "Old Man River" and "Cindy" to his tenor banjo accompaniment, earning seventy-five cents in three hours. His aunt Elsie Seeger, however, principal of the Dalton School, got him a job at a dance, where he earned five dollars and an invitation to repeat his performance at other private schools, among which was the progressive Little Red Schoolhouse, where Margo Mayo, founder of the American Square Dance Group, was on the faculty.

Mayo's square-dance group was at that point the center of New York City's folk song revival; Mayo's cousin, Kentucky mountain banjoist Rufus Crisp, showed Seeger the arcane mountain "clawhammer" or "frailing" style of banjo playing, a technique of West African origin nearly impossible to understand either by listening or watching alone, in which lay the secret of the folk banjo's driving, rhythmic sound. Seeger's adaptation of this technique, what he called his "basic strum," became his musical signature, and a versatile method for accompanying folk songs of all kinds. By stretching a resonant chord between the stakes of two sturdy notes, a melody note and a chiming note on the fifth string, Seeger gentrified the more percussive frailing style, with its vigorous forearm hammering and its percussive "rapping" of the fingernail on the banjo head.

This was of course precisely the moment that folk music was emerging into the culture of the Left in New York, whose principal preoccupation was the representation of a political idea, the idea of the People: not as a philosophical abstraction, nor even as the collective voice that speaks in the *Declaration,* but as a palpable reality, one that could be painted, photographed, interviewed and recorded, chronicled in novels, championed on the stage and screen, and celebrated in music and dance. The great Texas songster Huddie Ledbetter, "Leadbelly," whom folk song collectors John and Alan Lomax had brought to New York in 1934, was a People's hero incarnate; and so would be a few years later, in a similar way, Paul Robeson, not only as a singer, actor, and political spokesman, but, in Earl Robinson's "Ballad for Americans," as the rotund voice of "everybody who's nobody, the nobody who's everybody." 1938 had brought John Hammond's first Spirituals to Swing concert, Copland's *Billy the Kid,* and Martha Graham's *American Document*; in 1939 came the *Ballad for Americans*; in 1940 Alan Lomax's radio program "Back Where I Come From" made its debut, and Woody Guthrie arrived, shortly to appear in a "Grapes of Wrath" benefit for migrant workers and to record his *Dust Bowl Ballads.*

Literature had produced images of populist heroes in Sandburg's Lincoln and Steinbeck's Tom Joad, both of whom the folk song movement adopted as part of their iconography—Lincoln in Robinson's folk-music cantata "The Lonesome Train," in which Pete Seeger played a banjo part, and the Okie Tom Joad in Woody Guthrie's ambitious ballad, whose seventeen-odd stanzas, which he introduced at the "Grapes of Wrath" benefit, virtually retold the entire novel. "Woody Guthrie just ambled out," Pete Seeger recalled, "offhand and casual . . . a short fellow complete with western hat, boots, blue jeans, and needing a shave, spinning out stories and singing songs he'd made up . . . I just naturally wanted to know more about him."

Seeger himself, in fact, appeared with Guthrie that evening—his first concert performance—though stage fright, he says, deprived him both of the words to his song and the ability to accompany himself on the banjo. But his involvement with the heroes and heroines of the folk song movement was already intimate. Alan Lomax had introduced the fledgling banjoist to Aunt Molly Jackson, whom Seeger had heard on Library of Congress recordings, and to Leadbelly as well, from whom he took lessons on the twelve-string guitar. By the summer of 1939 his musical skills had improved sufficiently that he could travel as a banjoist and singer with the Vagabond Puppeteers, two of whose members had trained in the rural education campaign of post-revolutionary Mexico; this radical band offered to perform for the Dairy Farmers' Union in the midst of New York State's most violent milk strike. Seeger hadn't banked on becoming a soloist, which was anathema to him; but his audience of farmers was enthusiastic about his banjo, and asked to hear it—a crisis of self-consciousness which Peter resolved by coaxing the audience to sing along with him. By degrees Seeger was discovering his calling, whose moral tone was perhaps deepened shortly thereafter when a union steward who had offered his hospitality to the group was struck by a scab driver and killed.

Experience, especially very early experience, makes us, and makes us irredeemably. But to the extent that, in youth, we make our experiences, so we may be said to have made ourselves. As a boy Pete Seeger had watched volunteer squads from Communist Party unemployment councils replenish the shattered households of evicted tenants on the lower East Side; in the cold lofts of Greenwich Village, where the Composers' Collective held its meetings, he had heard Aaron Copland speak on the role of music in the class struggle. Still the impulse to remake himself by self-imposed rites of passage was irresistible: with Woody he set out for Oklahoma in Guthrie's new Plymouth—bought on credit—literally singing, not only for striking oil workers, but for haircuts, gasoline, lodging, and food; then in 1940 he set out on his own, hitchhiking and hoboing through Missouri, Wisconsin, South Dakota, and Montana, sleeping in a Salvation Army overcoat. He mangled his banjo in a leap from a moving freight train—and so hocked his camera for a cheap guitar and for money played Gene Autry songs in a saloon: a creditable narrative for a delicate boy. A month after his return he set out for Alabama, looking for Joe Gelders, a radical miner in whom he seems finally to have located the opposite pole of the social and cultural axis around which his career, and the entire folk revival, was to revolve. "You can have your Radio City Music Hall," he wrote, "your Hotel Savoy, your Hollywood Kleig lights, and your tuxedos, but as far as I'm concerned the best music I ever heard came out of that old shack in Townley, Alabama."

Seeger's late adolescence converged uncannily with an extraordinary historical moment, subjecting him to the influence of men and women of great personal amplitude and power, even of genius—Leadbelly, Guthrie, Lomax, Ruth Seeger, Molly Jackson, Moses Asch, after, of course, his own father, mother, and uncle Alan—around whom both the history and the prehistory of the folk revival had formed and was continuing to form, and which through these men and women may be said to have invested itself in Seeger's heart and mind. In the years of the folk revival many young people put on Seeger's identity in the hopes of making it their own. But Seeger's identity, while self-made, was not put on, but sought and won, a segment of a social and psychological arc which at its apogee worked an irresistible influence upon thousands of young people and altered their lives irrecoverably, and which, as Seeger approached his fiftieth year, returned, carrying the moral souvenirs of its remarkable transit, to the point at which it had begun.

Seeger is the type—and for the young people who encountered him in the 1950s and early 1960s, the original—of the fresh, untempered youth, who, dizzy with a sense of his own insubstantiality, despising the class and education which has made him, but filled with the romance of his class and education, projects out of his heart the adventure by which he will season himself, and in which he will discover the self that will authenticate him—or, more accurately, court the self which, if he is worthy, will accept him. All lives follow, like the energy that runs along a power line, a direction determined by the compass points of class, education, and the like, and defined by the particular terrain of personality and experience; all people carry in the energy of their being the resulting articulations of its flow which constitute the message of identity. For most of us, the life-force flows in one or two, at most three directions; experience follows, for most, a beaten track, and individuality falls readily into classes and categories. But Seeger, though in himself a point refined virtually out of existence, is the intersection of many such lines, each of which has left a betraying sign in him, each sign isolated from its own medium but nevertheless subliminally imparting its message, coexisting with other signs in a complex tension of mutual contradiction which can only be read, like a poem, and which, to people accustomed to making such painstaking interpretations, is a compelling mystery.

In the early nineteen-sixties, at the height of the commercial folk revival, the American Broadcasting Company declined to include Seeger on its short-lived television program "Hootenanny"—a fact particularly ironic because Seeger had introduced the word "hootenanny" into the national vocabulary, having learned it in Portland on a singing tour with the Almanacs. Blacklisting was in part responsible, of course, and fear of controversy; but as one producer noted, Seeger was "too slow and thoughtful" for the show (Spector 114). This was imprecise: what he might have said was that Seeger, to be understood and appreciated, demands not the mercurial television audience accustomed to monolithic television "personalities," but a slow and thoughtful audience, one that is willing to read the signs of a complex identity, most of which emerge in subtle textures and hues, in tones and overtones, to which the television screen is mostly insensitive.

That would be, of course, the college audience, among whom Seeger had most of his influence in the nineteen-fifties and sixties. In fact he seems to have something of the university about him. At his school concerts, in his knitted ties and rolled shirt sleeves, his bright red socks, he might be a physicist of the forties, engaged in some obscure way in the war effort; in his more familiar dungarees, work shirts and work boots, though these are ostensibly proletarian, he might be a geologist on a field trip. These clothes, in any case, even the tuxedo he wore at the Weavers' Carnegie Hall Christmas Eve concerts, never, when he is wearing them, quite fully assume their office; rather they hang upon his tall, delicate aristocratic frame like bunting, as much symbols of the realms of life to which they belong as artifacts of them. Seeger cannot dress at all, it seems, without making a statement.

Part of the cause is certainly that the awkwardness of his late growth—Seeger grew nearly a foot between the ages of seventeen and eighteen—has never really left him; always his ankles, wrists, and head seem to thrust out of his trouser leg, his shirt cuff and collar as if he had suddenly, in the night, shot up like a sunflower. And with this growth came, it seems, a late injection of masculinity which coarsened his jaw, enlarged his nose as if he had a permanent cold, and put gristle in his long, graceful limbs: caricaturing, but not effacing, his fundamental beauty—certainly the quality which recommended him for female roles at Avon Old Farms—which can be seen in its original purity and goodness in an early portrait of his mother Constance, whom he resembles, with her wide mouth, almost oriental cheekbones, and her large, watchful eyes. As a young man Pete still had her rosy complexion, and her fine, wavy hair, gleaming like chrome on the top of his head or hanging in a childlike ringlet over his temple. Craning his neck to sing, with his chin raised, his aerodynamic pompadour poised for highway travel, Seeger might have been a brazen college youth at the wheel of an open roadster, college pennant flying, speeding towards an Ivy League football game with a carful of girls singing the fight song; but he might have been, too, with his raw, innocent, uncouth face, an Iowa farm boy, with German parents perhaps, singing the national anthem.

When Seeger returned from a tour with the Army in the Pacific in 1944, he was, Bess Lomax remembered, "a very different man. He had matured physically and become a stronger singer. Now he was physically vibrant. He'd always been tense, lean, and bony, but the years of physical activity had put some weight on him. He was as hard as nails." This was the figure who—with outstretched arms and cuffs rolled, a man manifestly at work, as if at a union meeting or in front of a classroom—could set an entire auditorium singing with him in four-part harmony, summoning up what all the art and journalism of the 1930s could not do, an immediate, existential, auditory image of the People, a People not idealized at a distance but present, at once flowing out of and into the self, a personal and a supernal force, and bring to that experience a virtually religious sense of collective grace and purpose. His repertoire, with its global eclecticism reminiscent of Earl Robinson's American People's Chorus, leaped telephonically from an Appalachian ballad to an Indonesian lullaby to an African chant to a Woody Guthrie song, translating them all through Seeger's simple musical arrangements, designed for spontaneous choral singing, through his vocality, speech, indeed through his very being, into a familiar and authoritative cultural idiom.

Other concert singers such as John Jacob Niles and Richard Dyer Bennett had attempted to elevate folk song socially through, in Niles's case, melodrama, and in Bennett's, *bel canto* style—but this was merely an articulation of polite culture at the expense of folk song, moving it from enclaved to elite society and dispelling the cultural and political implications of such a movement. Seeger, on the other hand, suppressed all the *overt* signs of his cultural and social affiliations, and substituted, with his banjo, his proletarian costume, and so on, signs of a deliberate identification, in the iconography of thirties populism, with what were variously called workers, the people, or the folk. Those in his audience prepared to reject polite society, then, were disarmed; while overtly Seeger stood for the worker, the farmer, the black, he embodied, and tacitly and subliminally communicated, not mere *polite* society, with its bourgeois impulse to certify and enunciate itself, but hereditary caste, by Seeger's own embarrassed testimony "all upper-class." For however rustic or exotic his song, Seeger delivered it, not with the affected drawl of later folk revivalists, but in the honest accent of New England Protestant gentility, with its dignified, rotund vowels, every word articulate, and the raised voice of a scholar, lifted out of its element, projecting with the emphasis and drama of the elocutionist, as if out of a Latin primer, the folk song that through his mediation became always an artifact of high, indeed of the highest, culture, normally itself hidden in corporate boardrooms or behind the hedges of private schools and great estates. Seeger's performances are covertly a disclosure, and, in the archaic sense, an act of courtesy, in which he opens through folk song the ark of the social covenant to reveal what in a democratic society is the one treasure that individual initiative cannot win: privilege. *Real* privilege.

Europeans are familiar with the figure of the aristocrat-radical or reformer who from time to time appears on the social horizon. Allied with Seeger's physical resilience and social standing was the political radicalism with which he was increasingly, and to his everlasting detriment, identified and for which he was eternally vilified. Even at his acquittal for contempt of Congress in 1962 the presiding judge could not forbear referring to him as "one who may appear unworthy of sympathy." He had embraced radical causes at Harvard; in 1941 he joined the American Communist Party, sang at the opening of its headquarters in the Bronx and at lectures sponsored by the American Labor party, taught classes on labor songs at the Marxist Jefferson School of Social Science, helped to raise money for the *National Guardian,* and having led the People's Song movement in New York in the forties, traveled south in 1948 with Henry Wallace's Progressive Party campaign—these among many other leftist and Popular Front activities.

And yet, uncooperative as it appears to say so, Pete Seeger was not, strictly speaking, ideological. His sympathies and antipathies were powerful and persistent: but not the result of the conscientious embrace of a system of ideas quarried from texts, synthesized and refined through reflection and debate, re-embodied in memory and championed as an essentially textual description of reality. Seeger rather inherited his radicalism, as a boy, from his father and his father's associations, from the experiences that arose from them, as a streak in his temperament, just as the child of the Catholic, Presbyterian, or Jew inherits the social, moral, and cultural codes of these traditions even while he may not practice, or may consciously repudiate, the religions at the heart of them. Seeger's politics have much more the character of a creed, then, than of an ideology, rooted morally, as we have suggested, in a fundamentally religious sensibility which despises waste, ostentation, and worldly power, all the more so because his own origins lie in wealth and its prerogatives, and which emerges existentially in the original responses of his temperament to particular situations. Politically, then, it is an unsophisticated though often systematic opposition to commercialism and monopoly, especially in entertainment; socially it is a repression of the personal in favor of the collective and participatory; and personally it is his guarded asceticism sublimated by its identification with an idealized working people. "A person shouldn't have more property," Seeger used to say, "than he can squeeze between his banjo and the outside wall of his banjo case."

But the embodied, unarticulated, putative ideology—which strictly speaking is not an ideology at all, present only by inference—is far more powerful than ideology itself. Apart from direct political action, ideology has only verbal argument in which to advance itself and is therefore always vulnerable to argument; therefore the de-articulated "ideology," which is what Seeger's became after his blacklisting in 1950, had the power of innocence conferred by the brutal and self-aggrandizing provincialism of anti-Communism and the House Un-American Activities Committee. Arising only briefly and enigmatically in speech, never fully revealed in the unstable ambiguities of structures of words, but seeming almost mystically to inform every gesture and every word, bringing its moral energy into the music and elevating entire audiences with its communal spirit, Seeger's ideology is actually a silence which can absorb the meanings to which the ideas of his audiences, each person individually, incline them—a fact which accounts for the powerful allegiance, or revulsion, he inspired.

Seeger's radicalism, then, was a matter of desire more than of words, and hence for some more authentic, because less deliberate, than words; and the system of thought with which it was associated had been violently suppressed by the anti-Communism of the early fifties. He emerged, ultimately, as a system of paradoxes: masculine and feminine, patrician and proletarian, cosmopolitan and provincial, cultivated and un-cultivated, conservative and radical, hermetically private and gregariously public, a solitary wanderer and at the same time an entire movement—a richly heterogeneous, even contradictory cultural symbol eager for a re-articulation of itself. And herein lay his power: the power to arouse the need to speak.

In the 1940s, Pete Seeger sang for the labor movement; in the 1950s, after his black-listing, he took his music to schools and camps throughout the country and planted the seeds of the folk revival to come. He sang for the peace movement in the late fifties and sixties, in the civil rights movement in the early sixties, and in February 1968 sang his "Waist Deep in the Big Muddy," the anti-war song that CBS had suc-cessfully censored six months earlier, on the prime-time *Smothers Brothers Comedy Hour*. But the civil rights and anti-war movements were now dominated by young leaders, black and white, who openly advocated revolutionary violence. The youth counterculture, begotten by a ruthlessly exploitative commercial establishment upon the baby boom, waged a moral, and upon battlefields such as the Democratic Na-tional Convention at Chicago, a literal civil war against the political establishment, sadly polarizing families, classes, races, and sexes. In April Martin Luther King was assassinated, and in June presidential aspirant Robert Kennedy; race riots in Wash-ington, Chicago, Detroit, and Los Angeles set the ghettos burning throughout the summer. Without his leadership, King's Poor People's Campaign produced massive but ineffectual demonstrations in Washington, and foundered in the squalor of Res-urrection City, the tent city on the National Mall which, mired in mud and uncol-lected trash, and hung with the tear gas deployed by police against the firebombing of passing motorists by young demonstrators, was finally razed by bulldozers. Camped there with Toshi and his daughter Tinya, Seeger had helped other activists to lead the singing—but the blacks, native Americans, and others of the poor and dispossessed in the city could not feel, as Dunaway reminds us, that "This Land Is Your Land" applied to them.

But professional setbacks cannot terminate a career whose basis is a moral project. Twenty years earlier Seeger had anticipated what would shortly become the response to the wretched America of 1968 of thousands of young adults who, with their organic gardens, VW buses, and wood-heating stoves, paid him unawares the tribute of their imitation. Seeger had built, with the financial assistance of family and the contributed labor of friends, a log cabin on the banks of the Hudson near Beacon, New York. With its small woodlot, its garden, workshop, and fireplace, with the narrow clearing through which the river gleamed in the sunlight, the Seegers' cabin was a haven into which one might with dignity retreat from the physical and intellectual violence that now ruled in the political sphere. But the political sphere is where you find it: it expands with the consciousness of the political burden laid upon every aspect of ex-istence, dilating into moral and spiritual realms where "political" is only a metaphor—but a metaphor with a keen edge that is ever seeking to divide good from evil. Con-tending against evil was of course in the nature and tradition of the "old clergyman," as he once called himself, even in Beacon, where as recently as 1965 ever vigilant local conservatives had mounted a campaign to prevent him from singing in the high school auditorium.

Nineteen sixty-eight had sent Seeger, and half the counterculture with him, back to the land: and the land—specifically the Hudson River—became his new cause. Environmentalism was of course one of the political themes of the 1970s, one endearing itself to young activists now growing into their child-rearing and householding years, in spite of the fact that the history of environmental conservation lay largely with the upper classes. Hence it was disconcerting to his radical friends when Pete donned a Greek fisherman's cap—the kind that you can order from the back pages of *The New Yorker,* that you'll see around the wharfs of Vineyard Haven—and proposed to build a highly expensive replica of a nineteenth-century Hudson River sloop which would bring together "wealthy yachtsmen and kids from ghettos, church members and atheists" in the cause of cleaning up the Hudson.

Ever since his removal to Beacon, Seeger had been agitated by pollution in the Hudson, which flowed with everything from raw sewage to carcinogenic chemicals destined to poison the waters for a thousand years. Sailing in a small fiberglass skiff had provided a happy pastime in the years following the absorption of the folk song revival into the youth counterculture. With Toshi's administrative initiative, the Seegers raised sufficient funds from concert performances, local millionaires and historians, even from the Newport Folk Foundation, to build at last the half-a-million dollar sloop *Clearwater,* which with its several less expensively built progeny has become a symbol of one of the country's more successful environmental causes. Because his association with the sloop was a continuing source of controversy, Seeger eventually detached himself from the project; but to the children of the 1970s who never knew him in any of his earlier incarnations, Seeger will be remembered as the graybeard with the nautical chin, the fisherman's cap, the sailboat and the banjo who, with his crew of folk singers and schoolkids, brought back the birds and the fish.

"I am a product of my family and my childhood," Seeger told his biographer. "One thinks that one creates one's own life. So there I was at nineteen . . . going out to do what I thought needed to be done. To my surprise, thirty-five years later, I found that I was practically carrying out what my family had trained me to do." Seeger is eminently a man of his class and its traditions, with conscience, energy, and originality sufficient to realize the prerogatives and responsibilities of his class in ways sensitive at once to the historical moment and to the standard of courtesy belonging to that class and its tradition: a standard to which ideologues on the right and the left have been mostly blind. To the radicals of 1968 Seeger seemed to have lost touch with the Movement; but like the red-baiters of the early fifties, they had seen him only superficially, unable as ideologues always are to understand any complex human being— full of inconsistency and doubt, his ideas only approximately fitted to his experience, unable ever fully to know himself—as anything but a point on the map of their own thought. Personally remote, sometimes tiresome, childish perhaps, consumed with the perpetual inward struggle which is the psychological legacy of old New England Calvinism, often remorseful, self-chastising, despairing, occasionally given to intemperate outbursts of anger, Pete Seeger is nothing more or less than an imperfect mortal whose personal performance is of concern to himself and to his intimates alone.

To his public, however, he belongs with the religious dissenters and abolitionists who were his ancestors, and in time will perhaps join John Chapman, who shared his legacy, in that realm of memory, imagination, and speech where folklore, the realm in which Seeger has always sought to install himself, translates history into story and story into myth. The sound of Seeger's voice echoed long ago from the New England pulpit, the Lyceum and the schoolhouse, and the sound of his banjo from the circus ring and the minstrel stage; the sound of his axe, bedded in the hills above a river both blighted by civilization and touched with sublimity by art, recalls the isolated clearings of the first frontier. But Seeger's idea of life returns still earlier, to the primitive communities of Colonial America, where men and women thought to build in a wilderness a city without sin they called the New Jerusalem. And yet this man is no historical specter. Destined to go one way, he went another; favored with few natural advantages, he turned his many cultural advantages to a lifelong identification with people struggling to prove that we need not capitulate to the power that oppresses us, whether it proceeds from God, from nature, from history, from our parents, or from ourselves.

WORKS CITED

For biographical information and quotations from Pete Seeger I am indebted to David King Dunaway's engaging biography, *How Can I Keep From Singing: Pete Seeger,* McGraw Hill Book Company, New York, 1981, and to Joe Klein's rich and exhaustive *Woody Guthrie: A Life,* Ballantine Books, New York, 1980. I interviewed Ralph Rinzler and Roger Abrahams in January and February, 1986.

Blustein, Gene. "Moses Asch, Documentor," *American Music,* 5:3, Fall 1987.
Cohen, John. "In Defense of City Folksingers." *Sing Out!,* 9, Summer 1959.
Spector, Bert. "The Weavers: A Case History in Show Business Blacklisting." *Journal of American Culture,* 1982.

—Fall 1990

Eleanor Clark

Under the Sign of The Bison

The following is an extract from a volume entitled Tamrart: 13 Days in the Sahara, *an account of a camel trip in the southernmost part of that desert, the Hoggar, late in 1981. In the language of the nomads of the region, the Tuareg, vaguely honorific terms for the elderly are Amrar, male, meaning also Chief, and Tamrart, female: the author has adopted the names for herself and her husband. Entayent is the top-ranking of the four Tuareg guides; the French leader and organizer of the expedition is J.-L. Bernezat, known thereabouts as Bernouze. The town of departure and return is Tamanrasset, a long flight south from Algiers. Aside from the work force the party consisted of four of the author's family and three American friends who get names here like Kate and Bob, and a French unconnected pair of desert-lovers; nine in all. The camels come with the Tuareg and are their prize property.*

Third day out, one of the two out of our thirteen with no moving on. We'll sleep a second night in the same stunning spot, one of the trickiest, visually, of all our stopping-places only we were too sore to appreciate it on arrival yesterday. There is scale to it all right but of a peculiar kind, hardly a flatness of more than a few yards across, but every declivity and bump and angle is in a language of its own; with the slightest turn of your body you have to re-adapt inwardly to a new experience, a new set of expectations. Up over there is the ledge in the mountain wall where the youngest of our companions took his sleeping-bag last night. Across the opposite side of the sky is the stately peaked profile, a quarter of a horizon's worth, that I call the Mont St. Michel Affair. Altogether different from either of these, and from each other, are the lower stretches at any point between, gravelly sand and low brush here, great jagged rock bumps there, a red to ochre swell of very different rock smooth and silky as a quarter-mile of lady's bosom painted by Rubens.

Amrar (my husband's honorific name for the duration) is napping. Several have gone mountain-climbing with our guide and organizer Bernouze. Entayent is squatting alone by the last embers, seeing to the flat round bread, the galette, which must be done before the fire is stirred up for the evening meal. Not that it is ever brought to the kind of blaze we go in for in our campfires; the desert wood is extremely slow, long-burning and economical compared to most of ours; the cookery is over small diameter, high heat, no flame. This being a day or two before a voice from the mountains or some other power in the landscape ordained that this unworthy individual should be instantly and forever rescued from cigarettes, and having no matches, I join Entayent. He helps me get a light from the embers, and after murmuring the formality of a request—a bit of regal courtesy that puts the giver in debt for the favor of being asked, and to which anybody would nod assent as I do even if it were their very last piece of money or of bread or sip of water or cigarette—he lights one for himself.

His hands, very diluted cocoa in tint, are long and of great strength; a noble frame, and physiognomy to suit. There are small clouds here and there; it is not one of our skull-busting sun days. The lower folds of my companion's *chèche* are under his chin, a sign of quite relaxed informality, and I note that in that climate the color skin we call white is inappropriate to the point of ugliness; it seems an eccentricity and this Tuareg sand-to-umber the rightful epidermis for our species. You will hear them speak of the blacks, *les noirs*, some of whom were their slaves until not long ago; whether or not out of such ancestral dependence on menials, the Tuareg of upper degree, that is leaving out their serf class, are said to consider work debasing and to have no great habit of it in any form. Perhaps so. We would see nothing to bear that out and plenty to the contrary, but I believe the tribe, or it may have been two tribes, represented by our companions were altogether of vassal status. As such, impossible though it is to picture such a figure as Entayent in any subservient role, until this century they would not have been allowed to own either swords or camels, those being prerogatives of the nobles. The daily routines of encampment life, as described by our leader's wife Odette Bernezat in one of her two books on the region, are of more or less non-stop hard physical labor. Largely by women and children, it's true, but then the men are away on jobs for long periods, as they were also in the old raiding and trading days.

Entayent's French is excellent, only I have to get used to the intimate *tu* in any and all association. There is no other second person grammatically, no *vous* in that nomad society; you say *tu* to the police or the President or a visiting head of state if there should be one. Entayent wants to know how old I am. *"Quel âge as-tu?"* I can see that our conventional whimsicality about asking women that question would not go down, so I tell him. *"Et ton mari*? And your husband?" If he thinks we're both crazy to be there he doesn't say so. "I'm forty," he says. And already done for. *Fichu déjà."* His tone invites no questions about that or anything else of a personal kind. I had heard that he had recently taken a second wife, that number one had threatened to leave him at first but decided to stick it out, so he now had a town family, in Tam, and an encampment one in the desert somewhere. It might be true or might not. Until ten years ago he led some of the famous salt caravans from the great rock salt deposits farther north down into Niger and wherever else they went in central Africa, a trek of some forty days round trip, now lost to camels through the hard-top truck road. So except for wool and meat and hides, and the discomfort-seeking tourist trade represented by the likes of us, and for getting to certain places inaccessible by land vehicle but that not many people need to get to anyway, the camel has become obsolete, and this impressive figure of a man and all his people with it.

So it appears, as we hear and read of its appearing to be the case in every remaining intemperate or otherwise awkward piece of our planet, whether from dryness or wetness or ice or heat or heights of mountains. This hear-everything, go-anywhere world we've contrived is goodbye to our differences. If we survive we're going to be homogenized, look alike think alike talk and dress alike, etc. So many wiseacres I mean distinguished social scientists predicting it, it might as well have come about already. As in a way it has, while diversity increases fearfully along very different lines. Between Entayent and Bernouze there must surely be truer brotherhood than the Frenchman could feel for many of his compatriots. Or I for mine.

On a thong around his neck Entayent always wears a little flat leather container of nice workmanship, nothing ornate; I ask what is in it and he says the Koran, meaning presumably a passage or two considered crucial for guidance or protection in life, chosen either by himself or by some marabout, member of the priest class of his tribe. Later I would hear, how reliably I can't say, that such pious necklace texts may be pre-Islamic and that furthermore the wearer is supposed never to know the words. No risk in that respect for at least one batch of holy quotes, as women and camels too are similarly adorned, the thong in the camel's case having no utilitarian function outside of holding off evil spirits. Of those, the most publicized seem to be the Kel Essouf, mischief-makers related to the Arab djinn, who can wreak all manner of misfortune if not properly propitiated. They are easily offended, will have it in for you if you carry off the skull of a wild sheep, the *mouflon,* or other skeletal remains from their natural resting-place, and will do you no end of damage by getting into your head if you sleep with your mouth open.

Even so, they do less harm than a lot of what gets dumped nowadays into most heads where we came from. As with other sub-literate cultures, the Tuareg have long had a high art of oral recording and a faculty of memory that puts ours to shame and more so every day. One recent poll indicates that there are fewer Americans every year who can remember their own names, whereas it must be a rare targui who suffers any such cerebral hardship. Odette Bernezat reports that a few years ago, when the government made the Tuareg drop the "son of" form of surname and use one that could be passed on unchanged, their friends there had no trouble remembering the full names of their forebears for seven generations back.

For a while before their expulsion the French worked hard on a system of visiting schoolteachers for the desert nomad children. Independence may have been a step backward in that regard; some families manage to send children to town for a modicum of schooling but for many it is next to impossible. As I have been taught to read and have access to libraries, I probably know a little more about Entayent's larger family history than he does about mine, but that could be reversed in a couple of lectures, and what he heard he would never forget. What he knows of his own antecedents I try off and on to guess as we sit there, he and I, in the strange suspension of all purpose and progress that enchants our afternoon.

There will be happenings later, and have been some before. I think I was wrong about the mountain-climbing; the big expedition must have been in the morning, it is just a few of the indefatigables along with Bernouze who are off again now. I will wake Kate from a nap to come see the marvelous picture of the saddle camels, the privileged class, eating grain from a large cloth, four at a time, there not being room for more. They won't have any such treat every day; our stopping places each night are dictated by at least some minimal, miserable food supply for them—acacia thorns and a few tough leaves, twigs, brushy scrub, only once or twice the whole trip something really green and succulent. All right, and then water, always a happening in the Hoggar, and at this long day's stop a heavenly joy; that will be with Amrar and our little bucket and basin when he wakes up. The viper was last night, we two were already sacked out and didn't know until morning why there was some running and somebody came and zipped up our dufflebags. The snake was not in, just beside, Bob's sleeping-bag; he heard a little rustling. It was Entayent, whose motions are all of such a serenity now by the fireplace, who got over there like an arrow released from the bow and killed it, as soon as the word *vipère* was spoken. The clouds will get heavier, we'll be sprinkled for a few minutes, have to get out those raincoats we felt silly bringing. Bob's expensive new flask broke in his luggage, before any drop from it went to human throat, and the Tuareg subsequently walked a big circle past that bag to avoid being tainted by the aura. One swallow apiece for the eight of us who are indulging finishes our tiny supply of whiskey. For the next ten evenings alcohol consumption will consist of the prophylactic dash of pastis Bernouze shakes at dinnertime into our communal drinking-water pot.

Now, I'm still by the nearly cold mound of cinders, with Entayent whom I would like to understand yet do not feel in the least mystified by. The day of repose has sharpened vision, whetted the senses generally—a fool's paradise, there are plenty more aches and complaints coming. But now all that is magically in abeyance and I know why, I know my fairy tales, it is from that pure cool beautiful water I'll soon be pulling with a rope and my little red bucket from the secret cleft in rock half a mile away. The near rock facing me is shaped like the acoustical shell of a small outdoor concert stage, with a benchlike protuberance good for sitting or lying on, and on the more or less perpendicular wall above that, which bends to a lip of roof at the top, is the outline of a bison carved in the granite. Neolithic, they say, and I'm happy to believe it; if that particular one should not be genuine there are plenty of others around that are. Where our climbers went this morning there was an assortment, of different prehistoric animals, although the great art center—the Athens of the time, discovered only in the 1950s—was well north of the Hoggar in the Tassili.

Later we will meet an educated citizen, a resident of Tam, of somewhat sour and cynical bent, who will dismiss all such carvings and paintings in that vicinity as fakes, but that could be because he makes his living guiding scholars to stone-age artworks farther away. In any case, I'm in no mood to distrust our bison, or the little stone mortar Bernouze will shortly kick up out of the sand either. They give a time frame in which the Tuareg can move in comfort and in which we can get hold of a crux, or a sliver of one if that could be, about them, and I suppose equally about all people on earth who are called, less appropriately every day, primitive.

They will have lived along the same patterns, done the same things, in the same rhythms, made the same gestures, of love, of work and war and worship, for many centuries. . . . True? False? Both, maybe. These people are closer to ancestral grooves than most of us, which could be the secret of their sophistication in a world of transience and attendant jitters, but after all they see us, they see airplanes and may ride in them, they've lost their crafts, the camels' hobbles are plastic, they've done military service, helped build the Tam airport. Whatever their habits, their world does seem to have gone from prehistoric to nuclear, with very little between.

For one bit of very recent history, I'd love to know what memories Entayent has of that war of liberation that went on in his teens, 1954–62. Did he himself, I wonder, have to kill any French soldiers then? I don't know if the salt caravans continued in those years. Perhaps they did; the fighting as in previous milennia must have been mainly in the coastal strip, the Maghrib. But the Tuareg ware fighters, traditionally, fierce in the form of land piracy called the *rezzou,* and hardly less recently than that war for independence, in the carved bison time-scale, they performed a bloody feat of arms, of epic nature, that delayed the French advance southward by twenty years, until the turn of the century. As always in such matters, of course, what's valor for one mind is treachery for another. The date was 1881, the scene not many miles from ours that day, the outcome one of the most gruesome in French colonial annals at least in North Africa; in the Pacific or Southeast Asia or on or off the northeast coast of South America there may have been worse. But Algeria, right there in the back yard, must have hurt differently, and besides, this incident was of a kind conceivably to undercut the romance of the Foreign Legion. That much-fabled, ultra-disciplined corps of foreign mercenaries, not all of them runaway criminals or disinherited scape-graces, had been established fifty years earlier by King Louis Philippe to control French colonial possessions in North Africa. Not that the Legion, based much farther north in Algeria, was involved in this story.

Late in 1880 a colonel of some non-French lineage accounting for the name Flatters, left Ouargla, one of those oasis towns we would get a glimpse of from the air, with a mixed contingent of troops and guides. The idea, then and for long after, was to map a railroad route between the coast and French equatorial Africa. The French had been well entrenched then for thirty years along the northern edge of the Sahara, where Fromentin had come in on the mopping up, and longer than that in the fertile strip along the Mediterranean, so often coveted and grabbed and lost, but had yet no hold on the Hoggar. Obviously, in that vast, key area, aside from other factors of terrain and camel culture, they would never find the water spots, the *points d'eau,* on their own.

The Colonel was overbearing, as well as over-trusting, to the point of utter folly. That there could not have been a worse commander for the trek seems beyond dispute, which can be said for no other point in the narrative. Famous though the episode was and is still throughout the region among interested students and wayfarers, accounts of it vary greatly to this day, and whether an air of the scholarly about it warrants any more credence than the opposite is a good question, with sources mostly either unnamed or unreliable or both. Probably we can believe that the foolish, pig-headed colonel, setting out to cross Tuareg country, did so without any by your leave or other gesture of courtesy, having instead simply notified their top chief, the Ame-nukal, of his intentions. In a number of versions he acquired nevertheless the services of quite a few Tuareg guides, who rode along in a show of amity for several days before reaching a good place for a massacre. In a more circumstantial account, trust-worthy if you trust all academic credentials, the native guides were not Tuareg at all but for the height of folly, a band of their hereditary enemies the Chaamba, said to number thirty-one. In this and some other versions the party was made up of only ten French army officers, a couple of NCOs, and close to fifty Arab *tirailleurs.*

At a certain point, more or less where I'm sitting with Entayent beside the carved bison, somebody dressed exactly like him but with the *chèche* raised and the litham covering the rest of the face up to the eyes, approached on his camel with some companions and in friendly fashion offered to show the strangers the best way across the mountains. The Chaamba wanted to run for their lives. The poor foolish colonel accepted the offer and insisted on maintaining discipline—to the death as it soon turned out, and a pretty gory one. Any camels not in the line of fire were taken away.

Nobody speaks of Tuareg casualties; there must have been some, but there were not many on the other side left to tell the tale and indeed the figure for survivors, not at the immediate scene but after weeks of cannibalism and other extremities in the desert, is often given as one. One man, what was left of him, is sometimes said to have gotten back to Ouargla or some other settlement, and he was Chaamba, not French. One story has a fairly large group of starving survivors approached, to their surprise in amicable manner, by some Tuareg who give them a large sack of crushed dates. The Chaamba, so the tale goes, knew better than to touch them; the French who did were either poisoned to death or driven raving mad. The Chaamba cook came to be the one who picked and dispatched the next meat supply.

In another and quite persistent telling of the story, a badly wounded French officer was somehow dragged away, perhaps on donkey-back, by a *targuia*, whether of the tribe that did the killing or some other is not said, and nursed back to health by her over some weeks until he could make his way off to a French base, presumably with further help. He promised to write and send her presents to repay her kindness but never did, and twenty-odd years later, after the final defeat of the Tuareg at Tit and their acceptance of French hegemony, she was telling his name and asking for news of him from chance visitors and military personnel in the Hoggar.

There had in the meantime been developments not only of further French consolidation but of relations among the Tuareg tribes, often through the centuries far from peaceful and apparently further exacerbated just then by disagreement over the Flatters affair. Whatever the group ins and outs on that question and for that matter through their long fragmented history, a new balance of tribal power and a new Amenukal, top leader of all the tribes, were making for a rather different game before long. Perhaps if I had known the Flatters story then I would once in a while have cast a different glance at my friend by the fire, but of curiosity, hardly of criticism, as an offspring of anti-imperialist killers, or Minutemen, myself. We destroyed a cargo of tea, too, which no *targui* could be accused of.

But now look, my beautiful white camel Betsey and three others are eating their grain down on those upholstered bumps on their chests, front legs in the double-fold, hind ones out like a duck's in water, and that's when I see the fat crusty white worm that got rubbed off on the cloth. The nasty thing lives and breeds in all their noses, it makes them sick and may even kill them, but we're told the only known remedy is much too expensive and of only short-term benefit so nobody uses it, and that's why poor Betsey gives me such a time having to scratch her nose. If they took along grain for the pack camels too there'd have to be more camels to carry it, hence the class injustice.

The *point d'eau* at this stop is not one the camels can put their own mouths to, like some we'll come to, in the *oueds*. But they'll have their drink, for two or three days to come. It is patiently hauled up in a bucket and poured into a basin for them, over and over, until twenty-one camels have had enough from the invisible depths of the crevasse, where we too are doing our hauling and drinking and laundry and filling our canteens and in intervals of privacy bathing. The little clouds have moved away for the time being. In the great push and slap of the sun we strip and douse and soap and douse again, and drink, and drink some more, wash hair, wash underwear. The sense of luxury excites our skin from scalp to heel. The water is as cool as it is pure, every sip and splash is exquisite delight, and if there had been nobody to show us where it is we could have died of thirst standing almost on top of it, as any survivor of the Flatters incident could well have done, and plenty of other lost souls, martyrs not to their country's power greed, I mean altruism toward the under-civilized, but just to the human hunger for adventure, there or by other springs as hidden and as plentiful.

Last night's viper, we get to understand, might risk being a touchy subject in some company. Moussa, when it is mentioned, becomes a little defensive about it. "We don't see one every trip," he says stoutly. "There aren't that many. We might see one every ten trips." That remark struck me more for the large number of his trips than the small one, true or not, of vipers. Many trips, many trippers. Were we really being that unoriginal in our fine undertaking?

—Winter 1984

Terrence Des Pres

Self/Landscape/Grid

> *Miller owns this field, Locke that, and Manning the woodland beyond. But none of them owns the landscape. There is a property in the horizon which no man has but he whose eye can integrate all the parts, that is, the poet.*
> —Emerson
>
> *Every appearance in nature corresponds to some state of mind. . . .*
> —Emerson

I live in upstate New York, rural countryside and lovely hills, a place my neighbors like to call "the village." It's small, quiet, great for raising kids. Forty miles to the north, however, lies Griffiss Airforce Base, known locally as Rome, because Rome is the town the base uses. Out of there fly the B-52s that control our part of the sky. There too the Pentagon keeps its brood of cruise missiles. So nobody doubts, in this part of the country, that Rome (when it happens) will be the spot where the warheads hit. At one time we thought that the Russians had size but no technical finesse. That gave us a stupid sort of hope. An overshot might land on our heads, but if incoming missiles fell short, they would come down way north, maybe on Edmund Wilson's old stone house in Talcottville, and we, at least, would be well out of range. Now we are told that the Soviets have refined their delivery. Their guidance systems are on target, not least because the Russians have used American technology, computers, microchips, ball-bearings, made and sold by American firms. That, no matter how we look at it, is ugly news. And with Rome at the nub of a nuclear arc, we are resigned in our knowledge that things will start exactly forty miles away. How far the firestorm will reach is what we mainly wonder. We don't know, but we are counting on these upstate hills to block the worst of the blast. If the horizon works in our favor, we shall then have time to consider the wind. In the meantime, B-52s cross and recross above us. They gleam with their nuclear payload. Two or three are up there always, and once I counted thirteen. The air is creased with vapor trails, and in the afternoons, when the sun starts down, the sky looks welted with scars.

That, anyway, is the prospect I share with my neighbors, our part of the nuclear grid. Not a landscape of the mind, no inner weather sort of scene, it's just life's natural place for those who live here. Even so, the bombers overhead keep me reminded that this landscape possesses, or is possessed by, some other will, some demonic grand design or purpose not at all my own. Nor would that kind of death be mine. An all-at-once affair for almost everyone is how that death would come, impersonal but still no accident. That way of dying would be the ultimate instance of political intrusion, for that is what has brought us to this pass, politics, and by political intrusion I mean the increasing unsettlement and rending of our private lives by public force. We do what we can as citizens, but when it comes to nuclear war we can't do much. The hazard is before us and won't budge. How to live with it is our problem, and some of us, at least, resort to magic. We turn to words which give the spirit breathing space and strength to endure. As in any time of ultimate concern, we call on poetry.

I can read *Ecclesiastes* or *King Lear* for a language equal to extremity, but such language isn't of my time, not of my landscape perhaps I should say. I find a little of what I need in poets like Akhmatova or Mandelstam or Milosz, but American poetry? and among poets of the present generation? Not much, in fact hardly anything. I'm writing in early February (1983) and I've just gone through the recent issue of *American Poetry Review,* which offers forty-eight poems by twenty-one poets. Some few good poems, but only two touch upon our nuclear fate, which leaves forty-six in worlds elsewhere. In "Against Stuff" Marvin Bell follows the possibility—this is a night-thoughts poem—that all our forms and habits, including those of poetry itself, may have been wrong, wrong enough to bring us to "the coming instantaneous flaming" of all creatures and things "which could not suffer / that much light at one time." The poem spreads disquiet and resists reply, and in the following lines the pun on "not right" keeps the poet honestly uncertain:

> and, if we are shortly to find ourselves
> without beast, field or flower,
> is it not right that we now prepare
> by removing them from our poetry?

Under nuclear pressure, should poetry contract its domain? The other poem in *APR,* Maxine Kumin's "You Are In Bear Country," moves with wit and nice inevitability to the imagined moment when the grizzly attacks—and then jumps to this question in italics:

> *Is death*
> *by bear to be preferred*
> *to death by bomb?*

The question seems to intrude out of nowhere, and the poet closes by answering yes. The point, I presume, is that any thought of death, even one so unlikely, recalls the nuclear alternative. And grotesque though it would be, death "by bear" does seem preferable, one's own at least, and natural, part of the order of things and an order, too, as timeless as the wilderness. Bizarre consolations, but once the nuclear element intrudes, these are the sorts of ludicrous lengths to which we feel pushed. And the either/or is not even a choice, but only a preference. The absence of *a* and *the* before *bear* and *bomb* suggests two categories of death, only one of which is humanly acceptable.

After *APR* I went on to *Poetry,* where there was nothing relevant, and after that I rummaged randomly through the library's stock of recent journals and magazines, all I could manage in two afternoons. I am sure I read more than two hundred poems, most of them quite short, some very good, but none informed by nuclear awareness. I realize, of course, that any successful poem must authorize itself, must utter its world with self-certainty, but even so, reading so many poems one after the other left me rather shocked by the completeness, the sealed-up way these poems deny the knowledge or nearness of nuclear threat. The other striking thing about most of these poems was their sameness, and especially the meagerness. These observations are not original, of course. Lots of poetry gets written and published in America just now, and if one reads even a small but steady portion of it, one starts to see that the current talk about a "crisis" in our poetry is not unfounded. The trivialization, the huddled stance, the seemingly deliberate littleness of so much poetry in the last few years—how shall we account for it?

Perhaps the rise of the "workshop" poem has had something to do with it. Maybe also the new careerism among younger poets bent on bureaucratic power in the universities; those who, as Marx would say, have gone over to the management. And surely the kind of literary criticism now in vogue, hostile to the integrity of language, doesn't help. But these are as much symptoms as causes, and the larger situation comes down to this: In a time of nuclear threat, with absolutely everything at stake, our poetry grows increasingly claustrophilic and small-themed, it contracts its domain, it retires still further into the narrow chamber of the self; and we see in this not only the exhaustion of a mode and a tradition, but also the spectacle of spirit cowed and retreating.

The retreat has been swift because American practice invites it. Founded on Emersonian principles, our poetry has drawn much of its strength from an almost exclusive attention to self and nature. Typically we have conceived of the self *as* a world rather than of the self *in* the world. Things beyond the self either yield to imagination or else they don't matter, and the world becomes a store of metaphor to be raided as one can. The "strong" poet turns any landscape to private use, and solipsism wins praise as the sign of success. Emerson didn't invent these attitudes, but he was good at summing them up. "Every natural fact is a symbol of some spiritual fact," he wrote, and "the Universe is the externization [sic] of the soul." Thus the road was open for Whitman and poets to come, and thus Emerson delivered his mandate: "Know then that the world exists for you," and "Build therefore your own world." Partly, this is the mythology of our national experience, with its determination to deny social-political limits and focus instead on individual destiny. Partly, too, this is the American brand of Romanticism, part of a larger movement that on the continent peaked in its influential French example. Baudelaire called the world a "forest of symbols," and Mallarmé thought that everything external, *la cité, ses gouvernements, le code,* could be dismissed as *le mirage brutal*.

Stated thus, the whole business seems outlandish—but not really. The Emersonian mandate supports maximum belief in the poet's potency, not in itself a bad thing. Then, too, poets in our century have held some very odd convictions, Yeats for example, or for that matter, Merrill. But in one respect there is no doubting: American poetry has rejected history and politics on principle. Despite Lowell's example and more recent exceptions like Rich and Forché, our poets in the main have been satisfied to stick with Emerson, and few would find anything to take exception with in the following lines from Emerson's *Ode*:

I cannot leave
My honeyed thought

For the priest's cant,
Or statesman's rant.

If I refuse
My study for their politique,
Which at the best is trick,
The angry Muse
Puts confusion in my brain.

American contempt for politicians runs deep. As a sort of common-sense cynicism it allows us to go untroubled by crime in high places and, more to the point, it bolsters our belief that personal life exists apart from, and is superior to, political force and its agencies. But also, as Gunnar Myrdal demonstrated in *An American Dilemma,* our sort of political cynicism goes hand in hand with a remarkably durable idealism. We take for granted that governments are corrupt, then feel that some other power, providential and beyond the meddling of men, governs our destiny finally. Where there's a will there's a way, and everything comes right in the end. But does it? Even without the Bomb to put such faith into question, Emerson's example—Poland, for God's sake!—invites skepticism:

The Cossack eats Poland,
Like stolen fruit;
Her last noble is ruined,
Her last poet mute:
Straight, into double band
The victors divide;
Half for freedom strike and stand:—
The astonished Muse finds thousands at her side.

The Muse might well be befuddled, given the logic of Emerson's syntax. But of course, Emerson's faith in the future—disaster compensated by renewal—can't mean much to us. With the advent of the nuclear age there is no assurance that anything will remain for the phoenix to rise from.

We have fallen from the Garden, and the Garden itself—nature conceived as an inviolate wilderness—is pocked with nuclear waste and toxic dumps, at the mercy of industry and Watt, all of it open to nuclear defilement. Generations come and go, but that *the earth abideth forever* is something we need to feel, one of the foundations of poetry and humanness, and now we are not sure. That is the problem with nuclear threat, simply as threat; it undermines all certainty, and things once absolute are now contingent. To feel that one's private life was in the hands of God, or Fate, or even History, allowed the self a margin of transcendence; the dignity of personal life was part of a great if mysterious Order. But now our lives are in the hands of a few men in the Pentagon and the Kremlin, men who, having affirmed that they would destroy us to save us, have certified their madness—and yet their will determines our lives and our deaths. We are, then, quite literally enslaved, and assuming that this bothers poets no less than the rest of us, why do they so seldom speak of it? It is not too much to say that most poetry in America is written against experience, against first feelings and needs. Whether the Emersonian tradition is a trap or a last-ditch defense is perhaps a moot point. But the poetry of self still predominates, with nature as its cornerstone, despite Los Alamos, a lovely spot in the mountains.

Nuclear wipe-out is possible, perhaps probable, and every day I talk with people who are convinced it will happen. No soul is free of that terror, nor of that knowledge; and simply as a state of mind or way of knowing, it drastically alters how we receive and value our experience. Birth, for example, or one's own death; surely having children troubles us in ways not known before, and we need to feel that each of us shall have a death of his or her own, simply in order to feel fully possessed of our lives. These are common feelings, and it's clearer than it used to be that no man (no, nor woman neither) is an island. Our surface lives are individual and unique, but human existence itself—the being that all of us share and feel threatened—gives us our most important sense of ourselves and, I should also think, gives poetry its most significant themes. Can it be, then, that the shallowness of recent poetry reveals a desperate clinging to the surface?

I do *not* ask for poems directly about the Bomb or the end of the world, although with the Bell poem in *APR* as evidence, a theme of this kind can be as legitimate as any other. I don't expect poems of protest or outrage or horror either, although again, I can't see that they would hurt. I do, however, try to keep in mind that some subjects are more human, and more humanly exigent than others—Forché on Salvador compared to Leithauser on dandelions—and also that poets are often scared off by subjects which, precisely because of the fear, signal a challenge worth the risk. But what I'd mainly hope to see, in this case, is poetry that probes the impact of nuclear threat, poetry informed by nuclear knowing, poems that issue from the vantage of a self that accepts its larger landscape, a poetic diction testing itself against the magnitude of our present plight, or finally just poems which survive their own awareness of the ways nuclear holocaust threatens not only humankind but the life of poetry itself.

Nature, for example, remains the mainstay of our poetry. Natural imagery makes us trust the poem, suggests a permanence at the root of things, and every poem about nature bears somewhere within it the myth of renewal and rebirth. But from the nuclear perspective, these ministrations falter. Permanence? Rebirth? Emerson's response to nature was genuinely poetic, and the measure of our present loss may be judged by the degree of nostalgia rather than assent we feel when he says: "In the woods, we return to reason and faith. There I feel that nothing can befall me in life,— no disgrace, no calamity (leaving me my eyes), which nature cannot repair." Well, his notion of calamity isn't ours. And nature, for all its proven renovative power, could never repair the worst that might befall us. Nature suffers the same division we observe in ourselves and in the landscape generally. We are what we are, yet some deep part of selfhood has been invaded by forces wholly alien to personal being, political forces of which the worst is nuclear threat. In the same way, the landscape belongs to us and yet it does not. This concrete place we share is also a site on the nuclear grid. And when, therefore, Emerson tells us that "Every appearance in nature corresponds to some state of mind," we must inquire not only What state of mind? but also Whose mind?

No doubt the crews in the bombers are bored. And no doubt bureaucratic haggling keeps the commander of the base in Rome bogged down in mindless detail. The chiefs in the Pentagon, on the other hand, definitely share a state of mind which must, now and then, get rather dizzy with the glamour of their global strategy. What the Russians have in mind we don't know. But for all of them, we and the landscape are expendable; to think that way, after all, is their job. We cannot say, then, that the landscape corresponds to their minds and to ours in the same way. Rather, what expresses their state of mind, provokes and negates our own. In a traditional landscape, points of correspondence for us would be, among other things, the sky's infinity and the sense of permanence arising from the land itself. But exactly this kind of metaphor-making has been undermined by the transformation of the landscape into a sector on the grid. Or we might look at it this way: the military state of mind becomes an alien element *in* the landscape as we behold it, the B-52s, the proximity of the missile site, the grid and its planners. These forces have broken into our world, they have defiled its integrity, and the new points of correspondence between ourselves and the landscape are the condition of vulnerability and the threat of terminal defacement. Self and world, nature and landscape, everything exists in itself *and* as acceptable loss on the nuclear grid.

I've gone on at length about the landscape in my part of the country to suggest what Emerson's poetic principle—"Every appearance in nature corresponds to some state of mind"—might mean in the nuclear age. Every person has his or her own place, of course, and in a country as vast as ours the variety of landscape must be nearly infinite. The kinds of personal vision to which a landscape corresponds must also, then, be fairly limitless. But all vision converges in the fact that every landscape is part of the nuclear grid. I have the air base in Rome to remind me of this, whereas people living in, say, New York City are reminded by the city itself—its status as a prime target; the difficulty of maintaining life-support systems, water, energy, even in normal times; traffic's five o'clock entrapment every afternoon, not to mention the way the city is mocked by officials in Washington who suggest that in the event of an alert, nine million people will please evacuate the area. Then too, there are the nuclear power plants nearby; these are also targets, and when hit will spout radiation like the fourth of July. The citizenry can always avail itself of shovels, as another Washington wit has proposed, but no, there's no real hope. So that landscape too has its message.

Meanwhile, poets write about "marshes, lakes and woods, Sweet Emma of Preservation Hall, a Greek lover, an alchemist, actresses, fairy tales, canning peaches in North Carolina," stuff like that, to quote from the ad for a recent anthology. The apology for poems of this kind (triviality aside) is that by celebrating modest moments of the human spectacle—little snaps of wonder, bliss, or pain—poetry implicitly takes its stand against nuclear negation. To say Yes to life, this argument goes, automatically says No to the Bomb. And yes, a grain of truth sprouts here. I expect many among us read poetry that way in any case. The upshot, however, is that poets can go on producing their vignettes of self, pleased to be fighting the good fight without undue costs—except *the* cost, which is the enforced superficiality, the required avoidance of our deeper dismay.

Nuclear threat engenders cynicism, despair, allegiance to a mystique of physical force, and to say No to such destructive powers requires an enormously vehement Yes to life and human value. What's called for, in fact, is the kind of poetry we once named "great," and my suspicion is that today the will to greatness is absent. Great poems, Wordsworth's or Whitman's for example, confront their times; they face and contain their own negation. The human spirit draws its strength from adversity, and so do poems. Examples like *The Prelude* and *Song of Myself* incorporate and thereby transcend that which, if they ignored it, would surely cancel their capacity for final affirmation. And having mentioned poems of this calibre, I might also add that the "American sublime," as critics call it, has been missing in our poetry at least since late Stevens. The sublime, as observers like Burke and Kant and Schopenhauer insist, arises from terror, terror beheld and resisted, the terror of revolution for Wordsworth, of the abyss for Whitman, of nuclear annihilation for any poet today who would make a language to match our extremity.

I can see, though, why we try to avoid what we know. Terror will flare up suddenly, a burst of flame in the chest, and then there is simply no strength. Other times the mind goes blank in disbelief. The temptation to retreat is always with us, but where can we go, where finally? Sometimes I let it all recede, let silence be enough, and go for a walk through the fields and apple hedge above my house. The horizon then is remarkably clear, the sky is still its oldest blue. Overhead, the planes are half a hemisphere ahead of their thunder. It's hard not to think of them as beautiful, sometimes; humankind took so long to get up there. I wind my way through milkweed in the meadow and remember how Emerson, crossing an empty field, felt glad to the brink of fear. We know what he means, the elation that sweeps through us at such moments. And then I think of Osip Mandelstam and an old Russian proverb; life, he wrote, is not a walk across a field. We know what he means too, the inhuman hardship of centuries, the modern horror of being stalked to death. But it's all of this, isn't it? the grimness and the glory. Why should we think to keep them apart? We fear, maybe, that dread will undermine our joy, and often it does. To keep them wed is poetry's job. And now that the big salvations have failed us, the one clear thing is that we live by words.

—Summer 1983

Roald Hoffmann

Natural/Unnatural

At Millesgården, on the island of Lidingö near Stockholm, the work of the great Swedish sculptor Carl Milles is splendidly displayed. During a recent visit there I saw one sculpture group, the Aganippe fountain, in a new light. Its theme is classical in origin, but Milles's interpretation is idiosyncratic. The spring of Aganippe, on the slopes of Mount Helicon in Greece, was said to inspire artists and poets. Milles portrays Aganippe as a female figure, recumbent but in motion at the edge of the pool, and reflected in it. From the pool rise several dolphins, arched in mid-leap. Three of the dolphins carry men on their back, who symbolize Music, Painting, and Sculpture. Water rises from the beaks of the dolphins; this is after all a fountain, and Milles was a master designer of fountains. The Aganippe sculpture group always gave me pleasure when it graced a courtyard in the Metropolitan Museum of Art in New York. It has now been moved to Brookgreen Gardens outside of Charleston, South Carolina. At Millesgården one sees a replica, containing somewhat fewer figures. It remains lovely.

Fountains are about water, its motions, divisibility and reunion in flow. They are also about artifice, the real and the imagined, the natural and the unnatural. It is this last distinction that I want to explore in this essay, first by showing how the artist and scientist may confound this distinction for good reasons, and then by arguing that the distinction has some warrant after all.

One of the mounted figures that rises from the fountain represents Sculpture. It is a man, balanced on the dolphin's back. He is life-size, much larger than the stylized, diminished dolphin, and yet this disproportion doesn't matter. The man is dancing, and gravity's pull is light on him. Milles's art, his recurrent aim, was to defeat gravity. In bronze sculpture! The water, which emerges as several thin jets from the dolphin's snout, is angled upwards; it falls back, under the natural force of gravity, and sprays the young man. He reaches backwards, and on one outstretched hand rests (that's not the proper word for Milles's sculpture: more precisely "is balanced") a horse. The horse is small, the size of the man's forearm, but it is real, and galloping in the air. On the horse's head, in final defiance of gravity, another, smaller man is balanced, flying, falling, flying.

What is natural and what is unnatural about this work which is both a fountain and a sculpture? Like all fountains, it is patently synthetic, artificial and unnatural.

Someone has thought up a clever device, combining art and hydraulic engineering, to manipulate for aesthetic purposes one of the essentials of life and the earth, water. Fountains are sculpture with the unique feature that water is used as a sculptural element. And a substantial part of their interest derives from the tension of opposites between solid bronze or stone and moving, seemingly free water. How could these elements possibly be integrated? And yet in this kinetic sculpture they are.

The artifice is that the water doesn't "want" to run up, nor does it want to run in controlled channels, much less through dolphin beaks. We conspire to manufacture elaborate mechanisms to channel water, pump it up, so that it can flow down naturally, and in seeking its own level, in some places, even run straight up. Pumps, meters, gates, valves—God, all those hidden mechanics of the artificial! What could be more synthetic than a fountain?

The fountain's figures are cast in bronze, their mechanical elements made from other metals. The bronze itself is artificial. Or is it? Bronze is an alloy of copper and tin, perhaps with a little lead and zinc, an alloy of sufficient importance in the history of mankind to have an Age named after it. The alloy is both harder and more fusible than its component elements, which in turn are smelted from their ores, refined in a remarkable metallurgical process by men and machines. The ores of copper and tin— covellite, cuprite, cassiterite and others—are certainly natural. But they have not always lain in the earth unchanged. They came into existence under the action of forces operating on the one hand—by virtue of geochemistry—more weakly and over a longer period of time than they do under human metallurgical intervention, and on the other hand—in the nuclear transformations that occurred in the early seconds of the universe—more strongly, and in shorter time.

Thus here in Milles's fountain, natural ores, unnatural smelting and alloying technology, are used by natural man in the patently unnatural act of sculpture to manipulate the most natural of elements, water, and to construct images of natural man and horse and dolphin. And these are all perceived by my biological eye as a fountain that pleases me and that I can compare with Roman fountains I've never seen except through their unnatural images on natural but manufactured paper! Any imagined separation of the natural and unnatural can be confounded in the examination not only of Milles's fountain, but also in the careful analysis, aesthetic or scientific, of any object in our experience.

Scientists, especially chemists, will probably like this argument. They often feel beleaguered by society because they produce "unnatural" and often downright dangerous materials. A cursory survey of the media shows a consistent use of negative descriptive terms whenever chemistry is mentioned. Adjectives such as "explosive," "poisonous," "toxic," "polluting" are so closely conjoined with chemical names or nouns that they have become stock phrases. Whereas the words "natural," "organically grown," "unadulterated," etc., are given positive connotations, synthetics seem at best conditionally good. Yet they are widely manufactured and bought. For they do shelter us, heal us, make life easier, more interesting, and more colorful. Chemists encounter frustratingly conflicting signals from society—economic dependence and reward, coupled with an attitude from the media and some intellectuals that is abusive. I wonder if there are some parallels to the attitudes toward Jewish moneylenders in Europe in the Middle Ages.

One might advise chemists engaged in pure research not to take upon themselves the burden of guilt incurred by the often greedy, sometimes unethical producers and sellers of a dangerous chemical. But that is a subject that deserves its own extensive discussion—rightly or wrongly (I think both) many chemists feel that the media and society are negative not about businessmen but about chemistry and chemists.

One should also make the distinction between the words "manmade" (or "woman-made"), "synthetic," and "unnatural." Common language words are not insulated from the alternative meanings that usage has built for them. As one moves from "man-made" to "unnatural" the number of such other meanings, with their associated negative connotations, clearly compounds. Nevertheless I will use these words interchangeably, because I think they are so used in the dialogue around chemicals and people.

So the scientists will welcome what seems to me undeniable, that in any human activity, art, science, business, or childrearing, it makes little sense to separate the natural and unnatural. Both are inextricably intertwined, for there is an inherent ambiguity in any attempted separation.

The chemist will go on, as I will, to make the point that all substances—water, bronze, the patina on that bronze, Milles's hands, my eyes—all have a microscopic structure. They are composed of molecules. The component atoms, their arrangement in space, confer upon these macroscopic substances their various physical, chemical and biological properties. As subtle a difference as one molecule being the mirror image of another will decide whether it is sweet, or addictive, or a toxin. Much of the beauty of modern biochemistry is in the unraveling of the direct mechanisms of action of natural, biological processes—how precisely O_2 bonds to the hemoglobin in our red blood cells, and why CO binds better. That nylon replaced silk in women's stockings is not just a lucky circumstance—there are important similarities, on the molecular level, in the composition and structure (amide, carbonyl groups; pleated sheet structures; hydrogen bonding) of the two polymers. The singular intellectual achievement of chemistry in our time is the comprehension of the structure of molecules, covering the range from pure water to the alloy bronze or the protein rhodopsin in the cones in my eye.

But lest the scientist feel too comfortable, I will go on to defend the distinction between "natural" and "unnatural." No amount of supposed "rationality" will make the real intellectual concerns go away, and they persist for scientists as much as they do for other people.

In chemistry the natural/unnatural dichotomy has an interesting history. Early distinctions between organic and inorganic substances were swept aside by the demonstration, first by Wöhler in 1828 for urea, that naturally occuring substances could be synthesized from entirely inorganic, inanimate sources. Note the subtle difference of emphasis here—organic versus inorganic, not natural versus unnatural. Both organic and inorganic molecules required human manipulation to be shown to be identical.

The identity of substances remains to this day a subject of dispute and economic value. For instance, chemists will typically scorn health-food stores advertising (and selling at a premium) rose-hip vitamin C, as being different from synthetic vitamin C. The same chemist, call him A, will get very upset when a colleague, B, says that a synthesis of some molecule reported by A cannot be reproduced. What has probably happened is that a reagent in one synthesis contains some adventitious admixture of a catalyst, due to its mode of preparation. That "dirty" catalyst made the reaction go for A, but was absent from B's reaction flask. Pure vitamin C, synthetic, is identical to natural vitamin C. But a bottle of vitamin C made from rose hips is certainly not identical to a bottle of vitamin C made by a chemical manufacturer. At a parts per thousand level, I'm not implying that there are important differences, simply that there could in principle be differences in substances that are perforce impure.

Chemists might reflect on the fact that, despite the seeming irrelevance of the organic/inorganic and natural/unnatural divisions in chemistry, in their own language and social structure the dichotomy has a life of its own. For instance, people in the molecular trade talk of "natural product synthesis," i.e., the synthesis of molecules found in nature, to distinguish it from the synthesis of molecules never present on earth before. But, significantly, no chemist uses the term "unnatural products," except as a joke. The slightly guarded humor of the phrase "unnatural products" betrays, as humor often does, some of the ambiguous feelings chemists often harbor on this subject.

The chemist also distinguishes the discipline of biochemistry, which concerns the nature and mechanism of basic chemical processes in living organisms. Biochemists often aim to understand the mechanism of such processes by reducing them to a sequence of individual chemical actions. But the organic, inorganic, and physical chemists who study these individual fundamental steps would hardly be able to secure a job in a Department of Biochemistry! Synthetic chemists speak with approbation of *biomimetic* methods, i.e., synthetic procedures imitating natural ones. The prefix "bio-" obviously carries some psychological and social value. Such professional divisions and specializations persist in giving the natural/unnatural dichotomy life even within chemistry.

The personal conduct of scientists is also revealing. The scenario that follows is a composite of several recent experiences. Not long ago I was the guest at lunch of an executive of a major chemical company. I was prepared for small talk, platitudes, and some good science. Instead my host proceeded to unburden himself in an emotional tirade against a few young people, the American equivalent of the "The Greens" in Europe, who had given him a hard time at a press conference that morning. We were at a luxurious, recently opened restaurant, proud of bringing la Nouvelle Cuisine to this corner of America. The chairs were of light wood, delicately caned, and the napkins felt like fine linen. One could see the touch of someone with training in Ikebana in the fresh flower arrangements.

These young people (he kept coming back to them) dominated the public discussion after he had presented a plan for building a new agricultural chemical manufacturing facility for pesticides and herbicides. They asked him if the chemicals to be produced were adequately tested for mutagenicity, and questioned the company's control of effluents. They remind him, aggressively and, he thought, arrogantly, of a previous mishap at another facility of that company. He found their criticism full of fears, unscientific, and irrational. It seemed they doubted the need for the pesticide, a deterrent to weevils; they thought natural methods of pest control were adequate. The older man, a distinguished chemist and obviously a good businessman, was upset, perhaps because he could not allow himself to be upset at the press conference. He fumed about the confused anarchy of these people, and also hinted at organized political motives. The good wines, first a New York State chardonnay, and then a superb Saint-Emilion, did settle him a little. After the white wine he was able to joke about the then current Austrian wine adulteration scandal. In time, the pleasure of telling a receptive visitor about a find he had made in an antique store, an unusual Indian basket (we shared an interest in American Indian art), took over. After lunch we strolled in the gardens around the house, admiring especially the purple and black tulips then in bloom.

One does not need a business executive and a fancy modern restaurant for this scenario. I suspect that the strongest defenders of the lack of a separation of the natural and unnatural go home to houses with picture windows and not with large photographic enlargements of exotic landscapes in place of those windows. In their homes grow real plants, not artful plastic and fabric imitations. No solarium will substitute for their real Algarve tan; they will avoid plastic shingles on their house and wood grain imitations in their dining room furniture; they will complain about what the European Economic Community is trying to do to their beer. It seems clear to me that the scientist or technologist who complains about other "unreasonable" people not being able to see the impossibility of separating the natural and the synthetic, nonetheless testifies to the hold such a separation has on his or her own psyche in daily life.

So let us think about why it is that we prefer the natural, no matter who we are and what we do. I see many interconnected psychological, emotional forces at work—among them six that I can label: romance, status, alienation, pretense, scale, spirit.

Romance: In the second act of Tchaikovsky's opera "The Queen of Spades," a masque or pastorale, "The Faithful Shepherdess," is interpolated, which does not exist in Pushkin's original story. Daphnis and Chloe sing of the pleasure they take in nature, in a marvelous Mozartean duet. The tradition of the pastorale is as old as that of fountains, for romance derives from an unrealistic striving for what cannot be or no longer is, or even what one wishes to put at a distance. The irony of these unreal, unnatural, but entrancing constructions, supposedly about the natural, is that pastorales were fine for everyone except the people who had to make a living in the pasture. The courts are gone, but romantic traditions persist. A reaching out for nature, for real wood, the smell of hay, the feel of the wind in the sails, still determines our *desires*. It doesn't matter that the real stable smelled bad, or that train stations were dirty, noisy structures. I see Ingrid Bergman saying goodbye to Leslie Howard at the train station, and I know all train stations. I feel them within me. My mind's stable smells just right.

Status: The success of the synthetic is due to either some combination of lower cost, greater durability, more versatility, or even new capabilities, relative to some natural materials. This is the polymer century, when large synthetic molecules have replaced one natural material after another: nylon in place of cotton in fishing nets, fiberglass instead of wood in boat hulls. The replacement or new use (polyethylene as a food wrap, for example) is invariably a democratizing process, for a wider range of materials is made available more cheaply to a larger group of people. Sanitary water delivery and waste disposal, a wider spectrum of color, better shelter, the elimination of much death in childbirth and infancy are now available to many more than those who could enjoy such luxuries and essentials a hundred years ago. Although we still have a long way to go, this is what chemists and engineers can really be proud of having achieved.

But human beings are (nicely) strange. When they have some of anything, they want more. Or they simply want something better than their neighbors have. When the synthetic becomes inexpensive and available to all, a curious inversion of taste occurs: the arbiters of elegance decree that the "natural" carries more cachet. If a cotton shirt is supposed to feel more luxurious than a blend which is "permanent press," sure enough the shirt begins to feel that way. A wood floor is certainly perceived as being nicer than linoleum, and the rarer the wood the better. Perhaps I've been too negative here. Perhaps what we want is not so much to be superior to someone else, as to be somewhat (not too much!) different. The natural provides, in its infinite variability, that opportunity to be slightly different.

Alienation: We are distanced from our tools, and from the effects of our actions. We see it in routine work on an assembly line, in selling lingerie, even in scientific research. We work on a piece of something, not the whole. To be efficient we work repetitiously, so that we may even lose interest in the whole. Mountains of paper insulate us from the human beings affected by our actions. Around us proliferate machines whose workings we don't understand. I doubt that there are many among my colleagues who could do what Mark Twain's Connecticut Yankee in King Arthur's Court could do, that is to reconstruct our technology from all those partial differential equations we know. We press buttons and elevators come (or don't come). Worse, we press buttons and missiles are launched, and only the victims see the blood.

The synthetic, artificial and unnatural, is almost always a factory-produced multiple, inexpensive because mass-produced. To be mass-produced it must be stamped, cast, or pressed repeatedly. The objects so made appear identical. In principle their design could be good, in practice design is sacrificed for economy. The typical mass-produced object shows little of the history of its making, neither in design nor in execution. Tetracycline antibiotics, for instance, are isolated from a culture of living organisms, chemically modified, purified, and packaged by remarkable, inventive tools and devices. But a bottle of fifty tetracycline pills hides the ingenuity behind that multiple product, its manufacture by human beings using tools of their own design.

There is something deep within us that makes us want to see the signature of a human hand on a product. Yet there are clever ways to individualize mass-produced items. I think of the color variations on the prints of F. Hundertwasser (hardly inexpensive) or the cheerful ceramics that Stig Lindberg designed for Gustavsberg in Sweden in the fifties. They should be encouraged.

Pretense: The false has a negative connotation in all things of significance to human beings. To tell a lie, to pretend to be what one isn't, is not to be good. Much of the synthetic world of chemicals is not only unnatural in the sense of being man-made, it also often pretends to be what it is not. In part this is a natural consequence of replacing something familiar with something else, not very different, but stronger, more resistant to heat, etc. So plastic plates carry the patterns of porcelain, and sheet plastic in furniture often imitates the wood grain. Napkins emulate linen, lace, and embroidery. There is the ancient profession of marbling. I was once told by a young man who was apprenticed in this honorable craft, that to be good at it one should not only study marble but also think, while painting, of the geological forces that shaped it. Now some of this is fine, but too much imitation, a dissembling that accumulates, inevitably leads to revulsion. One longs for the authentic, the real.

Scale: There can be too many of one thing, and too many, period. The first plastic ashtray, or titanium jewelry, or (in the USSR) portrait of Lenin, looks interesting, but as more and more of them invade our visual environment, they quickly begin to bore us. The repetitive nature of its production (the key to its economic success) is often the only feature that a mass-produced object then stylistically communicates to us.

Sometimes the very superabundance of artificial objects in our environment, rather than the repetition of one and the same one, repels us. The typical American motel room, for instance, offers us little respite from the artificial. The variety of plastics and synthetic fibers in the furnishing of such a room is astonishing and even intellectually interesting, as an exemplar for a course about polymers, or in thinking of the problems such a room will pose for future archaeologists. But one is hardly attracted to that setting.

Spirit: What makes scientists, indeed all of us, because scientists are no different from other people, seek out the natural? No simple psychological or sociological explanation suffices. I believe that our soul has an innate need for the chanced, the unique, the growing that is life. I see a fir tree trying to grow in an apparent absence of topsoil, in a cleft of a cliff-side of Swedish granite near Millesgården, and I think how it, or its offspring, will eventually split that rock. The plants trying to live in my office remind me of that tree. Even the grain in the wood of my desk, though it tells me of death, tells me of that fir tree. I see a baby satisfied after breastfeeding, and its smile unlocks a neural path to memory of the smiles of my children when they were small, to a line of ducklings forming after their mother, to that tree. As A. R. Ammons says, "My nature singing in me is your nature singing."

These six overlapping, interpenetrating categories seem to me to contain some of the many reasons for asserting a claim to the primacy of the natural. Some arise from the weaknesses of human beings, some from their strengths. What still seems to bother some technologists and scientists is that the separation of the synthetic, artificial or unnatural from the natural, and the assignment to it of negative connotation, is made by some of their fellow human beings on the basis of some irrational (to the straw-man technologist I've set up) *fears*.

So we must talk about fear. Nature is certainly fearful, and often hardly benign. The need for shelter and protection from natural forces, perfectly neutral but for that very reason inimical to anthropocentric us, is one of the primary motives in development of technology. Fear of nature, its real or imagined dangers, is also a source of religion and literature.

Fear is an emotion. If we should want to alleviate it, or remove it, reason or knowledge play a certain role, but far from the major one. The person who is afraid must also feel that he or she gains control. Compassion is essential. For example, most of us, especially city dwellers, would be afraid to be alone and lost, on a dark night in the forest. We have read as children what happens in dark forests. We hear signs of the forces out there: if those forces are inherently mysterious, and we cannot control them, they seem all the more threatening. If a woodsman then tells us that the animals are not really dangerous, but can't explain just why they are shrieking so, we aren't much comforted.

Let us turn to a fear of what we as men, women, scientists, and technologists have added to what is already fearful in nature. Why do some scientists, who (sometimes) know how to deal with the fears of their own children, refuse to recognize the real fears that people have of nuclear war, pollution, ecological disasters, or manmade threats in general? Need I rehearse the disasters which form the real basis for such fears? Affectations of superrationality are not the way to respond to such fears. Telling a person who worries about the carcinogenicity of certain ubiquitous food additives that the risk to him or her from drinking a glass of wine (the source of another carcinogen) is ten times larger, is about as comforting or psychologically perceptive as telling a child who has woken from a nightmare of being run over by a locomotive, "Don't worry about runaway locomotives, the chance of a dog biting you is much greater."

Over thousands of years we have come to terms with the dangers of nature. We fear it less, and this is to the credit of science, for science has helped us understand it a little better, from the behavior of wolves to spring floods. Of course, in its random, lively way, nature shakes us up, now and then, with a volcanic explosion or AIDS. But we have added to its repertoire of dangers our own man-made ones: Chernobyl, thalidomide, Bhopal, lakes ecologically destroyed by acid rain. These dangers are not only real, but have a hold on our imaginations that magnifies that reality, just as the books we've read on dangerous forests or ghost stories do. Because these man-provoked disasters occurred under the control of people who were supposed to be rational and expert, the authority of experts in general is undermined. And the danger is regarded as insidious, since it is out of the control of ordinary people. No wonder that the next infusion of the synthetic or man-made is viewed with fear, and the word "unnatural" causes such negative connotations.

I would argue that the irrational fear which some scientists see behind opposition to the synthetic or artificial can be seen as a rational response, or at least accepted as an understandable reaction of thinking and feeling human beings. The fear manifests itself in a separation of natural and unnatural, and a further typecasting of the unnatural as bad. It leads to ambivalent attitudes towards the producers of the unnatural, and also towards the unhampered extension of knowledge.

I think the response to that fear must encompass at least (1) reason; (2) empowerment (granting people control); and (3) compassion. Understanding and empowerment derive from education; obviously scientists must explain to people more of what they do. Science is observation and common-sense logic; it can be taught. Although some scientists think it's more difficult and requires greater intelligence and creative inspiration to acquire new knowledge than to teach it, perhaps just the reverse might be true.

Scientists are badly served by the assumption that they, and they alone, speak for reason. First of all, it's just not true: the wide variety of modes of personal behavior associated with success in acquiring knowledge within science speaks against it. So does the range of political or ideological beliefs of good scientists. Second, a claim to stand for reason alone is dehumanizing and impoverishing. The creative forces behind the new and the deep in science or art, are sparked by other features of our psyche. Emotions, the irrational, matter just as much as cool reason.

Empowerment requires access to knowledge *and* a democratic system of government. The best of present systems of governance are just an approximation to the ideal of democracy. Still, no amount of knowledge, no matter how skillfully and widely taught, will assuage fear of the synthetic unless people feel that they have something to say, politically, in the use of the materials that frighten them.

I suspect empowerment plays the dominant role in personal risk assessment. We feel safer driving a car rather than flying in an airplane, despite accident statistics to the contrary. Why? Because it is we who are driving, but someone else is flying the plane. Much of the fear of nuclear power generation and of other technological dangers, real or unreal, derive not so much from ignorance of the processes as from the feeling that we are not near control.

Compassion is easy to extend to children and the bereaved, less so to an adult worried about a hypothetical disaster. Scientists confronted by fear of technology often neglect to react with compassion. Instead, they tend to argue the points one would focus on in the laboratory: for instance, whether the analytical procedure showing the presence of a pollutant at a certain level is reliable or not. The scientist who responds this way only succeeds in sounding defensive. There is a place for rational discourse on analytical procedures, but *after* one gains the confidence of the worried person through sympathy. Compassion and empathy must be the first response.

Scientists need to stop thinking that negative responses are based on "irrational fear," since this only provokes anger. I believe they can do it in a dialogue into which both science and art are drawn. The natural/unnatural distinction is obviously undermined by much great art. The discussion of the Aganippe fountain makes this clear, as would an analysis of a Japanese ceramic or Tchaikovsky's "Queen of Spades." Compassion, empathy, understanding will also come if scientists muse a little as to why one part of themselves is drawn to the natural, while another part argues that the natural and unnatural are inextricably mixed.

—Summer 1990

Jonathan Holden

Postmodern Poetic Form: A Theory

To appreciate the difficulty a critic faces when trying to find any kind of continuity in contemporary American poetry, one need only thumb through the third edition of A. Poulin's anthology, *Contemporary American Poetry*. It would seem at first glance that the poems of John Ashbery and Imamu Amiri Baraka would have nothing significant in common—no more, certainly, than the graceful, late-modernist, domestic verses of Richard Wilbur have with the chants of Allen Ginsberg—both featured in that anthology—or the male boastings of James Dickey have in common with the recent work of Adrienne Rich. Critics have, of course, tried to locate a pattern in this diversity; but their efforts have been either too tentative or not thoroughly enough thought out. Jerome Mazzaro, for example, in his preface to *Postmodern American Poetry*, gives us the following, vague prognostication:

Without the technical language of the structuralists, the formulation of the essential differences between "modernism" and "postmodernism" becomes: in conceiving of language as a fall from unity, modernism seeks to restore the original state often by proposing silence or the destruction of language; postmodernism accepts the division and uses language and self-definition—much as Descartes interpreted thinking—as the basis of identity. Modernism tends, as a consequence, to be more mystical in the traditional senses of that word whereas postmodernism, for all its seeming mysticism, is irrevocably worldly and social. Rather than T. S. Eliot's belief that poetry "is not the expression of personality, but an escape from personality," postmodernists propose the opposite.

Mazzaro's statement that "postmodernism accepts the division" simply ignores the poetry of Robert Bly, Galway Kinnell, James Wright, Gary Snyder and other contemporary poets working in the romantic tradition which Paul Breslin has aptly named "psychological pastoral." When, for example, at the close of "Late November in a Field," James Wright says:

> I have nothing to ask a blessing for,
> Except these words.
> I wish they were
> Grass.

he is, to use Mazzaro's language, "proposing silence or the destruction of language." In short, Mazzaro's formulation simply does not apply to a significant segment of postmodern American poetry. More troublesome, however, is Mazzaro's assumption that the character of poetry is determined primarily by epistemology, by the way in which the poet "conceives of language." Nowhere in the paragraph above does Mazzaro suggest why the conception of language "as a fall from unity" is more significant for a *poet* writing in verse than for any other educated user of "language."

Harold Bloom's approach, in *The Princeton Encyclopedia of Poetry and Poetics* is, like Mazzaro's, epistemological. According to Bloom, "The *stance*" of "the strongest and most characteristic poetry of the late 1960s and early 1970s, a transcendental synthesis of the various native strains," ignores the "bogus" issue of whether to write in closed or open "phrased fields," and, "in order to escape the fall into the confessional," performs "a deliberate curtailment of the revisionary impulse toward an endlessly journalistic scrutiny" of the self, "while simultaneously [a la Emerson] asking the fact for the form." Bloom then adduces some poetic instances and remarks: "every passage, whether in tone, in cognitive aim, or in human stance, shows the same anxiety: to ask the fact for the form." If we translate Bloom into plain English, he means to say that the mainstream of postmodern poetry shuns confessional, strives toward organic form, and is therefore transcendental, part of a tradition that goes back to Emerson. Leaving aside the fact that the confessional mode is very much alive and, in the hands of poets like Carolyn Forché and Louise Glück, important, Bloom's thesis, while it embraces Ammons, Ashbery and a few other poets, ignores so much of our best poetry and so radically misunderstands the creative process—a process which is not, as Bloom would portray it, inherently philosophical—that it is largely unconvincing.

Postmodern American poetic form, from the political invective of a Baraka to the elegant assemblages of Ashbery, is *not* founded on epistemological anxiety; nor is it primarily "organic." It is *analogical*. Deprived by the modernist revolution of any sure sense of what poetic form should be, poets have increasingly turned to non-literary analogues such as conversation, confession, dream, and other kinds of discourse as substitutes for the ousted "fixed forms," substitutes which in many cases carry with them assumptions about rhetoric which are distinctly anti-modernist. Indeed, it is through deployment of such relatively "personal" analogues as conversation and confession that a substantial number of our poets are attempting to recover some of the favorable conditions for poetry which had seemed to obtain before the triumph of modernism.

In order to fully appreciate this analogical impulse behind much contemporary poetic form, one must understand why and in what ways the advent and eventual institutionalization (in universities) of "modernism" has rendered the poetic vocation so much more diminished than it once was. How relatively complacent that vocation had been—how reasonable the assumptions behind it had sounded—is vividly evident in the late Robert Hillyer's aesthetic will and testament, the book-length essay *In Pursuit of Poetry* (1960). Hillyer, born in 1895, in East Orange, New Jersey, was eight years younger than Eliot and ten years younger than Pound. Like Eliot, he attended Harvard. Like most of the founders of American modernist poetry, he spent time in Europe: he was an ambulance driver with the French army from 1917 to 1919. But he remained a traditionalist. It was well after the period which has come to be known as "High Modernist" when the *Collected Verse of Robert Hillyer* (1934) received the Pulitzer Prize for Poetry. And when in 1944 Hillyer retired as Boylston Professor of Rhetoric and Oratory at Harvard, he was considered a major American poet.

A striking aspect of *In Pursuit of Poetry* is the bitterness with which Hillyer attacks modernism. He deplores the modernists' specialization of poetry, evidenced to him by the rise of the New Criticism, and he laments their usurpation of the genteel tradition to which he, himself, belongs:

Though the symbolism of T. S. Eliot's poetry and the incoherence of Ezra Pound's Cantos have served as damaging models for young men, the more nearly complete sterilization and confusion of recent American poetry were accomplished by the New Criticism.

He attacks the modernists' formal innovations such as "free verse," comparing it to "a river the banks of which are removed so that it spreads out without restraint into a marsh," and he rejects what might be termed the pessimistic vision of most modernist poetry, chiding Eliot for his "*self-pity,* a dreadful element in any art," and Auden for being, in such poems as "Miss Gee. A Ballad," "completely *heartless*":

This general rejection of humanity, this stripping away of a mystery and aspiration is the result of a materialistic, mechanistic point of view so closely allied to the self-destructive elements of the age that the poet's continuous complaints about them become a colloquy between the pot and the kettle. . . . To mention the human soul in the presence of such poetry would be embarrassing.

The traditionalist conception of poetic form which Hillyer proposes has a cut-and-dried quality which any postmodern poet might envy; for Hillyer's conception of the universe provides the very model for traditional poetic form, for meter:

Intricate though verse seems, it is a more natural form of expression than prose. Verse means a turning, and since the turn must come full circle on itself, we speak of it as a repeating, or recurrent, rhythm, just as in music. Prose rhythm is non-recurrent; hence, verse is more natural because it is closer to the rhythms of the universe—and note that universe means a concerted turning . . . we are metrical creatures in a metrical universe.

Hillyer's notion of poetic form and his defense of what we now call the "fixed forms" follow immediately from his view of a "metrical universe:"

The main forms . . . have developed through centuries and are the result of endless experiment. Their roots go as deep as the languages, and those that we still have with us are so natural that they might almost be cited as examples of Darwinian survival of the fittest. How foolish it is for defenders of free verse to maintain that these metrical structures are not natural. Free verse has no roots at all, and is itself an unnatural departure from the ebb and flow of all things.

Hillyer classifies the language of poetry into two styles, "the *rhetorical,* heightened and dignified, and the *conversational,* informal and familiar. . . . Each has its dangers as well as its virtues; the first may become bombastic, the second prosaic." The poet's choice of a style must be governed, Hillyer says, by the idiom that is "considered most appropriate for the expression of his idea." Similarly, if—as Hillyer suggests—poetry may be loosely classified into "epic, dramatic and lyric," then certain meters are appropriate to certain modes: blank verse to the English language epic and dramatic modes, "three- or four-stress verse and divided into stanzas" to "pure lyrics." Hillyer sees rhyme as "the one string we have added to the Greek lyre;" whereas "it enriches the harmonies of purely lyric poetry, and it makes verse easier to remember by heart," it "remains . . . an adornment and is not essential to poetry, as is demonstrated by the great body of our poetry that is written in blank verse."

Hillyer's conception of the role and the mission of the poet follows, likewise, from his view of the universe as an orderly and essentially benign entity:

A good poet is at home in his countryside and his world, and at one with the spirits and traditions of the past. These truths, however, are but aspects of the one truth that poetry is the highest expression of what is most natural to man in every phase of his life. The single idea of the poet is to create from disharmony, harmony; from formlessness, form. . . .

As an illustration, Hillyer says that "the majority of the modern poets" who give him "satisfaction," poets such as "Bridges, Frost, Robinson, Hodgson . . . Yeats, Stephens, and Gogarty, regard life, in spite of its dissonances, as essentially a harmony in which they are a part. They are at home in this world."

The posture of alienated romantic, for Hillyer, is very nearly a disqualification from poetry. His metaphor for the sensibility that brings harmony from dissonance is a Wordsworthian one, imagining not the sensibility of an isolated and extraordinary individual but a communal sensibility, collectively attained:

the poet is the stained-glass window that transmits sunlight just as ordinary windows do, but colors it as it passes through. And the poet should rest content with that; no man is great enough to be both the window and the sunlight. And no man should be so perverse as to be merely a distorting glass.

Implicit in this figure is not only an appeal to tradition, but also the sense of a congregation to share that tradition. Perhaps this is the most enviable aspect of Hillyer's conception of poetry:

All art, in spite of many modern tendencies to the contrary, is more or less enduring as its intention is more or less communal, granted that the receptive community is the intelligent and responsive part of the general population. That is a minority and always has been.

Elsewhere, Hillyer remarks, rather poignantly:

There is so little reading of poetry nowadays. One reason for the decline of appreciation is the fact that poetry is so seldom read in family groups any more, or among teachers and pupils as a recreation rather than an assignment. And then, of course, so few people know how to read aloud.

The "decline of appreciation" which Hillyer remarks—the apparent end of a tradition in which a family might, instead of watching television, spend an evening reading aloud from Stevenson's *Home Book of Verse*—is nowhere more tersely described than in Edward Mendelson's introduction to *Early Auden*:

Among the historical crises faced, and, in part invented, by modernism was a breakdown in what might be called the symbolic contract, the common frame of reference and expectation that joins a poet with a finite audience, and joins both with the subjects of his poem.

Lionel Trilling is more explicit than Mendelson. He suggests that the debunking of the very communal kind of art that Hillyer defends was a deliberately conceived element of the cultural politics of the modernist overthrow:

Any historian of the literature of the modern age will take virtually for granted the adversary intention, the actually subversive intention, that characterizes modern writing—he will perceive its clear purpose of detaching the reader from the habits of thought and feeling that the larger culture imposes, of giving him a ground and a vantage point from which to judge and condemn, and perhaps revise, the culture that produced him.

Would any of today's really important poets in America accept Hillyer's comforting view of a metrical universe? Unlikely. But few of them, I suspect, would not envy Hillyer's pre-modernist image of the poetic vocation—of a world in which poetry enjoyed some general popularity, in which the poet could deploy with confidence a repertoire of fixed poetic forms. One cannot, of course, deny the desirability of many aspects of the modernist tradition. One need only open any copy of *Georgian Poetry* to observe that the rhetorical tradition against which the imagists reacted was far staler and more exhausted than Hillyer admits. Moreover, while the great modernist experiments were being conducted, it was inevitable that the experimenters see themselves as specialists, and it is no accident that the metaphor at the heart of Eliot's "Tradition and the Individual Talent" is drawn from chemistry: it required "scientists" to synthesize the new compounds, the new "art-emotions" that would replace the old. But the resulting losses were immense and have not yet been fully tallied. Just as Hillyer complained, the revolution has left the poet in America a bureaucratic specialist isolated in a university as in a laboratory, conducting endless experiments with poetic form, and in an adversary relation to the general culture.

Postmodern poetic form in American poetry is best understood as a reaction to the situation I have described; it is, however, variously also an attempt to recover, or at least pretend that there could now exist, favorable conditions analogous to those which Hillyer so intrepidly took for granted. Such form is not, as critics like Bloom would have us believe, Emersonian. That is to say, it is not "organic;" for Bloom's notion that a poem "ask the fact for form" is no more than the conventional organic theory of poetic form, a restatement, for example, of Denise Levertov's dictum that "form is never more than a *revelation* of content," a restatement in which Bloom has substituted "the fact" for "content." Perhaps oddly, the true notion of form which underlies our postmodern poetry, regardless of whether a given poem is in free verse or accentual-syllabic meter, is quite similar to Hillyer's pre-modernist conception of the "fixed forms." It refers to a category. When "form" is conceived and applied as a category, in conjunction with the word "content," "content" must, likewise, be restricted so as to refer to a category of subject matter. Thus the "form" of a poem is a container; the poem's "content" is what is contained. But, it will be immediately objected, the form of most contemporary poems does not fit any known category. My answer to this is that our poems *do* fit formal categories—categories which poets are quite aware of but which, because the aesthetics of modernism has generated so much (often deliberate) mystification, have remained implicit. One of Allen Ginsberg's longest poems, for example, is called a "sutra." Some of Richard Hugo's poems are in the form of "letters." Much of William Stafford's poetry is a mimesis of conversation. Poets like Louise Glück or Carolyn Forché often resort to a rhetoric, a "form" which, in all its details, resembles psychological and religious confession. Certainly some of Galway Kinnell's poems are attempts to imitate something like "primitive song," a sort of scream not from a specific individual but from an archetypal, prehistoric human.

Whether it pretends to be a sutra, a letter, psychiatric confession, talk, primitive song, or whatnot, when a poem uses some non-literary analogue as a basis for its form, the name of the analogue becomes, in effect, the name of a category of form. To talk sensibly about postmodern poetic form, instead of resorting to vague, "organic" mystifications, all we need do is: 1) *to recognize that postmodern poetic form is predominantly analogical;* 2) *to extend the range of categories by which we refer to poems, using the analogues to name these categories.* In fact, if an analogical poem is any good, the name of its formal "category" will tell us far more about the poem than even a term like "sonnet" or "villanelle." Consider the following poem by Gary Gildner:

First Practice

After the doctor checked to see
we weren't ruptured,
the man with the short cigar took us
under the grade school,
where we went in case of attack
or storm, and said
he was Clifford Hill, he was
a man who believed dogs
ate dogs, he had once killed
for his country, and if
there were any girls present
for them to leave now.
                    No one
left. OK, he said, he said I take
that to mean you are hungry
men who hate to lose as much
as I do. OK. Then
he made two lines of us
facing each other,
and across the way, he said,
is the man you hate most
in the world,
and if we are to win
that title I want to see how.
But I don't want to see
any marks when you're dressed,
he said. He said, *Now.*

I suggest that the term "conversation" poem will tell us a great deal about "First Practice." It tells us that the author is speaking in his own person, directly to the reader. It tells us that, if the poem is going to be a successful mimesis of conversation, the prosody will have to seem relatively artless, yet be pronounced enough to lend the poem unity—be blank verse or very skillful free verse. It tells us that the subject matter of the poem will be relatively quotidian, and that the poem's authority—what holds our interest in it and commands our respect—will have to come not, as in confession, from the speaker's unusual suffering, not, as in a mimesis of primitive song, from the grand claims of the unconscious, nor from the speaker's literary expertise, but simply from the speaker's way of telling, his ethos, his sheer inventiveness (for this reason, the conversational analogue, though the most prevalent one in the early '80s, is the most difficult one, because it places extreme demands on the speaker to be casually brilliant).

"First Practice," then, is, in form, a "conversation poem" whose content is a reminiscence about high school football. Without the notion of an analogue, however, it is nearly impossible to describe this poem's form at all, let alone account for it. Is it a "lyric"? No, not in any conventional sense of that word, although it is around the length of a lyric, and its line-length, though irregular, is about that of trimeter, a meter which Hillyer conventionally associates with "lyric." Because there is no category which will simply identify this poem, we must, in order to describe it, begin by enumerating its characteristics. It is narrative, in two stanzas, in the first-person singular, past tense; it is rather short, in free verse and in conversational diction. The more we list characteristics, the more we implicitly regard the poem's "form" in what Robert Pinsky would call a "nominalist" manner—not as a category but as a unique thing-in-itself—and are drawn toward an organic conception of the poem's form. Our analogical account of its form, however, is far more accurate (as well as economical) both as to the poem's intention and final result than an "organic" account could ever be, and the reason is simple. The very term "form" as Bloom deploys it or as organicists such as Levertov do acquires such a range of reference that it becomes meaningless.

An ideal example of the limitations of the organic position is Denise Levertov's essay, "Some Notes On Organic Form." Levertov begins as follows:

For me, back of the idea of organic form is the concept that there is a form in all things (and in our experience) which the poet can discover and reveal.

She then suggests that "poets who use prescribed form" believe that "content, reality, experience is essentially fluid and must be given form" whereas poets "who look for new [forms]" have "this sense of seeking out inherent, though not immediately apparent, form. . . ."

A partial definition, then, of organic poetry might be that it is a method of apperception, i.e., of recognizing what we perceive, and is based on an intuition of an order, a form beyond forms, of which forms partake, and of which man's creative works are analogies, resemblances, natural allegories.

For Levertov, poetic composition happens as follows:

. . . first there must be an experience . . . or constellation of perceptions . . . felt by the poet intensely enough to demand of him their equivalence in words. . . .

So—as the poet stands . . . contemplating his experience, there come to him the first words of the poem: . . . The pressure of demand and the meditation on its elements culminate in a moment of vision, of crystallization in which some inkling of the correspondence between those elements occurs; and it occurs as words. . . .

According to Levertov, as the process of composition proceeds,

. . . content and form are in a state of dynamic interaction; the understanding of whether an experience is a linear sequence or a constellation raying out from and into a central focus or axis, for instance, is discoverable only in the work, not before it.

Levertov's account describes very accurately what certain stages of composition in free verse feel like. The main strength of her argument lies in her attempt to be, at all times, as specific as possible—for example in her distinction above between "linear sequence" and "constellation;" but her very willingness to be specific reveals the impossibility of the organic argument. Consider, for example, her remarks on the sonic aspect of composition:

Rhyme, chime, echo, reiteration: they . . . often are the very means, the sole means, by which the density of texture and the returning or circling of perception can be transmuted into language, apperceived. A may lead to E directly through B, C, and D; but if there then is the sharp remembrance or revisioning of A, this return must find its metric counterpart. It could do so by actual repetition of the words that spoke of A for the first time. . . . Or it may be that since the return to A is now conditioned by the journey through B, C, and D, its words will not be a simple repetition but a variation. . . . Again, if B and D are of a complementary nature, then their thought- or feeling-rhyme may find its corresponding word-rhyme.

Levertov then summarizes all the specific formal possibilities so painstakingly enumerated above:

In organic poetry the metric movement, the measure, is the direct expression of the movement of perception. And the sounds, acting together with the measure, are a kind of extended onomatopoeia—i.e., they imitate not the sounds of an experience (which may well be soundless, or to which sounds contribute only incidentally)—but the feeling of an experience, its emotional tone or texture.

Her conclusion: "Form is never more than a revelation of content."

Levertov's argument has immense charm; but for us to wholly accept it requires inordinate faith. If, as she implies, each experience were unique, then each poem—which is the organic crystallization of an experience—would have a unique set of formal requirements for its expression, requirements which could not be anticipated. There would be an *infinite* number of ways in which "A may lead to E." This is one reason why organicists invariably use the word "form" as a blank check that can refer to *any* element of a poem. In a good poem, there are too many factors at work to be spelled out. But that is not the only reason. The organic argument, *per se,* is so extreme that, tested against any specific poem, it will not stand up. If we actually examine one of Levertov's strong poems—a poem written around the time when she conceived "Some Notes On Organic Form"—we see that, although elements of its form *do* reinforce its content, that its "form" and "content" are by no means indissoluble, that we can always discover arrangements of the poem which do not substantially alter its

content. We discover, in fact, that its "content" is rather abstract. Consider, for ex-
ample, her poem "Losing Track":

> Long after you have swung back
> away from me
> I think you are still with me:
>
> you come in close to the shore
> on the tide
> and nudge me awake the way
>
> a boat adrift nudges the pier:
> am I a pier
> half-in half-out of the water?
>
> and in the pleasure of that communion
> I lose track,
> the moon I watch goes down, the
>
> tide swings you away before
> I know I'm
> alone again long since,
>
> mud sucking at gray and black
> timbers of me,
> a light growth of green dreams dying.

After the initial reading our attention is directed entirely toward the question of the
poem's "content" rather than toward questions of form: we ask, "What is the poem
about?" If the poem is the "crystallization" of an experience, what is the *type* of that
experience? Implicit in this question is the assumption that each experience, although
in many senses unique, may fit into a recognizable category; for indeed only to the
extent that a poem admits the categorization of experience can it become a public
rather than a wholly subjective utterance. With another reading, we conclude that
"Losing Track" is about a love affair, the speaker's dazed paralysis, her helplessness,
her enchantment by the intermittent sexual "communion" with "you," so that even
when he is gone, she is preoccupied with him, passive: she waits for the tide to come
in, the boat to return. But we also see that this "content" would be just as recognizable
if the lineation of the verses were different, if the text were written in prose, if the
stanza breaks were eliminated, if the order of the sentences were different, or even if
some of the diction were changed. In other words, the poem's content is largely
(though not entirely) independent of its form.

   It will immediately be objected that when Levertov says "Form is never more than
a *revelation* of content," she means by "content" something roughly akin to "feel-
ing"—that the essence of poetry is its ability to transmute directly into language the
emotional tone of experience. True enough. The problem is that Levertov's organic
argument overstates its case by focusing *exclusively* on the particularity of an experi-
ence and therefore treating "content" as if content consisted exclusively of ungener-

alizable "feelings." No one would argue with Levertov that unless "the feeling of an experience" has, by some mysterious process, been transmuted into language, the verse format will seem to lack a raison d'être and the resulting poem will be a failure. "Losing Track" succeeds marvelously. With its repeated vowel-sounds, its line-breaks that make the voice crack, make the breath catch in an almost-sob, it moans and sings like blues, while its archetypal imagery of "tides," "moon," and "water" evokes the depth of the speaker's awakened sexuality, which connects her physically, like a pier, to the earth, to the sea, to the rhythms to the universe, to the world's body. We might be correct to say that in "Losing Track" prosody is no more than a "revelation of emotion;" but also to claim that its "form is no more than a revelation of content" is to blur crucial distinctions.

Although organicists such as Levertov doubtless believe in the organic argument while they compose, "organic form," like the "conversation poem," is best regarded as a prescribed type of form rather than as a method of invention. A poem whose form is "organic" is an imitation of a recognizable, indeed almost conventional type of psychic process, one that is non-rational, affective, intuitive, and (paradoxically) sub-verbal. The finished organic poem must, therefore, display the predictable tokens of such a process: it is often in the present tense, in the "lyric" radical of presentation, with the speaker talking or musing to him- or herself; its prosody is apt to be flexible; its overall shape is apt to be rather plastic, and its diction is apt to be unstudied. In short, it must conceal its artifice.

"Organic," then, is itself the name of a category that can be applied to a kind of rhetoric—a rhetoric of artful spontaneity and one which is commonly associated with the traditional lyric, such as "Ode to a Nightingale," in which the speaker, overflowing with sub-verbal "feeling," sings to himself or herself. Another good contemporary example of this type of poem would be Ted Kooser's "A Summer Night:"

> At the end of the street
> a porch light is burning,
> showing the way. How simple,
> how perfect it seems: the darkness,
> the white house like a passage
> through summer and into
> a snowfield. Night after night,
> the lamp comes on at dusk,
> the end of the street
> stands open and white,
> and an old woman sits there
> tending the lonely gate.

As in the Levertov poem, here, too, because the poem's content consists of feelings which are predominantly sub-verbal, we find a heavy reliance upon imagery to evoke the unspoken, subliminal deathliness as well as the profound melancholy of the evening. Tone and emotion are not, as in Gildner's "First Practice," conveyed primarily by means of voice and line-break but rather as they have to be, by means of imagery;

for imagery, as Stanley Plumly has pointed out, is voiceless. It is this voicelessness which, together with the countless past echoes that make up the lyric tradition, gives the speaker of lyric his or her oddly generic quality.

"Lyric," then, like "conversation poem," is a category of poetic form, one that carries with it certain assumptions as to the nature of the speaker, type of subject-matter, and type of rhetoric. Whereas Gildner's conversational analogue dictates a persona who is a particular (and rather ordinary) person, a quotidian subject-matter and a conversational rhetoric, the "lyric" category dictates a generic persona, sub-verbal subject-matter and an organic rhetoric deploying a high degree of imagery. Indeed, it is as hard to imagine Kooser writing "A Summer Night" without knowing in advance what general type of poem he had in mind, as it is to imagine Gildner writing "First Practice" without having decided in advance to make his poem a mimesis of conversation. It is in this sense that our poetry is still "fixed form." Analogues, each with its strictures as to decorum, have replaced "the fixed forms."

This analogical basis for poetic form is what characterizes postmodern American poetry, if we take "postmodern" to name a literary period beginning after World War II. Historically, it is apparent that whenever the raison d'être of "fixed forms" is in question, poets wistfully propound impossible "organic" notions of poetic form to replace the seemingly dead fixed forms, while instinctively reaching for non-literary analogues as a fresh basis. The romantics, we recall, were attracted both to organicism and to analogical poetic forms: "conversation poems," precisely, or "lyrical ballads." Similarly, it is hardly an accident that Pound, wrestling in a later age with the amoebic growth of the *Cantos*, would invoke the analogies of "fugue," and "ideogram," that Eliot's *The Waste Land* invokes the collage as a formal analogy, that *The Four Quartets* invokes a musical analogy, or that *Paterson* would contain a high proportion of un-digested, non-literary material. Indeed, analogical poetic form may be regarded as a manifestation of a general literary principle: the further a poem deviates from fixed-form conventions and a traditional prosody, the more it will be compelled to seek, as a basis for its form, some non-literary analogue. The self-evident quality of this principle may be appreciated if we reword it slightly. If a work of literature does not invoke, as the basis of its form, literary conventions, then, if it is to have a form, by definition that form will have to be non-literary. Thus, for example, before the "novel" in English was sufficiently developed to be the name of a genre, it tended to be a mimesis of something else, such as journalism, romance, epistolary correspondence, spiritual autobiography. Thus it is that, in any epoch, in proportion to the degree that free verse becomes normalized, the analogues underlying poetic form tend to become non-literary.

Just so, *postmodern* poetic form is *analogical* poetic form with a vengeance: though on the one hand it represents a refinement of the analogical approach to form implicit in poetry of the High Modernist period, on the other hand it evinces considerable dissatisfaction with the impersonality of modernism. Postmodern formal strategy consists, therefore, not only of extending the range of formal analogues, but also of clearly favoring "communal" analogues such as confession and conversation over such impersonal analogues as the "fugue," the "ideogram," and the "vortex." We can, in fact, order the prevalent formal analogues along a scale, to borrow Al Poulin's term, of their degree of "personalization." In the admittedly over-schematic taxonomy that results, the outlines of three domains emerge distinctly and in a significant arrangement. Near the middle of this scale, we can locate and define a large, stable body consisting of a rather conservative type of poem that is "lyric"—a poem like Levertov's "Losing Track" or Kooser's "A Summer Night," spoken by a generic, literary "I" and deploying a traditionally "organic" rhetoric. The generic quality of the "lyric" voice may be regarded as an implicit norm, rejected on the one hand by modernists such as Pound and Eliot as being too personal, modified, on the other hand, by such post-modern "confessional" poets as Lowell, Hugo, and Berryman so as to incorporate a broader, more particularized and more topical range of personal experience. To one side of the lyric norm, in the direction of greater personalization, may be located two types of poem—the "confessional" and, furthest from the center, the "conversational." The "confessional" poem, as its very name would imply, is a poem whose form is derived by analogy from the ritual of "confession," a ritual which, in its religious aspect, is Roman Catholic and which, in its secular aspect, is psychoanalytic. It is a mimesis of testimony, in which the speaker either addresses the reader (often defiantly) or addresses some other person. The sense in which "confessional" may be regarded as a greater personalization of lyric may be appreciated if we imagine a blasphemous version of Keats's "Ode to a Nightingale," in which the speaker explicitly complained, in the first person, about his sexual needs, his medical problems, his *thanatos*. By particularizing the agenda of the inner life, placing its items in history and attributing psychological cause and effect to feelings—feelings traced back to specific origins, as elements of a unique autobiography—the speaker would lose much of his generic quality and, because the subject-matter was no longer subverbal, would be no longer singing to himself, but complaining aloud to a listener.

Whereas the authority of the lyric voice finds its source in tradition, the authority of the confessional voice finds its source in the authenticity of the speaker's testimony—a testimony which must, however, transcend the narrowly personal: to some extent, the persona's story must acquire, like a saint's life, a mythic significance. The persona must become a ritual scapegoat. Carolyn Forché's long poem "Return" might serve as a paradigm of how, when the confessional analogue is successfully applied, the poem negotiates these paradoxical demands. The poem's journalistic "witnessing" for conditions in El Salvador has authenticity; yet for all the particularity of exposition, Forché is able, at the end of the poem, to convert her individual suffering into a prophetic stance:

> Your problem is not your life as it is
> in America, not that your hands, as you
> tell me, are tied to something. It is
> that you were born to an island of greed & grace
> where you have this sense of yourself
> as apart from others. It is not your right
> to feel powerless. Better people than you
> were powerless. You have not returned
> to your country, but to a life you never left.

Just as lyric modulates into confessional, so does confessional modulate into conversation. To the extent which the persona of confessional relinquishes the claim to mythic status and extraordinary suffering, he or she becomes further particularized. The conversation poem such as "First Practice" is at once the most personal and, because its subject-matter is quotidian, the most difficult type of poem to write. Its authority depends not on tradition or on authenticity but entirely upon the artistic inventiveness of the poet who, speaking in his own person, must sustain brilliant conversation. Gildner's "First Practice," a narrative conversation poem of voice, is a good paradigm of what Stanley Plumly has labelled "the prose lyric." To the degree that a conversation poem abandons narrative, it becomes discursive, modulating into the mode which it is now fashionable to call "meditative," a mode often shown to its best advantage by such poets as Marvin Bell, William Stafford, William Matthews, and Jorie Graham.

To the other side of the lyric norm, in the direction of impersonality, may be grouped respectively and in descending order of personalization those types of poems which, in various ways, elaborate and extend the modernist impulse to produce poems as objects which can exist independently of their author's implied biography. Immediately to the impersonal side may be placed what, for convenience, I will call "deep-image" poems. The "deep-image" mode, like the "imagist" movement fifty years before it, may be seen in part as a reaction against personalization in poetry, recalling, in its revulsion from confessional, T. E. Hulme's earlier dictum to the "romantic" poet to "End your moan and come away." The deep-image poem attempts to treat of the self, but of a self even more generic than the self implicit in lyric. The persona of the deep-image poem is, in fact, scarcely human. The three most prevalent analogues underlying "deep image" poems are: (1) that of a modern man screaming a prehistoric, primal scream; (2) that of a modern man dreaming in prehistoric symbols; (3) as some of W. S. Merwin's poems purport to be, that of the earth itself, speaking through the poet. All three of these analogues recall Galway Kinnell's well-known formulation: "If you could keep going deeper and deeper, you'd finally not be a person either; you'd be an animal; and if you kept going deeper and deeper, you'd be a blade of grass or ultimately perhaps a stone. And if a stone could read, [poetry] would speak for it."

Within the "deep-image" tradition, the same paradox that underlies lyric—that of rendering sub-verbal material by means of language—becomes increasingly acute the further we modulate from lyric in the direction of the inhuman. By far the best poetry in this tradition is by Kinnell—poems which, like "Under the Maud Moon," deploy what I would call "primitive song" as a formal analogue. The less human, the less personal the formal analogue, the weaker deep-image poetry becomes. Consider, for example, Robert Bly's "The Hermit," a poem which deploys archetypal dream-vision as its formal analogue:

Darkness is falling through darkness,
Falling from ledge
To ledge.
There is a man whose body is perfectly whole.

He stands, the storm behind him,
And the grass blades are leaping in the wind.
Darkness is gathered in fold
About his feet.
He is no one. When we see
Him, we grow calm,
And sail on into the tunnels of joyful death.

Like a dream, the poem presents images. But whereas images in actual dreams have a powerful affect, a "numinosity" which, according to Jung (Bly's model), is proportional to the charge of "psychic energy" which they carry, such images, dried out on the printed page, are reduced to abstractions. Because language cannot render the feeling of numinosity, the poet tries, futilely, to tell us what to feel—"calm"—as we read.

The least successful formal analogue in the deep-image canon consists of the mimesis of the earth's "speech" itself, a wordless speech which is articulated verbally by the poem, with the poet, who does not appear directly, serving as a passive medium. Such a poem is W. S. Merwin's "Eyes of Summer:"

All the stones have been us
and will be again
as the sun touches them you can feel
sun
and remember waking with no face
knowing that it was summer
still
when the witnesses
day after day are blinded
so that they will forget nothing

The vocabulary of the earth is elemental to the point of dullness. Translated into human words, it has the force of stale, romantic doctrine.

All three of the principal "deep-image" analogues, "primitive song," "Jungian dream-vision," "Voice-of-Earth," deal with a single type of subject matter: they purport to put us back in direct touch with a primeval mode of consciousness. As all analogues do, these carry with them certain obvious requirements as to prosodic and rhetorical decorum. Primeval consciousness, approached directly instead of through the medium of civilized institutions, does not express itself by means of heroic couplets, in a polysyllabic, abstract vocabulary or in subordinate clauses, but through free verse, through what Paul Breslin has called "a studied plainness of vocabulary," through archetypal dream-symbols, and through simple (in the case of Merwin's poem, deliberately suppressed) grammar. The decorum dictated by deep-image analogues is that of an organic rhetoric carried too often beyond the point of diminishing returns. Kinnell's "Under the Maud Moon" is successful precisely because it avoids the fallacy of imitative form. Instead of insisting on an innocence of vision commensurate with a primitive analogue, it accepts the paradox inherent in the very notion of rendering sub-verbal subject-matter in language. It deploys the primitive-song analogue as a nostalgic but *sophisticated* commentary on the human fall. Kinnell takes up his analogue longingly; but his best poems implicitly criticize the very analogue they are imitating. Consider, for example, the following passage from "Under the Maud Moon":

> The black
> wood reddens, the deathwatches inside
> begin running out of time, I can see
> the dead, crossed limbs
> longing again for the universe, I can hear
> in the wet wood the snap
> and re-snap of the same embrace being torn.
> The raindrops trying
> to put the fire out
> fall into it and are
> changed: the oath broken,
> the oath sworn between earth and water, flesh and
>   spirit, broken,
> to be sworn again,
> over and over, in the clouds, and to be broken again,
> over and over, on earth.

In this passage, Kinnell's attitude toward the purely physical world—that world which Bly and Merwin purport to accept, without qualification—is far from comfortable. The speaker's longing for it is counterbalanced by fear of it, and his sense, hunched before the fire, of being in a starkly elemental position, is counterbalanced by his clear consciousness of how far *outside* natural process (epitomized by the fire) he stands. Bly's "The Hermit" and Merwin's "Eyes of Summer," on the other hand, by taking too literally the epistemological demands inherent in their formal analogues, lack the tension generated by the necessarily paradoxical nature of achieved poetic form.

Continuing to extend our taxonomy, we may locate, contiguous with the deep-image category but in the direction of greater impersonality, poems whose forms are based upon what might be regarded as "literary" analogues: narrative poems such as Louis Simpson's Chekhovian pieces, in which the speaking voice resembles that of a novelist; dramatic monologues such as Robert Pack's recent work, in which the poet's voice vanishes altogether; and late-modernist "essay" poems such as Richard Wilbur's famous "Love Calls Us to the Things of This World," highly crafted pieces, rich in literary diction and allusions, displaying conspicuous literary artifice, and spoken by a literary expert, a specialist. Whereas even in Merwin's "Eyes of Summer," the author retains a faint, vestigial presence as a character in his own poem, in the three types of poem above, the poet has removed himself fully as a character, and we are conscious of him only as a peripheral presence, as "The Author"; and it may be noted that, once an author has removed himself from his poem the requirements regarding prosodic and rhetorical decorum are simplified. No longer does the speaking voice have to take into account such factors as the need to sound spontaneous, sincere, "authentic." The ethos of the author is no longer directly on trial. Whereas poems based upon non-literary analogues present acute epistemological paradoxes—requirements for calculated spontaneity, for sophisticated primitivism, for mythologically resonant banal detail, for ordinary conversation with the force and staying power of art—the conventions associated with literary analogues render these modes of discourse far easier to manipulate without committing the fallacy of imitative form.

At the farthest end of the scale, absolute in their impersonality, may be grouped poems which are spoken by *nobody,* poems in which our sense even of the author's presence as a central consciousness all but disappears. These are poems in the so-called "post-modern*ist*" mode, for example, many of Ashbery's—poems which are asserted as objects and whose forms depend *entirely* upon analogues, in that they passively recapitulate all the possible modes of discourse, literary or otherwise. Such poems, placed beside the achieved conversation poem, reveal, in stark outline, the fundamental choice confronting the poet working in America today. It is a choice between analogues, between forms which, as we have seen, range from the communal to the impersonal. Curiously enough, this choice ends up being not an epistemological one but an ethical one: whether to trust the self and presume to impose upon the world, by sheer force of character, an individual aesthetic and ethical order, or to continue the modernist hegemony of Eliot and Pound, to retreat in an elitist disgust from modern civilization and indulge in the facile despair of the parodist, recapitulating all the bad languages that comprise our environment, holding our own civilization up before us as if the sad facts could only speak for themselves.

—Fall 1983

Philip Levine

The Holy Cities: Detroit, Barcelona, Byzantium

What follows is the story of a passion, or perhaps I should call it a faith, for anarchism is as much a religion as it is a political system. I'm not sure where the story begins. I suppose like most of the stories which make up my life or which I make up out of the events of my life, it has no beginning or ending; rather it has high points and low points, crests and troughs in the little seas of my awareness.

Let me begin with my growing up in the 1930s in the city of Detroit, a city choking on the ills of the Great Depression, though it was no worse off then than it is now, despised and avoided during the glory days of Reagan-Bush economics and racism. The first political event I recall with clarity was the presidential election of '32 which pitted the upstart Franklin Roosevelt against Herbert Hoover. My father, an immigrant from Tsarist Russia and a deserter from the British Army during the first World War, was then a partner with my grandfather in a small but lively automobile replacement parts company located near the ball park. He had also transformed himself into an ardent Republican. My grandfather had come to the U.S. during the first decade of the century in order to avoid military conscription for the Russo-Japanese War; his only politics were to avoid getting shot at protecting someone else's property; since he could not read English he was unaware of the fact that the leading conservative journal of the day, the Literary Digest, had picked Hoover in a landslide. He and my father bet on the election; I don't know the size of the bet, but it was enough to arouse passion in Zaydee's heart. My grandfather's political intuitions were keen: "With a voice like honey you don't lose." (Years later he won a fortune betting against Dewey, who he knew could not win because "right after Hitler the American people don't elect a little schmuck with such a moustache.") The family sat at the dining room table long after dinner listening to the returns come in as I played war with my lead soldiers under the table, hearing my father groan as each state reported the Republican defeat. My father was a good loser, and my grandfather generous in victory, so the evening ended without strain, although my father predicted bad times for business with this new president. Zaydee chuckled, "How much worse could they be?"

A year later in an art class in kindergarten I had my second political experience. We were assembling armatures for a sculpture the class was building, and for it we used wadded hunks of newspapers and paste we made ourselves out of flour and water. I was sitting next to a teacher's aide when I noticed an odd picture in the Sunday rotogravure section; men in uniforms bearing armbands with curious symbols on them were rounding up civilians. The symbols were swastikas, the men brown-shirts, a militia of the National Socialist Party of Germany; the civilians were Jews. The photograph and its caption froze me, and as I started to read the article below it the teacher's aide, who was a college student at Wayne University, covered the text with her hand. "You don't want to read that," she said. "Why are they wearing those things on their sleeves?" I asked. Slowly she pulled the paper away from me and repeated her ominous warning, "You don't want to read that." "Why are they doing that to us?" I asked. Immediately I recognized that she was far more upset by my discovery of the photograph than I; her hands were trembling, and she shook her head from side to side. "Please," she said, "you don't want to know any of this." Immediately I shut up, knowing I could get the truth from my mother.

Although I was born into the middle class, my father died before I was old enough to enjoy my station. My mother found work as a stenographer and, later, office manager. Although she always provided for us, my memory includes a succession of moves from first a house to a series of ever-shrinking apartments. Something had been suspect about my father's life insurance policy, and the company refused to pay the full value. Money became the chief topic of meal-time conversations, money and especially the lack of it. Curiously, my older brother seemed not the least fazed by our difficulties. He demanded a clean shirt for every school day, and amazingly he got one. Some days he would return from school, check himself out in the bathroom mirror, decide his shirt was dirty, and immediately change to another one even though he was going to do nothing except practice the piano or study his text books. When I questioned my mother about this, she merely informed me that he was the first born.

In the evenings my mother would return home from work exhausted but never dirty. I learned from Belle, my mother's younger sister, that this was significant. Once, before Belle took me on the bus downtown to buy a new pair of shoes for the beginning of the school year, she made me first take a bath and then change into my only clean knickers and of course into clean socks. I questioned her about the sense of all this preparation. "We may be poor," she said, "but at least we're clean." "We're poor!" I demanded. She hedged. No, we weren't exactly poor, we just didn't have any money, and that was why it was important to be clean, so no one would mistake us for the poor. Clearly it would be terrible to be mistaken for the poor. We had enough money, for example, to buy me a pair of shoes for the new school year. She held up the battered ones I'd been wearing all summer. "These are way too small for you, and look at them." She stretched the sole away from the rest of the shoe and let it slip slowly back like a fatigued spring. "People with money don't wear clothes that are falling apart, and they don't have to spend an afternoon going downtown to save a dollar on a pair of shoes." Later at Hudson's Department Store, a massive structure that occupied an entire square block, Belle argued ferociously with a salesman who claimed that the sale did not include the shoes she wanted for me. Belle was fearless; she just kept pushing the ad clipped from the *Free Press* in his face and repeating, "It's right here in black and white." Finally the salesman relented and gave us the hideous brown, heavy "English" walking shoes at the sale price. On the way home she confided in me one of the principles by which she purchased: "The English make the best shoes." The little jerk of a salesman had been trying to pass off an American pair on her. I left the shoes in their box, afraid to wear them until the first day of school. I'd learned how quickly the gleaming surface of the soles could be eroded simply by sliding on the pavement, an exercise that was always tempting. A week passed before I took them from the closet; I discovered that the box clearly declared they'd been manufactured by union labor in Brockton, Massachusetts. Immediately I lost all affection for them, though I never revealed to Belle the profundity of her error.

Entering the second grade that year, I began to notice for the first time how differently we students dressed, and at the same time how many of us wore the same clothes. There were four boys in my class aside from me who wore sweaters which bore the figure of a stag knitted in white against a maroon background. It too had been on sale at Hudson's, the maroon a dollar cheaper than the navy blue. There was one boy who wore far more elegant sweaters in subtle hues of brown and fawn; even his checked socks were in matching colors. He was always neatly combed, his nails never bitten down, and they gleamed as though they had been polished. I noticed too that my teacher seemed to defer to him, to call on him only when he raised his hand and clearly knew the answers to her questions, whereas she was continually trying to make fools out of the rest of us. This boy, Milton Journey, was always driven to school in a long white LaSalle convertible, which I learned belonged to his older brother who attended a nearby junior high school. On winter days after school, Milton would wait in his long blue overcoat inside the main doors until his mother stopped and honked from her sedan. Milton would toss back his straight blond hair, shrug, and go out into the weather to accept his privileges.

Another boy, Fred Batten, disgusted me. When he spoke to me he had a habit of sticking his face as close as he could to mine as though he were trying to swipe my breath; perhaps he truly meant to, for his own breath smelled awful. Unfortunately he had some sort of affection for me and continually pursued me. One day I noticed that the skin behind his ears and around his neck bore dark smudges. I realized Fred Batten didn't wash; his hands too were always filthy. With a shock I realized he wore no socks, and often that winter the skin of his ankles was raw and swollen. One day he caught me staring at his bare ankles, and he turned away from me in silence. I began to notice several other boys and girls who bore these same "wounds" at wrist and ankles, and I did my best not to stare at them.

Winters in Michigan were fierce, but I never left for school without a warm jacket, socks, a cap that covered my ears, usually by means of some sort of hideous flap that fastened below the chin, gloves, and a scarf. Not once did I go off without a sacked lunch, nor were lice ever found in my hair, though weekly I had to bow for the health officer's inspection. Many of my classmates were not so fortunate and were taken off for their "treatment" and returned, heads bent and reeking of kerosene.

Lunch times grew particularly difficult, for many students had nothing to eat except the free carton of milk that was provided by the school. By the age of ten I'd decided that it was easier to walk the mile back to our apartment and eat my lunch in privacy than to bear the envious glances of many of my school mates. In autumn especially the tree-lined streets were lovely, and since my mother was unable to buy glasses for me until I was fourteen, in those early years I was walking through a city invented by an impressionist painter.

Often I'd make the walk home with a classmate, Martin Peters, who though shorter than I was actually two years older and lived with his family in a "halfer," a second story apartment that was divided into two separate units both of which shared the kitchen and bathroom. Suddenly during a particularly cold week in January Martin stopped coming to school. I didn't see him for three weeks. The word was he was suffering from pneumonia, but when he returned to class he shared his secret. His mother had been keeping him home because he had no heavy jacket or coat. His father was out of work, the gas bill had not been paid, so the heat had been shut off. Martin had spent most days in bed, under the covers, listening to the radio. During those weeks he'd become an extraordinary source of the comings and goings of his favorite soap-opera characters, and now the need to return to class was depriving him of more of their adventures.

Something was very wrong with the world, and I was powerless to do anything about it. When my father died in his middle thirties I was assured that it was due to the rules of God: the good died young so that they could be close to Him. That did me and my family absolutely no good, for we were doomed to spend the rest of our lives deprived of this lovable man. Poor men came to our doors daily, and we had to turn them away for lack of anything to give them. To and from school I would walk past blocks of stately mansions. I experimented. In the back seat of my grandfather's Hudson, I would imagine myself equipped with a repeating rifle and opening fire on every Cadillac, LaSalle, Lincoln, or Chrysler we happened across. This was my battle against the forces of injustice and greed. My bullets equalized nothing, but they made me feel better.

Meanwhile I was growing up in a viciously anti-Semitic community in a particularly anti-Semitic era. From Royal Oak, Michigan, a suburb of Detroit, the rantings of Father Coughlin were broadcast every Sunday, and those rantings blamed the Communist Jews for every social and moral problem and urged our expulsion. For reasons I still fail to comprehend, my family often tuned into international broadcasts of Hitler's speeches. When the Italians invaded Abyssinia, when the Japanese moved into China, when Hitler annexed the Rhineland, I saw the motive as revenge against the Jews.

When I was seven my mother hired a hill woman named Florence Hickcock to clean, cook, and look after us, especially during the summer, when we were out of school and my mother worked all through the season as a stenographer. Florence was one of those uncompromising Americans who believe in militancy, a fair wage, and the never-ending battle against the excesses of capitalism that all decent working people were obliged by God and common sense to carry on until their last breath. Tall, gaunt, weather-beaten, with a cigarette burning in the corner of her mouth, at the breakfast table she'd read through the morning Free Press muttering, "The bastards are selling us down the river." She hadn't the least doubt that the European "Democ-racies" and America as well were run by and for the rich. By "us" she meant, of course, all those who had to work for a living, whose labor created the wealth that ironically imprisoned them. From the Black Hills of the Dakotas, Florence claimed to be of the same blood as Wild Bill, who she assured us was also a red. (In those days independent working Americans were proud of being red, which did not mean membership in the Communist Party: it merely meant struggling with the common people against the exploiters. No matter what you've been told to the contrary, we reds knew the differ-ence between the totalitarian, brain-washed CP members, the professional Commu-nists, and ourselves, the reds who wanted not to be encumbered with another hier-archy of bosses.)

Then occurred one of the epic events of my young life; I was eight years old during the summer of '36 when the generals rose up to overthrow the Spanish Republic. The American right-wing press called it a battle between the Nationalists and the Com-munists, but even then I knew it was the legally elected people's government versus the fascists, the ancient repressive forces of church, army, and the great landowners. Florence had no doubts, and when the United States, France, and England refused to sell arms to the Republic even though the Nazis and the Italian Fascists were sending men, tanks, and warplanes, she showed not the least surprise. "They're selling us down the river. You watch, Philip, France will be next. They'd rather lose to the Nazis than to the working people."

Immediately young men from my neighborhood were being recruited to join the Lincoln Brigade and fight for the defense of the Republic. Before long one of my classmates told me that his parents had received a telegram the night before saying that his older brother, whose name was the same as mine, was missing in action. I was puzzled by that expression, "missing in action," and asked my friend exactly what it meant. "He may be a prisoner of war," little Irv said, "but my uncle told me they aren't taking prisoners, so I guess it means he's dead." Out on the playground in the already chilled autumn air, we sat on the bleachers just behind the baseball diamond while Irv told us how scared he was to go home. His mom was just wrecked by the news; she'd begged her oldest not to go. To us Philip was a hero: in some curious way we envied his sacrifice.

In those days baseball cards were not the only prizes available with the purchase of bubble gum. You had the option of choosing "War Cards," which until then had featured the bombing of Abyssinians and the beheading of civilians in Shanghai by hunks of plate glass blasted from the windows of modern European-style hotels. But now the Spanish Nationalists in their chic uniforms and tasseled caps were attacking Madrid on one card and on another holding out for over two hundred days against the Communists, with the aid of Moorish troops. I never saw it, but there must have been one that celebrated the death of the commander of the Anarchist Durruti Bri-gade, shot in the back on the road to Madrid. I don't doubt that it existed in the lurid colors of the day, depicting a thick-waisted brutal man brought to a brutal end; the friends of our enemies seemed to own every avenue of communication except word of mouth, which became the only one we trusted. Soon the cities with their holy names fell to Franco, one after the other, Granada, Malaga, Madrid, Alicante, Valencia, and lastly the great outpost of our people, Barcelona. That was in the spring of '39, and before that summer was over Florence's prediction proved true: fascism was sweeping everything before it. Poland was sliced in two by Hitler and Stalin; their non-aggression pact was sealed. The Nazis were one giant step closer to Detroit.

In D'Angelo & Ferrente's Dry Cleaning & Tailoring Shop, around the corner from where we lived, the two proprietors argued continually with each other and with their employees regarding the political truths of the day. D'Angelo was medium height, slender, and dressed with what he considered a studied elegance. It was a rare day on which he appeared without his suit coat; a lover of Verdi and Puccini, he considered himself several cuts above his squat little Sicilian partner, who never failed to assure me of his love for FDR and his loathing of Mussolini, who had plunged a knife into the back of his neighbor. They paid me a quarter for each delivery I made on foot, and while I waited for the parcels to be readied I often conversed with the tall, slender presser whose name I have forgotten. Because of the heat he'd work in pleated trousers and a sleeveless undershirt which revealed his scars—a gift of his years of imprisonment for his loyalties to the anarchist cause. He and the Bulgarian tailor ("a whiz at trousers," Ferrente claimed) never spoke to or even acknowledged each other. Thick, gray-haired, and balding, the Bulgarian saw what was coming even in the winter of 1940 and legally renamed his sons Leonard and Stanley (they had been Lenin and Stalin). Because of his resemblance to another anarchist who shared his faith in the Spanish working people, I shall call the presser Cipriano. He was the first anarchist I met who knew he was an anarchist. He was by far the most reserved and self-contained member of this informal debating society. Perhaps because he had actually fought the battles in body and spirit, he seemed to have no need to carry on verbally, and his only response to the Bulgarian's Marxist rants was a silent shaking of the head. A tightly built muscular man with deep set dark eyes and long black hair, he went about his work with an alarming suddenness, as though he were not a pants presser but an actor playing the role of one. I read in his movements not a disregard for this work but rather the affirmation that all work was worth doing with elegance and precision and that necessary work granted dignity to the worker. For me he was both a pants presser and the most truly dignified person I'd ever met, one of the unacknowledged legislators of the world. He never lectured me; instead he shared his views on the unending struggle for equality and independence that each of us must wage against the forces of government and private ownership, for it was only by owning nothing that each of us would come fully into possession of the gift of the self. In spite of all his defeats he was animated by an amazing optimism. "Some day this will all be ours," he said into my boy's wide eyes, "someday you will see." Pared of all excess, he seemed to me the perfect embodiment of the human spirit.

During the summer of 1942 I was working in a soap factory on the outskirts of town, wheeling huge racks of sliced soap chips into the ovens, where they dried, yellowed, and curled until they resembled some rare, unworldly pasta. The heat was extraordinary, and I had to hop to it not to succumb, but for 35¢ an hour I did my best. (The ironies were lost on me; in '42 in Detroit we did not know about the other ovens nor the transformation of Jews into soap.) I was saving for a good pair of trousers—hopefully created by the Bulgarian Marxist—in which I could return to school in the fall. On Saturday afternoons I'd stop by D'Angelo & Ferrente's and make whatever deliveries were needed. And one day Cipriano was gone, replaced by a short, wizened black man. No, he hadn't been fired, he hadn't called in sick, he hadn't even collected his last check. He had just vanished into America, and except for me no one seemed to care. I hoped that wherever his life had taken him, he was sharing his vision with some other kid. Also, that summer Florence Hickcock accidently stumbled across her childhood sweetheart, Peg, at the zoo, where he fed and looked after the big cats. After a few weeks of spooning, they thought they'd try life together in the West, for Florence's lungs were bad after a lifetime of chain-smoking and a particularly severe bout of pneumonia the previous winter. My teachers were leaving, and I supposed it was time for me to become a man. I was fourteen, walking the avenues with eyes lowered, having discovered the sculptured beauty of women's legs and suddenly aware of the fact that every handsome woman knew I was looking.

That autumn I found poetry. After dark, ambling the deserted streets, I would speak to the moon and stars about the emotional revolution that was raging within me, and true to their natures the moon and stars would not answer. My most intimate poems were summoned by the promise of rain in the air or the odors of its aftermath. Night after night I spun and respun these poems—if poems they were—none of which I ever committed to the page. I was learning to love solitude and to discover the power of my voice to deprive it of terror; I was learning how to become one man in a sea of men and women who by some mystery came together to form a brotherhood and sisterhood of all those beings with souls. At that age I knew of almost no beings without souls; certainly trees had them and the wildflowers that sprung up in the undeveloped lots and the tall grasses I lay down in for shelter. Even the hum of traffic on the distant Outer Drive had a kind of intelligence, as though it too spoke for some human yearning, as though each separate car were on some quest whose goal was love, for all I knew love of me. Once the dark took over, nothing was impossible. Each night that I labored joyously at my new craft and art, I sang out to the city and the larger world beyond the city, and no one was the wiser.

✳

The more I consider these events the more sure I become that I cannot write about the development in me of a faith or a passion. I don't actually understand why for so many years I lectured my friends on the virtues of anarchism and then suddenly stopped. I doubt that it had anything to do with my desire not to bore them. Perhaps some of my hesitancy sprung from the events that followed my being tossed out of the house my wife and I had been renting for fourteen years. That was 1973, a time when millions of Americans were intensely aware of the evils of the American state, and so many of the young were into a kind of rock or punk anarchism. All around me I perceived the truth of that basic anarchist tenant that property is theft. My wife and kids and I would drive into the nearby Sierra Nevada mountains for informal hikes only to be greeted by bullet-riddled signs announcing "No Trespassing," signs that made it clear that violators would be prosecuted or worse. All my growing up I'd been told about the immense wealth I'd inherited merely by being born an American, and now nothing was clearer than that my inheritance had been stolen. In my own life I was stealing nothing from anyone: I had clothes (two pairs of shoes now), a record player and records, a few hundred books I'd gathered over the years, a car, a house full of odds and ends of furniture. I had my poems also, but by its very nature a poem is something you hope to share with others, even to give away if need be. And suddenly our security was shattered by an order either to purchase a house we'd been living in for fourteen years or to hit the road. We chose to look elsewhere, but since rents were rising steeply and a poetry grant from the National Endowment gave me enough for a down payment, and since my wife happened across exactly the house she wanted—a small California farm house on an enormous lot dotted with orange trees and with room for a large garden—and since walking through the place on a blazing July afternoon the thought came to me so clearly I declaimed it—"I can write here"—and the price was reasonable, we bought. I've never regretted that act, though it deprived me forever of the right to say, "Property is theft." No doubt all my friends were relieved, and in fact even I was. My lectures ended, but though silent I did not stop believing the lessons I'd derived from my heroes.

So let this be a story of my heroes and the story of how a particular poem grew out of the homage I tried to pay to those heroes. And in the spirit of fairness to the complexities of experience let it also become the story of the poem I did not write and never will write, though all the material is there stored in my memory, textured scenes I hope never to forget, peopled with those singular individuals who enter our lives only on those days during which creation has deemed us worthy of the highest gift, the clarity inspiration gives us. This shall be the story of the poem I wrote in 1978, "Francisco, I'll Bring You Red Carnations" and the poem I did not write ten years later when I fulfilled the promise in the title of the written poem.

*

For the sake of fullness let me return to an earlier me. In the spring of 1965 my college, Fresno State, granted me my first sabbatical leave. My sense of Fresno State is that as schools of higher education go, it's not much (my best student once referred to it in print as "Wind & Dust State"), although the student body represents the community far more accurately than most schools, certainly far more than Yale represents New Haven or Harvard represents Cambridge or the University of California represents Berkeley. The overriding problem is the bureaucracy of the entire state university system as well as our local administration. We teachers are required to spend twelve hours in the classroom each week, usually in four different classes, each with an average of thirty students, for someone has to pay for the army of mediocrities we are saddled with, administrators with titles like Dean of Steam or Vice President of Non-academic Affairs and Non-sexual Relations. These people with huge salaries and no function determine the priorities of the place, and they couldn't care less about the arts, the sciences, the humanities, the teaching of something so esoteric as poetry writing. The last time I saw our president in public he was on TV hawking private suites at our football stadium at thirty grand a year; we've gone into competition with the Dallas Cowboys.

A dear colleague urged England on me, reminding me how Frost's work took off during and after his English years. I seriously considered England. In April of '65 I took part in a writing conference at U.C. Santa Barbara; there I met the poet and fiction writer Yascha Kessler who assured me that England was far too cold and too stuffy for my temperament. He'd recently returned from a year in Europe, most of which he'd spent in Italy. When I told him how much money I had, he said, "Spain, it's the only place you can afford." He described a wine he'd bought for ten cents a liter in a Spanish bodega near Malaga; the richness and delicacy of the wine were still with him, though he'd forgotten the name. "What about Franco?" I asked. "You don't bother him, he won't bother you." I returned to Fresno a few days later and presented the idea to my wife. In her youth she'd spent a large part of a winter in Paris and England, and she knew how cold northern Europe could be; she was all for Spain.

She took up the study of the Spanish language while I began to grapple with Spain's history, both ancient and modern. I taught summer school and a writing conference in San Francisco and put aside as much as I could. Could a family of five make it for a year on less than $8000? I was scared, but I was also excited to be making this break with teaching, with Fresno, and with the United States, now well into its exercise in imperialism in southeast Asia. I wrote almost nothing that summer, but I read an enormous amount, and it was during a rereading of Orwell's *Homage to Catalonia* that I made the final decision. The book begins with a scene in the Lenin Barracks in Barcelona; it is December of '36, the anarchists are still in control of the city, and no one publicly says "Señor" or "Don" or even "Usted," Orwell tells us. They say "Comrade" and "Thou"; instead of "Buenas dias" they say "Salud." Tipping is forbidden. "Practically everyone wore rough working class clothes. . . . All this was queer and moving . . . but I recognized it immediately as a sate of affairs worth fighting for," wrote Orwell, some seven months later. But what moved me most in the book was what moved him most: an Italian militiaman he saw the day he too joined the militia. "He was a tough looking youth of twenty-five or six, with reddish yellow hair and powerful shoulders. His peaked leather cap was pulled fiercely over one eye. He was standing in profile to me, his chin on his breast, gazing with a puzzled frown at a map which one of the officers had opened on the table. Something in his face deeply moved me. It was the face of a man who would commit murder and throw his life away for a friend—the kind of face you expect in an Anarchist. . . ." I too knew that face, or at least one of its many million incarnations. I had not seen it in almost twenty-five years, I had not felt its singular power to rouse and inspire. I would search for it again in the capital of anarchism, in the streets of Barcelona.

Mid-September, 1965. We entered the great city under a shroud of smog as heavy as any I had ever seen. In spite of the heat, we had avoided the coast road in order to save time. This took us through a dozen industrial towns which spilled into each other to form one seamless misunderstanding. We passed miles of cheap high-rise apartment buildings with that raw, unfinished look one associates with post-war Italian films or photographs of the third world. The truck traffic was extraordinary, and every time we got stuck behind one of the big diesels our windshield darkened with tiny spots of filth. And the noise! Scooters and two-cycle motorbikes weaved in and out of the stalled traffic, loudspeakers blared from every square as we crawled toward our new home. We had traveled half way around the world to discover this Detroit of Europe. My wife and kids bravely accepted the fact: we would live here for a year, we would make the best of it.

The next morning I wakened early in a hotel room twelve floors above Barcelona's Rambla de Cataluña and descended by elevator into the streets to find someplace that served coffee and rolls. The air was surprisingly cool and fresh; it was before 7 A.M. and people were still on their way to or from work. I sat for over an hour in a bar watching the men in their blue cover-alls embracing and chatting before going off to their separate jobs or their apartments. It was as though I'd known these men before I saw them, these men in their wool caps, smoking and hollering in their hoarse voices. Their faces unshaven, rough, spare, worn down but not worn out, these were the men of my boyhood and my growing up. In spite of or perhaps because of the decades of Franco's repression, their anger was palpable and fresh. Little wonder this city had become the birthplace and burial ground of one of the world's most daring experiments in self-government.

✳

The beginnings of Spanish anarchism are usually traced to the arrival in Spain in the fall of 1868 of Giuseppi Fanelli, an Italian supporter of the Russian anarchist, and theoretician Mikhail Bakunin, who had financed the trip from Geneva to Spain. His arrival there should have signaled a total fiasco; for one thing he spoke almost no Spanish, and for another he was constantly running out of money, but somehow wherever he went he was able to express his loathing of social injustice and the profundity of his libertarian ideals. (Those who write about anarchism have begun to avoid the very word because the popular press has managed to transform it into a synonym for bomb throwing and assassination.) By January of the following year he had helped found an International Working-man's Association in Madrid of twenty-some members. Urged to stay, he decided to leave, for, as he put it, these groups had to develop "by their own efforts, with their own values." On his way home he stopped off in Barcelona and there too made a few key converts. He returned to Italy and his life as a professional revolutionary, preaching his ideals in small villages, sleeping in railroad cars, impoverished, until his death eight years later of TB at the age of forty-eight.

What was "The Idea," as it was later called, that was now to spread throughout much of Spain, reaching its glory years in the 1930s? As Murray Bookchin, the historian of this era, writes, "anarchist ideals are difficult to fix into a hard and fast credo. Anarchism is a great libidinal movement of humanity to shake off the repressive apparatus created by hierarchical society. It originates in the age-old drive of the oppressed to assert the spirit of freedom, equality, and spontaneity over values and institutions based on authority. This accounts for the enormous antiquity of anarchistic visions, their irrepressibility and continual reemergence in history." Little wonder "The Idea" spread wildly in the rich, once Christian soil of Spain, for as Bookchin notes, "The slaves and poor who flocked to Christianity saw the second coming of Christ as a time when 'a grain of wheat would bear ten thousand ears,' when hunger, coercion, and hierarchy would be banished forever from the earth." Throughout its history Spanish Anarchism remained a people's movement. In spite of the most severe efforts to suppress it, it flowered in a country of the basest poverty and inequality, and not only in the industrial centers, but also in the mining country of the north and in agrarian Andalusia, though in each region it produced its own particular character. By the 1930s the largest trade union in Spain was the anarcho-syndicalist CNT (National Confederation of Workers), which had almost two million members.

The history of Spanish Anarchism is also the history of terrible repressions under the monarchy, the dictatorship of Primo de Rivera, and even under the Second Republic. Perhaps the most famous was the "Tragic Week" of July 1909, which was touched off by the governments attempt to call up the military reserves to deal with the Riff uprisings in Morocco. There were very few workingmen who wanted to risk their lives to protect the colonial holdings of their employers. Workingmen of all persuasions banded together in what was largely a spontaneous uprising. As one observer wrote, "What is happening here is amazing. A social revolution has broken out in Barcelona and it has been started by the people. No one instigated it. No one has led it. Neither the Liberals nor Catalan Nationalists, nor Republicans, nor Socialists, nor Anarchists." After the army brutally put down the rebellion, one of those singled out for execution by the military to pay for his "crimes" against the state had absolutely nothing to do with the event. He was not even in Barcelona when the uprising began and had spent the previous month nursing his sister and caring for her daughter on his farm some fifteen miles outside the city. Francisco Ferrer y Guardia was famous not as a revolutionary but as the founder of what was to become the most influential school in modern Spain, the *Escuela Moderna,* which by today's standards may hardly sound revolutionary, but at a time when most young Spaniards were the students of clerics and were subject to terrible physical punishment and humiliation, he established a school that would promote "a stern hostility to prejudice" and create "solid minds, capable of forming their own rational convictions on every subject." His aim was to bring together not only the sexes—a thing unheard of in Spain—but young people of all social classes so as to create a "school of emancipation that will be concerned with banning from the mind whatever divides men, the false concepts of property, country, and family." A man known for his gentleness and humility, Ferrer was none the less a marked man, and when the authorities got their chance at the end of the tragic week, they took it. After a farcical, rigged military trial of one day he was sentenced to death, and on the morning of October 13, 1909, in Montjuich prison (which shares the Mountain of Jove or Mountain of Jews—there is disagreement on the source of the name—with the great cemetery of Barcelona) he was executed by a firing squad. It is reported that he faced his death calmly, and that as the soldiers aimed their rifles he cried out, "Look well, my children! I am innocent. Long live the *Escuela Moderna!*"

The other two historical figures, Buenaventura Durruti and Francisco Ascaso, were to become the two most famous Spanish anarchists, the central agents in the mobilization of the working class against fascist dictatorship and the ancient exploitations of church, army, and state. The biographer Abel Paz describes their first meeting in Saragossa in 1922. The two men were then in their twenties, and Ascaso had just been released from prison for his part in labor organizing, which was forbidden during the reign of Alphonso XIII. At the time, Ascaso was the better known of the two, having gained attention for his extraordinary courage, his shrewdness as an organizer, and also through his theoretical publications. Paz states that from the beginning the two were drawn to each other's person and thought. "The differences in their characters only brought out better the resemblances between the two men. Ascaso, small, thin, nervous; Durruti, athletic and calm. Ascaso with his strained and suspicious glance, seemed unlikable at first sight; Durruti on the contrary radiated sympathy. Icy calculation, rationality and mistrust in one; passion and optimism behind an apparently calm exterior in the other . . . once a complete climate of confidence had been established great projects were born from the dialogue between the two revolutionaries."

The two men spent much of the rest of the decade in exile, working together as organizers in Latin America and Europe, spreading "The Idea." Once their activities were discovered by the authorities, they were imprisoned or forced to move on, and by the end of the decade there was almost no country that would have them. The two lived quietly in Brussels from 1929 until 1931 when a general pardon was granted by the new Spanish Republic. Within a few weeks of their return they were speaking at anarchist rallies to enormous crowds, and before a month passed Durruti was in prison on old, trumped up charges. Soon released, he threw himself with all his ferocious nature into his work. The rest of the story is, as they say, history. On July 19, 1936 the generals rose against the republic, and the terrible civil war began. In Barcelona the workers, largely under the leadership of the CNT, were able to seize the initiative, put down the uprising, and declare a revolution in Catalonia. It was on that day, July 19th, that Ascaso died leading the charge against the Atarazanas barracks in Barcelona.

There were many who saw in the death of Ascaso a foreshadowing of all disasters that were to follow, the deep divisions within the left, the betrayal of the revolution, and even the struggle against fascism by the communists. (As we know from eye witness accounts, Orwell's and others, the communists did everything within their power to brand as pro-fascist all those on the Republican side who refused to follow the commissars, and they did not stop short of assassination.) One of the most moving tributes to the particular gifts of Ascaso and the beauty of his friendship with Durruti is found in Robert W. Kern's *Red Years, Black Years,* a political history of Spanish Anarchism from 1911 to 1937:

Seen from our age, which is cynical about such things, their friendship can only be summarized as a revolutionary partnership, an incredible voyage by a pair of Spanish peasants through the politics and crime of Latin America, Western Europe, Africa, and Spain. In many situations there was something of the *picaro* about them, not in the sense of Lazzerello de Tormes, but more in remaining what they were, of not craving publicity or seeking a large following, of constantly working for a goal while staying very much as they always had been. Peasant rebels in an urban, industrial century, as political individualists representing the collective revolutionary dream of the countryside, unfettered by vanguardism or any of the other rigorous dialectics of the modern Left, they had a certain roguish quality. One survivor who remembers Ascaso called him "one of the last nineteenth century libertarians," a radical thrown up by the great upheavals of the early capitalist era when everything was much more black and white than in the 1930s.

Above all else, above even the sacrifices and the terrible martyrdoms, it was this friendship and the fellowship of working men and women it suggested that inspired my poem. In some way I cannot explain, I had chosen since boyhood to live vitally in the Spain of that era, to take part in the struggle for a new world.

Francisco, I'll Bring You Red Carnations

Here in the great cemetery
behind the fortress of Barcelona
I have come once more to see
the graves of my fallen.
Two ancient picnickers direct
us down the hill. "Durruti,"
says the man, "I was on
his side." The woman hushes
him. All the way down
this is a city of the dead,
871, 251, *difuntos*.
The poor packed in tenements
a dozen high; the rich
in splendid homes or temples.
So nothing has changed
except for the single
unswerving fact: they are
all dead. Here is the Plaza
of San Jaime, here the Rambla
of San Pedro, so very death
still has a mailing address,
but since this is Spain
the mail never comes or
comes too late to be of use.
Between the cemetery and
the Protestant burial ground
we find the three stones
all in a row: Ferrer Guardia,
B. Durruti, F. Ascaso, the names
written with marking pens,

and a few circled A's and tributes
to the FAI and CNT.
For two there are floral
displays, but Ascaso faces
eternity with only a stone.
Maybe as it should be. He was
a stone, a stone and a blade,
the first grinding and sharpening
the other. Half his 36
years were spent in prisons
or on the run, and yet
in that last photograph
taken less than an hour before
he died, he stands in a dark
suit, smoking, a rifle
slung behind his shoulder, and glances
sideways at the camera
half smiling. It is July 20,
1936, and before the darkness
falls a darkness will have
fallen on him. While
the streets are echoing
with victory and revolution,
Francisco Ascaso will take up
the hammered little blade
of his spirit and enter for
the last time the republics
of death. I remember
his words to a frightened
comrade who questioned
the wisdom of attack: "We
have gathered here to die, but we
don't have to die with dogs,
so go." Forty-one years
ago, and now the city stretches
as far as the eye can see,
huge cement columns like nails
pounded into the once green
meadows of the Llobregat.
Your Barcelona is gone,
the old town swallowed
in industrial filth and
the burning mists of gasoline.
Only the police remain, armed

and arrogant, smiling masters
of the boulevards, the police
and your dream of the city
of God, where every man
and every woman gives
and receives the gifts of work
and care, and that dream
goes on in spite of slums,
in spite of death clouds,
the roar of trucks, the harbor
straining the mother sea,
it goes on in spite of all
that mocks it. We have it here
growing in our hearts, as
your comrade said, and when
we give it up with our last
breaths someone will gasp
it home to their lives.
Francisco, stone, knife blade,
single soldier still on
the run down the darkest
street of all, we will be back
across an ocean and a continent
to bring you red carnations,
to celebrate the unbroken
promise of your life that
once was frail and flesh.

✴

"We carry a new world here in our hearts. That world is growing this minute."
—Buenaventura Durruti

In the spring of 1988 we returned to Spain for the first time since I wrote the poem some ten years before. It was a very different Spain we found under the governance of the Socialist Felipe Gonzalez, and a very different "Catalunya," as we found it spelled in Catalan, now one of the legal languages of the region, though banished during the reign of Franco. A hipper, richer, more swinging, more exciting Barcelona, though the city had never fallen as heavily under the thumb of fascism as the rest of Spain. One of my reasons for going to Barcelona was to fulfill the vow made in the poem, to bring to the grave of Francisco Ascaso the red carnations I felt were the least tribute I could pay him for leading a life dedicated to anarchist principles, a life I could not lead but which had inspired me for over twenty years.

I should explain that while the poem is true to my feelings about my visit to the cemetery, it neglects to mention the most dramatic encounter I had with the three graves, which took place during my second visit. I went there in the company of my wife, my oldest son Mark, and his friend Geraldine Pontius, an architect. Geraldine had brought to Europe an expensive rented 16 mm movie camera, and for the previous few days she had been filming the work of the great Catalan mystical architect Gaudí. In order to find the graves we drove to a small office, a registry of graves, and there I asked for the location of the grave of Ferrer; I knew the exact date of his burial. A young woman looked up the date in an enormous and ancient tome, but she could find no Ferrer nor could she give me any hint as to the whereabouts of the grave. Finally I told her that the three graves were side by side, Ferrer, Ascaso, and Durruti. "*Ah, los anarquistas!*" she said, and she summoned a uniformed official. He asked if we had a car. Fine, I could follow him. Noticing a 35mm still camera in my hand, he remarked that I must take no photographs of the grave. Did I understand that? I assured him I did. Two civil guards sitting in a corner seemed to take no notice of us but went on smoking and chatting. The man in the uniform mounted a motor scooter, and we followed up and down some small hills over very narrow roads that were more like cart trails than anything else. Less than a half mile later he motioned us to park in a small open area. Before us were the graves, overlooking a road below that led up to the main portions of the Catholic cemetery; beyond the road in the haze we could see the roofs of warehouses, industrial buildings, and beyond them blocks of tenements. Beyond all that was the sea. As I had been told by my friend Flavio Costantini, the Italian anarchist painter, the original gravestones had been removed, and before us were three large slabs with nothing incised upon them, but, as I note in the poem, the names of the dead heroes were written with chalk and marking pencils, and there were a few flowers and other objects left for decorations or tributes.

My son Mark is not a temporizer. He went immediately to the trunk of the car and removed the Bolex and its tripod and began to film the scene. Not to be outdone, I took a few photos of the gravestones, one of which appears on the cover of my book *7 Years from Somewhere,* the book in which the Francisco poem first appeared. I stood there musing on the sacrifices of these three men, on the fact that so few of us knew they had lived and died in titanic struggles to liberate the human soul and mind, when suddenly I heard the roar of motorcycles. Before we could gather our wits, the two civil guards from the registry office were upon us. As the men approached me, I noticed that Mark had dropped the Bolex in the tall grass beside a path that led downward to the road. Without removing his helmet the taller of the two *Guardias* approached me. "You were told not to take any pictures." "Yes," I said. "And this?" he said, pointing to the tripod Mark had set up. "Yes," I said, "we were thinking of taking some pictures." He nodded sadly at my folly, and then he and his colleague began searching the area, and within a few minutes they turned up the Bolex. "And how did this get here?" he asked. "I put it there," I said, "when I heard you coming." I didn't know if he knew I was lying. "It was my fault." Then I offered to remove the film and give it to him. No, he did not want the film, of what possible use could such film be to him? No, the film was totally without value. Then he asked me a curious question: "Do you ever suffer from insomnia?" I wasn't sure my Spanish was up to it; I thought I must be misunderstanding him and asked him to repeat the question.

"Do you ever suffer from insomnia?" This time I answered, "Yes, sometimes I cannot sleep." "Next time you cannot sleep, look at this film a few times, and it will put you to sleep." And then he and his sidekick roared with laughter. I was being let go, and there followed a stern warning, which—believe me—I took seriously. We were ordered to pack up and leave immediately, and we did so. We had lived in Spain during the Franco era and knew the limitless powers,of the *Guardia*.

So it was on a Sunday morning in April of 1988 that my wife and I purchased a huge bouquet of red carnations on the Ramblas, the great boulevard of Barcelona, one of whose *ramblas* is the Rambla de Flores, where flowers are sold seven mornings a week. We decided that it would be most fitting to take public transportation to the great cemetery of Montjuich, and after much questioning and searching we located what we thought was the proper bus stop. The presence of several women carrying small bouquets of flowers suggested we'd found the right one. To make sure, I asked an old man in a heavy tweed suit if I could get the bus here to the cemetery at Montjuich. He told me which bus to take and then asked if we were going to the unveiling of the monument to Luis Companys (pronounced comPANCH), whom I knew to have been the first president of Catalunya under the Republic. I told him I had not known of the ceremony, and that my wife and I were taking flowers to some old heroes of ours. He asked if I had been a *Brigadista* (a member of the International Brigades that fought in Spain on the Republican side during the civil war). I told him I was too young to have fought in the war, which ended when I was eleven. He, it turned out, was a veteran, having fought on the Republican side. He had lived thirty years in exile in Southern France before he had been allowed to return to Spain without fear of reprisal. A small, stiff, formal man, he spoke without bitterness, but like so many older Catalans he was very reserved, though also very considerate, for when we arrived at the cemetery he directed us toward the office of grave registrations. There I encountered a different young woman. This time I did not ask for the graves of Ferrer, Durruti, and Ascaso, believing it was better not to mention them so as to avoid any interference. Instead I asked for the location of the Protestant cemetery, thinking I could orient myself to their graves from that point. The Protestant cemetery turned out, however, to be far larger than we had remembered, and we wandered for almost a half hour without finding the least sign of the little alcove that housed the graves of our heroes.

On the upper border of the Protestant cemetery, I found two motorcycle cops. The larger of the two cops politely removed his helmet, saluted me, dismounted his bike, and asked if he could be of help. He was an enormous man by any standards, but especially large by those of Spain. (In 1965 I was informed in a clothing store in Barcelona that they had in stock nothing that would fit a man of my size, and I am under 5'10" and weigh 160 pounds.) No doubt his black boots and heavy leather jacket made him seem even larger. I asked him if he knew the location of the graves of the three famous anarchists. Yes, he did, he could tell us how to get there, but he could not lead us there because he had this other duty. "Do you see those people in the distance?" and he pointed across an open meadow to where a few hundred people were gathered in front of what looked like an enormous stone. "They are here for the dedication of a monument to the memory of Luis Companys, the first president of Catalunya. They are mainly old people, those who survived the war, and it is my job to protect them. I don't think there is any danger, but it is better to be careful, you never know. . . ." Then he told us how we must find a particular foot path and descend it, taking each turn to the left, and go all the way down to the end of the path, and we would be there. Seeing our puzzlement, he said something in Catalan to his silent comrade who never lifted his eyes from the distant group. "Come, I will show you," and he began to lead us in the direction of the path, but every few strides he took a worried look back over his shoulder to observe the distant group. Finally he found the path. "I cannot go any farther," he said, "but if you will descend, taking each turn to the left, always to the left, until you get to the end of the path, you will find them. OK?" We assured him that it was OK, and he gave us a wonderfully full and open smile and shook our hands and hurried back. What a Spain, with policemen whose main concern was ordinary people. I wondered if he were merely human or some magical presence out of the Spanish Poet Rafael Alberti's great book *Sobre Los Angelos* (on the theme of angels), the Angel of Protectors become a Spanish cop.

We did our best to follow his instructions, but after descending to the end of the path we still had not come upon the little alcove we were seeking. I decided to start over—there was nothing else for it—and we returned to the grave registry office and this time asked for the location of the graves of the three. The woman knew where they were, she assured me, but even with the aid of a cemetery map she had difficulty showing me exactly how to locate them. She phoned for help, and a middle-aged man with steely gray hair arrived, dressed in casual wear. Could I wait a few minutes? If so he would be glad to drive us there. On a stone bench my wife and I waited outside in the soft, dusty light, curious once again what "a few minutes" might mean in Spain and growing ever more impatient to complete our mission.

True to his word, he reappeared within less than ten minutes and directed us to a state car. It was the same ride we had taken years before behind the man on the motor scooter. This very amiable man asked if I'd been a "Brigadista," and once again I answered that I had been too young to fight in the war. He remarked that I didn't look it, and I had the sense that he was merely being objective and meant no offense. There were, he informed me, many *Brigadistas* buried in the cemetery. Americans? I asked. Oh, yes, Americans, English, French, Germans, men from everywhere who had come to fight for the Republic and had given their lives for the people of Spain. Like many Spaniards, he seemed to have no trouble rising to a moment of eloquence in praise of courage. I was somewhat surprised how easily he made his sympathies known in the presence of strangers. I remembered that in 1965 the easiest way to stop all the busy voices in a bar was to ask a question about the Civil War. And then quite suddenly we were there. He showed us the road below, which we could take to get back. "You are sure you can make your way back to the bus?" I assured him we could and thanked him, and after the formal handshakes he left.

Then came the laying on of the carnations. This time there were real gravestones, each bearing not only the names and dates of the man but also some small tribute. Ferrer was identified as one who had begun a school which long before its time was teaching the principles of liberty, and for this he had been persecuted and finally killed. Durruti's most famous quotation marked his stone: "We carry a new world here in our hearts. That world is growing this minute." Ascaso was identified as the great anarchist who had led the assault on the Atarazanas barracks during the first hours of the Civil War, a man who had given his life for the working people of Spain. My wife fanned out a dozen carnations on the stone of Ascaso, and there were some left for the other two stones, which once again bore flowers and tokens brought by others. Then we stood back in silence. Below us in the distance was the same view I had described in the poem, the smog perhaps a little thicker, for now there were even more cars in Spain and much more commercial activity on a Sunday.

This was a day of celebration for Companys, who had once worked as a lawyer defending members of the CNT. It was he who, after the military uprising had been put down, had invited the anarchists along with the other parties of the Left to take part in governing Catalunya and waging the war. Durruti accepted for the CNT, and thus the anarchists joined the government and for some months dominated it.

Before the year was over the Durruti column would distinguish itself in desperate fighting on the Aragon front and Durruti himself would die in the defense of Madrid. A half million people—one of every four citizens of Barcelona—would turn out for his funeral, which was an incredible jumble since no one led the crowd and two bands played at the same time and in different tempos. The coffin, carried on the shoulders of men from his column, surged back and forth for hours. The cars bearing the mountain of wreaths had to drive in reverse. An observer wrote, "It was an anarchist funeral—that was its majesty."

Fifty-six years later, the noon sun falling evenly into the little incised gutters of their names, I wondered if the wounds ever healed, or if the wounded merely passed from the earth to be replaced by new generations of the wounded. I took a photograph of each of the graves to show my son Mark. We allowed ourselves the luxury of a long silence, and then hand in hand my wife and I descended to the road, returning just in time to catch the bus back to the center of the city. It was the same driver we'd had earlier in the day, and he smiled at us in recognition. Even then, on the ride back, I knew I would never write the poem of this day. For one thing I was no longer an anarchist. "Property is theft," I had said so many times I'd tired of hearing my voice. Now I owned a house. I even voted for the impossible losing candidates the Democrats presented us every four years. For another thing, this was all too improbable. These dark marble stones with their beautiful brief inscriptions topping the graves of my heroes were merely tokens of the incredible changes that had come over this country as it advanced on the road toward the 21st century. All day I had been meeting people who openly expressed their thankfulness to those who had died in the struggle against oppression. And the police were now my friends. Two nights before two cops had shown us the proper way to walk to our favorite restaurant so as to avoid the junkies who hung out in the Barrio Chino and preyed on tourists. We must be careful, they told us, the junkies are dangerous. What I had said to Ascaso was true, his Barcelona was gone, but so was mine, the Barcelona in repressed rebellion and fear under the thumb of Franco. This was a new world, though not the one Durruti claimed to carry in his heart, not the anarchist ideal. How certain he had been back in 1936 in the first flush of victory over the fascists. "We are going to inherit the earth," he had said. "We have always lived in slums and holes in the wall." Within a few weeks, he believed, they would be fighting and winning the crucial battles of the war, and they, the workers, could rebuild the palaces and cities that the bourgeoisie would blast and ruin before they left the stage of history. Had they not built them in the first place? They, the workers, would inherit the earth. "There is not the slightest doubt about that," he had said.

On a bright spring morning the roads heading south were clogged with BMWs, VWs, Seats (the Spanish version of the Fiat) loaded with Sunday crowds heading for the beaches at Castelldefels and Sitges and the new bedroom communities of Barcelona. I knew how packed the trains would be, having taken them on just such a day as this. The workers and their children packed in as tightly as the worst parody of a NYC subway train at rush hour, and because they were Spaniards, crazy and daring young men would ride outside the cars holding on to the frames of open windows with all their might and howling with mad fear and glee as the train raced through the black tunnels. And after an afternoon of sun, sea, picnic, and siesta, the whole crazy process would be repeated on the way home.

Walking aimlessly on the Ramblas that afternoon, I found representatives of almost every Spanish and Catalan political party. Below their colorful banners the men and women sat at long tables pushing their pamphlets, buttons, bumper stickers, and membership forms. To my surprise there was even a table representing the CNT and FAI, now fighting for legalized abortion, the rights of women and gays, an end to nuclear power, a new vision of Spain's ecology. Two young anarchists smiled at me as I purchased a number of items to help finance their work. The younger of the two seemed utterly shocked to discover I was an American from the USA. "Do not forget," I said to this slender woman still in her teens, "we have a great tradition of anarchist struggle in the USA."

"In the United States of America," she said, shaking her head in total disbelief.

"Yes," I said, "it began in the 19th century and came to its greatest fruition before and after WWI. You must have heard of the Wobblies."

"Wobblies?" she said, mispronouncing the word.

"Yes, the International Workers of the World, who organized all over the western states of the USA. They were especially effective among the miners, and they took hard stands on behalf of working people. This was before most of the major industries of America were unionized."

She looked at me in disbelief. "In the United States of North America the major groups of industrial workers have formed trade unions?"

"Yes, of course," I went on, "but even before that there were the International Workers of the World, a truly international union of workers who saw that their cause involved all the workers of the world. Many of them chose prison rather than serve in WWI. They felt a solidarity with workers in other countries and none with the American state."

She turned to her male comrade, a young bearded Catalan; he was wearing a down vest and a baseball cap with a CNT logo stitched on it. Did he know there were once anarchists in the United States of North America and they were called Wobblies? A short, squat man of no more than 25, he rose slowly from his folding metal chair to shake my hand. Like a character in a comic strip he seemed visibly to be thinking. At last he nodded sagely. This was certainly possible. After all, anarchism was a great ideal capable of inspiring men and women for centuries. "It is possible that even in the United States of North America people could awaken to the limitations of capitalism and the monstrosity of private ownership. Yes, this is possible, even in the United States of North America."

I assured them both that we in America had our martyrs to the cause of the anarchist struggle. I was thinking specifically of Frank Little, who had once organized a free speech in downtown Fresno and was later hanged for organizing miners in Idaho. "Yes, we've had our heroes," I said. "Men and women of the courage and dedication of Ascaso and Durruti." They both nodded without enthusiasm. I told them about finding the graves years ago and returning this morning with red carnations for the new grave stones I'd discovered.

"Why would you do that?" the man said. I told them I did it to fulfill a promise. "A promise to whom?" he asked. I explained it was a promise I'd made in a poem, a poem that dealt with the life and death of Ascaso.

Across the way the elderly, well-dressed members of the Communist Party of Catalunya were folding their tables and repacking their pamphlets. The day's politics were ending. Down the way the General Union of Workers were preparing to make their departure. "Ascaso and Durruti," the young woman said, "You know who they were? You know they were *pistoleros,* you know they believed in 'Revolution by the Deed,' what now we call terrorism?"

"They were important men in their time," the bearded man said. "We do not dispute that. But you should also know they were willing to take part in the government. Durruti asked his followers to risk their lives for the government of Spain, for the Republic, the same government that had jailed him. He compromised all those members of the CNT, he spoke of fighting the war first and only when it was over resuming the revolution. He even urged his old friend Federica Montseny to take a cabinet position." I knew the old arguments, how the anarchists had betrayed their principles by working for victory before revolution, how Montseny had defied her own father, had risked what he called "the liquidation of anarchism." "Once in power you will not rid yourself of power," her father had told her, and true anarchist that she was, she had agonized over the decision.

The shadows were lengthening along the Ramblas. The music of the Sardana, the ancient traditional dance of Catalunya—banned during the Franco years—drifted in from the great plaza. Another Sunday was coming to an end. Through the eyes of these two young workers for anarchism, I saw myself in the year 1988, a befuddled elderly man with powerful sentimental attachments to the past and—for a North American—a curious knowledge of their own history. Tomorrow morning the work week would begin again for all these, a routine I no longer took part in. We smiled at each other one last time and shook hands. "No doubt your Wobblies were sincere people, as were our *pistoleros,*" said the bearded man. "No doubt they labored with great dedication." No doubt, I agreed. He offered me as a gift a bumper sticker which proclaimed in Catalan a refusal to employ nuclear power. These young, somber anarchists had an entirely new agenda. Their civil war seemed more a part of my history than theirs. What could I do but accept the gift and thank them.

✳

"All things to end are made."—Thomas Nashe

Two years passed. In the spring of 1990, I went to the University of Massachusetts to deliver the annual Troy Lecture, which I was told should "go beyond the parochial interests of English Professors to interest the larger academic community." The year before I'd been invited to the Folger Shakespeare Library in Washington D.C., to speak in a series concerned with "socializing the private vision," and I had not given a talk on the relationship between poetry and anarchism, which had animated so much of my writing life. Instead I attempted to make clear that living American poets did not need on the one hand elitist critics and on the other socially conscious, well-meaning, unimaginative drones telling them what to write. I had hoped to make clear that our obsessions and concerns came to us and not we to them, and that whatever poets are given to write should be accepted as a gift they can only regard with awe and modesty. Curiously enough, it was not my choice to repeat this lecture. At the Folger and on one other occasion I felt the talk was misunderstood, and I was tired of presenting it and tired of myself for not writing something new. But the essay had recently been published in a literary review, and I had been asked specifically to read it. And it gave me an opportunity to see my friend Paul Mariani, who teaches at U. Mass., and who surely arranged for me to be that year's lecturer.

Years before in an academic setting I'd given a talk that arose out of my obsession with the Spanish Civil War and concerned the translation of historical events into poetry. I'd chosen to examine the assassination of a hero of the Spanish working people, an event that led directly to the Civil War. In doing so I'd made my politics clear to a group of "good old boys" at the University of Cincinnati where I was that year's Elliston Poetry Professor. The exchange—it was not a talk because before I could get underway I was interrupted several times by the outraged academics—took place in a marvellous house built by Frank Lloyd Wright. The more abrasive they got the more radical I got until I suggested their marvellous suburbs in which they took so much pride might better be turned over to the working people of Cincinnati. It ended with my silent host driving me back to my dim apartment and another solitary night in the retirement home in which the English Department had lodged me. For years I had thought it better not to repeat that mistake. Now I was not so sure.

The night before the talk Paul had met me at the Hartford airport, and leaving the darkened terminal I was amazed by how warm the night winds felt; even in the darkness I could tell there were still some scraps of snow on the ground, but at 11 P.M. the odor of the earth and its return to life were thrilling. I had left a California which seemed in perpetual spring and returned to the drama of my Midwestern boyhood. Before we retired that night, Paul asked me if I'd be willing to visit his modern poetry class the next day, and I had agreed to do so. The poet under discussion was Yeats.

Awakening the next morning I found what looked like the return of winter. At breakfast Paul did his best to make me feel I'd come to New England at the most glorious moment of the year. Outside his kitchen window a great variety of birds collected at the feeder including bright tanagers and finches I never see in California. In the fields beside the rain-slickened road from Montague to Amherst he pointed out a little pale bloom of a crocus dying of loneliness. I started to tell him about the overpowering perfume of orange blossoms that filled my house two nights before, and then, realizing my rudeness, I stopped. I recalled a good-natured argument between my mentor Yvor Winters and that amazing critic Kenneth Burke. Burke had come West in the spring of '58, and Winters tried to overwhelm him with the profusion and variety of California trees. Burke countered by claiming that nothing he'd seen in Winters' garden rivalled in nobility his beloved Northeastern apple trees. Winters, whose bent was toward the plain style in life and poetry, had to concede.

In Amherst the huge campus hunkered down under a cold wind and a leaden sky that promised more rain, which was already arriving in little frozen spurts. Paul's classroom was the usual: low ceiling, hideous artificial lights that suggested a bus station, four rows of desks facing the "business end" of the room, where Paul and I seated ourselves behind the protection of a battered oak desk. The students filed in, a friendly looking crew of all ages. Dressed as they were in gear suitable for hiking, most of the men bearded or unshaven, none of the women wearing makeup, they reminded me of the people I get in my classes at Fresno State, the students I've grown comfortable with.

Paul proved a skillful lecturer; without notes he moved easily from one period of Yeats' work to another, bringing the relevant Irish history to bear. The students already seemed familiar with Yeats' cosmology and its special vocabulary. After a muscular, impassioned reading of "The Second Coming" the class sat for some moments in silence. Paul was clearly waiting for a response, and so I asked him, "Aside from the glory of the writing, what do you think of the poem?" And of course he asked me, "What do you think?"

I answered that I was dazzled by Yeats' ability in 1919 to forecast the rise of totalitarianism in Europe and the nightmare of WWII. But I was deeply offended by his notion that the best lacked all conviction while the worst were full of passionate intensity, then or now. For me the great lesson of the 1960s was that those who dared to stand in the way of America's war machine did so out of a genuine and passionate commitment to the deepest human values. Underneath all the commercially viable styles in music, dress, and drugs, I'd seen for the first time in my life millions of our young and no longer young willing to pay an enormous price for their beliefs. What was it that animated those who were able to face the batons of the police, the censure of their families and friends, and finally exile, prison, or worse? Perhaps through the flawed lens of my anarchist beliefs, I saw the old vision that the earth belongs to no one, that we all come for a little time to act as stewards of the place, obliged to do our best to leave it in as good shape as we found it. And why did so many Americans find it intolerable that these Asian stewards were being killed in their name? Perhaps they believed that we are all one being and as such the children of God, as anarchism teaches.

As for those lacking all conviction, I recalled a colleague and office mate who accompanied me to a protest march on campus; one moment he was beside me, and the next he had vanished. When it was over and none of us was hurt, though clearly our identities had been noted, I found him back in the office, immersed in the silent study of his books. Surely he was not the best among us. No religion puts the fence sitters in heaven.

I didn't mean to suggest that all self-styled anarchists are devoted to the well-being of the human animal; anarchism has its pure theorists. Back in 1980 when I was living in a small apartment in downtown San Francisco two young anarchist thinkers came to interview me. One was very disappointed to discover that I had not worked in factories in Detroit to help form cadres of the working class; that my aim had been to make enough money to live on. Finally he interrupted a long spiel of mine on the heroism of Durruti and Ascaso to tell me that most young people would find my interest in those men "tacky." "Tacky?" I asked, "why?" "It's just so extreme," he said, and I realized that he did not mean most young people, he meant himself. My tackiness was not really the point anyway. What he had discovered was that I was irrelevant, for I was far more obsessed with the men and women who had lived and died for anarchism than the theories that motivated them. He had discovered the truth: I was in love with those people and therefore untrustworthy.

Paul moved on to a discussion of "Sailing to Byzantium." Struck by the fact that I was the same age Yeats was when he wrote the poem, struck and humbled also, I felt it was ridiculous of me to be vexed by the poem (even the verb is Yeats's). Paul was fascinated by the presence of the Grecian goldsmiths and saw in them the image of the "artificer," the model for the poet Yeats aspired to be.

Once out of nature I shall never take
My bodily form from any natural thing,
But such a form as Grecian goldsmiths make
Of hammered gold and gold enamelling
To keep a drowsy Emperor awake;
Or set upon a golden bough to sing
To lords and ladies of Byzantium
Of what is past, or passing, or to come.

"Once out of nature" Yeats chose to entertain the master of a hideous slave society so rigid that no one escaped the station of birth. He would sing to the lords and ladies of the place, perhaps for his supper, if golden birds eat; he would sing to the very people who in real life I would like to strangle. Once out of nature I knew I would be nothing or at most a remembered voice, hopefully the voice of my poetry, and if that poetry proved worthy perhaps a voice as authentic and powerful as the voice of my lost Cipriano, who seemed even in his living flesh to be pared down to the essential. No one else I'd ever known either in his physical or spiritual presence came so close to being "out of nature." He dared each day to live for the sake of "The Idea" and if need be for the sake of it to surrender the little that was left of him. In a poem written years before I had implored him to return to me and rekindle my faith.

> Come back, Cipriano Mera, step
> out of the wind and dressed in the robe
> of your pain tell me again this
> world will be ours. Enter my dreams
> or my life, Cipriano, come back
> out of the wind.

Of course for a poet there is something wonderful in Yeats's notion of being transformed into a magical bird, one who might sing with the perfection denied the living writer. But why sing to the courtiers of a vanished world? In his poem "Winds of the People," the great Spanish poet Miguel Hernandez also imagines himself transformed into a singing bird. He accepts his death in battle against the tyrannical forces of Franco's army but asks to remain an inspiration to his comrades,

> for there are nightingales
> above the rifle fire
> there were our fight is, singing.

Before he moved on Paul noted how original it was of Yeats to choose Byzantium and to avoid Rome and Jerusalem, the traditional holy cities of European poets. A young, studious-looking man directed a disturbing question at Paul and me. For the sake of the poem had Yeats deliberately avoided those aspects of Byzantine culture which did not suit his purposes? I started to answer that that was exactly what he'd done—though a hierarchical society would hardly have offended Yeats the way it would offend most young Americans—and then it struck me that I was simplifying what I had no right to simplify, for like Yeats I'd chosen a holy city and my allegiance to it was far more powerful than anything I'd managed to express in my poetry. I'd made my pilgrimage to Barcelona over and over and unquestioningly accepted all its lessons. I'd made certain of its heroes the high priests of my life. I needed my Barcelona, I needed to uncover somewhere in the history of the failed attempts of men and women to create a decent society an experiment that worked, and having half-found it in the violent struggles of Spanish Anarchism, I'd clung to it no matter what, no matter that Ascaso probably assassinated the archbishop of Saragossa, no matter that he and Durruti robbed banks to fund their exploits, no matter that Durruti's "discipline of indiscipline" was a military disaster, no matter that "Propaganda by the Deed" was terrorism. I recounted for the class a passage from Hugh Thomas' monumental history of the Spanish Civil War in which Thomas describes the anarchists of Barcelona killing "as if they were mystics" in order to crush the material things of this world, choosing indiscriminately anyone who displayed a bourgeois past. Victims were trucked thirty miles down the coast to be shot overlooking the dazzling Bay of Sitges. "Those about to die," wrote Thomas, "would pass their last moments on earth looking out to sea in the marvelous Mediterranean dawn. 'See how beautiful life could have been,' their assassins seemed to be saying, 'if only you had not been a bourgeois and had got up early and had seen the dawn more often—as workers do.'"

The class was stunned by this fragment of anarchist history as well as by my allegiance to such a movement. Of course the centuries of violence done to these workers had to produce an equal violence. The students were unconvinced. A hushed atmosphere invaded the room. I was no longer a sixty-two year old "smiling public man." In recounting the events I felt a portion of my old pride in the worthiness of the anarchist vision and the totally uncompromising behavior of its adherents. Had I apologized for anything it would have been my failure to live as an anarchist, having so long ago discovered "The Idea."

The time has come to bring this tale to an end, but since as I wrote earlier most of the stories that make up my life have no beginning or ending, I shall have to compose one. So let the class turn their attention back to the poetry of Yeats, this time to my favorite poem of his, "Lapis Lazuli." Let the students bow their heads to attend to their texts as Paul reads aloud with serenity and passion. Let all those present, teacher, students, guest, allow the words to enter their minds and hearts, let them be momentarily overwhelmed as the poem sings to its extraordinary ending.

Every discoloration of the stone,
Every accidental crack or dent,
Seems a water-course or an avalanche,
Or lofty slope where it still snows
Though doubtless plum or cherry-branch
Sweetens the little half-way house
Those Chinamen climb towards, and I
Delight to imagine them seated there;
There, on the tragic scene they stare.
One asks for mournful melodies;
Accomplished fingers begin to play.
Their eyes mid many wrinkles, their eyes,
Their ancient, glittering eyes, are gay.

Somewhere bells sound the noon hour. The students file out in silence and, once released from this odd encounter, resume their usual lives. Now their good-natured chatter echoes down the halls. Paul packs up his books and papers. The guest stares out the window. The sky is lifting, and high above, the sun seems for a moment about to peep through. All their adult lives these students of poetry have climbed between heaven and earth and, wearied, have stopped to look down "on all the tragic scene." Let the guest realize that no matter what he has climbed toward he has never left the world below, that tangled mess he would escape only at his own peril. And what has he climbed toward? Perhaps a "lofty slope where it still snows," perhaps a sky unsullied by our human blunders, perhaps the holy cities of the world and of the imagination, Detroit, Barcelona, Byzantium, stained with our blood.

—Spring 1992

Samuel F. Pickering

Taking the Night Plane to Tulsa

When folks feel good in Tulsa, they stomp on the floor and holler "shit." In Hanover nobody ever feels good. New England will turn any man's Blue Bird of Happiness into a Turkey Buzzard. I ought to know; I've been here nine years. Soon, though, everything's going to change. They next time a jet engine whines I'll be traveling west. An acquaintance argues that my dissatisfaction is not New England's fault. Corn and crows, he says, can't grow in the same field. Perhaps, but there is not much corn grown in New England, and I'm not a crow—no, not even a towhee or a chickadee, although if I stay around here much longer surrounded by lads with necklaces, purses, and tight pants I just might become one.

Have you ever heard of a town without a used car lot? Hanover, New Hampshire, is such a town. Used car lots are the signs of dreams. A man sees a rainbow, hurries to the used car lot, buys a chariot of hope and wheels over the hills and far away. In Hanover the rainbow, like the Dodo, is extinct, and there is no market for used cars. The town fathers have banished used car lots. Even worse, no one ever comes to town, suddenly sees a shaft of golden light, sings "oh, happy day," and sells his car. Like cattails in a wet wasteland, parking meters stand where green vineyards once grew. And pinched foreign cars with their windows tight scrape through the streets, then are sealed in garages whose fronts button down like double-breasted suits. In Tulsa used cars shine on every corner. Tulsa is full of folks ready to shift gears and pursue their dreams. People whose eyes glitter like diamond stickpins in the neckties of Baptist preachers crowd the streets.

New England would bore the ass off an elephant. This past winter a debutante in Tulsa canceled her ball at the last minute because she came down with a sudden case of worms. Such things don't happen in New England. I understand that the worms have almost been wiped out at Wellesley. An admissions officer swears to me that there hasn't been a serious case there in the last three years. More's the pity because those folks in Massachusetts need something other than George McGovern to stir them up. Intellectually New England is as complacent as a Bible Christian in a poker game with two aces up his sleeve. New Englanders worship the meaning of words, not words themselves. In the beginning was the word, not the sentence gummed with meaning. Joy in the word is the creative spirit, and New England priding itself upon possessing truth or upon stoic terseness is deader than integration in Boston. The celebration of silent gentility is nothing fancier than the worship of death. In a society in which gaps fill pauses in conversation and genteel silence smothers the controversial, quasi-theological writers thrive. Only New England could worship Emerson preaching self-reliance when anyone with any part of an eyeball in his head or a whitlow on his thumb knows that this world has had too much self-reliance. What we need is a little more relying on each other. In contrast to the doily-bound reticence of New England is the creative garrulity of the Southwest. Words, accompanied by a steaming, whistling train of rich malaprops, rush to fill pauses in conversation. Style is more important than content; joy in the word flourishes and literary creation blossoms brightly.

If a New Englander ever does talk, he makes one want to be in church listening to a five hour sermon on Presbyterian missionaries. Some say Old Man Know All died last year, but if he did, he was resurrected in New England. Once a New Englander gets going, he sounds like a bumblebee in a sugar barrel. There's a lot of noise but not much traveling. Everybody up here is busy getting close to the soil. That's fine with people who groove on Annie Dillard and think that trees are for poetic inspiration and not lumber. God made trees for monkeys to climb and men to chop down. Monkeys get coconuts and men get houses. Of course Vermont is doomed. The state is little more than a suburb of New Canaan and Greenwich. Rumor has it though that these two country clubs are about to be sold South. I've heard that oil money plans to dismantle them brick by brick, clapboard by clapboard, polo field by polo field, and ship them to Philadelphia, Mississippi, where they will be reassembled as retirement homes for rich Choctaws. I have also heard that they are going to be bulldozed, dumped into freight cars, and used for a landfill in Plaquemines Parish, Louisiana. An environmentalist will probably prevent this. One look at all those psychiatrists' bills and "how-to" books and the water moccasins would shed their skins and head for high ground. Can you imagine the problems of an alligator who swallowed a personalized Connecticut license plate which read "Super" or "Marvy"?

The mineral money in the southwest is developing new art forms and new ways of living. No right-thinking southwesterner wants to refurbish a battered Saltbox infested with roaches, earwigs, and history. He wants his house clean and new. Not long ago I visited a dentist friend in Lubbock. Over the fireplace was a family portrait. My friend and his wife were both naked. Like a good little woman, the wife sat demurely while he stood proudly erect. Gainsborough didn't do the painting, but the artist tried to capture my friends' innocent glory. And the painting was certainly more interesting than the hand-me-down portraits of bearded horse thieves and preachers one sees in New England. The southwestern imagination is expansive not reclusive, communal not individual. The Brazos is the American Nile and the gritty soil of the southwest has something in common with the dunes of Egypt, for its sons raise pyramids to their own greatness. No southwesterner would be satisfied like Emily Dickinson with an orchard for a dome. Instead the southwesterner builds the Astrodome. Instead of a bobolink for a chorister, he flushes a covey of Dallas cowgirls and keeps the Sabbath, not by staying at home, but by joining his friends at the stadium. Stretching above Tulsa is the two hundred foot prayer tower of Oral Roberts University. With steel girders jutting out as a symbolic crown of thorns, the tower strikes horror into the minds of second-generation Episcopalians. Yet, Oral Roberts University is reaching toward something, through vulgarity to an unknown beyond. The highest point on the campus of Dartmouth College is the tower of Baker Library. On top of the tower is a weather-vane, an emblem that makes no statement about life and serves no practical purpose. Why put a weathervane on the tower when everyone knows the weather is always going to be "mostly bad"?

Like the weather, religion in New England is sorry. It can't flourish in towns called Hebron, Canaan, Lebanon, Bethel, and New Haven. It does best in places with heathen names like Skiatook, Pawhuska, and Tishomingo. Often the name is the thing. And when a town is given a heathen name, its inhabitants realize that part of their nature is bad and they try to do better. That's not so in New England. When it comes to low-down, hypocritical meanness, folks here are not just green, they are ripe. Like copperheads in the Blue Ridge Mountains, New England is crawling with Unitarians. It has been said that the Unitarian church in Norwich, Vermont, doesn't even have a Bible, much less religion. I'd just as soon pray in the YMCA. Of course, you can't find one of those around here either. The YMCA in Norwich is now a health food store, filled with skinny kooks, sitting around like a flock of tom-tits chewing sun flower seeds and God knows what else.

Religion in the southwest is creative. Baptists have tried so hard to stifle the imagination that they have created worlds alongside of which Sodom would seem dull as ditchwater. My Aunt Sally, the one with the spayed pup Polly, writes that recently there has been a great commotion in her church. One of the maiden ladies testified on Rogation Sunday that she was with child and said that the Second Coming was only a few months away. It seems that this maiden had been seen after the church picnic walking with the nice, new, young preacher Brother William. Most of the congregation believes that Sister Rebecca is a chosen vessel. But my Aunt Sally who went to Sweetbriar has her doubts and writes, "when the Lambs of God meet together, they will play and divert themselves." When I go to Tulsa, I'm joining Aunt Sally's church. It has a full-immersion baptismal font with a glass front. Baptisms are important events, although sometimes things get a little out of hand. Once a bad boy caused a hollering among the sisters when he dumped a bucket of bullfrogs in amongst the saved. Another time a hard case dropped in a couple of black leeches, who when they are hungry can stretch out a yard or two. Aunt Sally tells me that so many folks were possessed by the spirit that day that the chiropractor next door complained, saying the shouting was ruining his business.

Aunt Sally's church is not air-cooled, and the doors like the hearts of the people, she says, stay open during meeting. One Sunday last July while the congregation was praying up a storm and not rolling their eyes around like they do when old Deacon Griffiths preaches, a donkey wandered in. Before anybody could stop him, the donkey had high-stepped it on up to the front of the church and commenced to eat the lilies which Sister Lucille had given in memory of her dear departed Franklin. Kneeling before the altar and praying so loud that he could be heard in the next county, that nice young William didn't hear the chewing going on behind him. The choir saw it all right though, and it threw them right off of "Nearer My God to Thee" and onto a fit of whooping. This irritated the old donkey and he must have figured he could do better. When he finished the lilies, he threw up his head and let out such a bray that Brother William jumped up like he had been shot. Later he said he thought Balaam had ridden down for the service, but Aunt Sally says she reckons he thought that Sister Rebecca's daddy had finally caught up with him.

In Oklahoma folks don't worry about mending walls. Everybody's got a gun. Guns make people normal. Living up here is like living in an out patient clinic next door to a mental health center. Come spring most people are ready for white sport coats, the kind with the wrap-around arms. A little more lead and a lot less talk would do people hereabouts a wheelbarrow full of good. This is not a normal place. You might not credit what I have to say, but it's true. Bend over up here to tie your shoelaces and only the good Lord knows what will happen to you. In Tulsa a horny toad might run up your leg but that's about all. Things are so normal in the southwest that there's a big Baptist school down near Waco that says in its faculty handbook that teachers can be fired for "gross abuse of trust in faculty-student relationship." Hot-damn, during my vacations, I'm traveling to Waco. When a school has to print a rule like that, there must be some old-fashioned religion going on. I wouldn't be surprised if nice William didn't hear the call and join the faculty in Waco. The southwest's the place for love. Not long ago when I was flying from Nashville to Dallas, a pert red-head plopped down next to me. She was Miss Tommy Tricksy, an exotic dancer who had just appeared in the Pussywillow Club in Nashville. We got along like a banjo and a fingernail. When we parted, she gave me one of her promotional photographs. It was slick; she didn't have much on and was half-turned around peeking over a bottom that was as white as fine alabaster.

If you want to play house, go to the southwest. The ladies out there remind me of Tammy Wynette's voice. Tammy's voice is smooth as velvet but every once in a while there's a gulch in it. Love ought to be filled with gulches. Passion ought not to flow like molasses out of a jug. Men like stumbling into gulches and then climbing out cut and bleeding. Many nice women in the southwest make a handsome living on alimony. In New England, the judge like as not will award it to a man. Not only that but women up here look like they were dragged right off the ark. I met a graduate of Wellesley the other day who had enough suet on her hair to keep all the starlings in Vermont well-fed during February. In Tulsa things are different; they have beauty parlors. The bouffant is still stylish. And when a lady goes walking, she looks sweeter and cleaner than a strawberry ice cream cone.

Love in New England just isn't any fun. Nobody here has to gallop out the back door praying that the old man's shotgun will misfire. Here if you get caught, you are offered scotch and soda. Next comes a discussion of human needs and individual fulfillment. Values are laid on with a trowel. And then, and this does take all dog, the aggrieved husband suggests that the three of you form a more intimate relationship. I'd rather be a bug with a bee martin after him than be caught gallivanting in New England.

Folks in the southwest haven't read Emerson and they season their recollections with lies. Stories told in bars will make a man swallow his grin and fetch a howl. In all my years in New England, I've not once heard anyone talk about Henry the hare-lip and his mean mammy Mary Lou. Nobody hereabouts has ever been to the side-show and seen Henry's cousin Billy Bob the birth-marked boy. In Wetumka you'll hear things they have never heard in Woodstock. Some of what is said might be banned in Provincetown, but most of it is all right. Speaking of Wetumka, I once saw quite a fight there. I don't know what started it but a big man in a red and orange shirt grabbed a little man in overalls and started to squeeze him. He squeezed the little man so hard that the little man's eyeballs bulged like a bullfrog serenading his sweetheart. The little man didn't fight back. You would have thought he was asleep. This discommoded the big man, for he was used to people biting, scratching, and praying. He asked the little man why he didn't struggle, saying he was fixing to apply his famous Chickasaw squeeze, one which, he added, had almost popped out more eyeballs than the goings-on in Waco. And that, dear hearts is saying something, for I have just received another letter from Aunt Sally. She writes that nice William has moved to Waco. It won't be long, she adds, before he becomes a pillar of the community, spreading the good word and sowing the gospel seed far and wide.

Anyway, the little man yawned when the big man addressed him. Then he allowed as how he was getting ready to fight, but he liked the people in Wetumka and didn't want to damage their property. Before he fought, he explained, he had to look around to see where he could throw the big man and not hurt any houses. So he could see better he was bulging his eyes. He was about through, though, he added, and he told the big man that he could soon expect to be bouncing across the prairie like a hop-pergrass ahead of a fire. These words fell on the big man like a two by four and he lit out like a hound dog with a polecat after him. Some say he crossed over to Arkansas and is lying low in Fayetteville, hoping the little man doesn't look his way. In any case he was last seen high-balling it through Tallequah heading for the state line.

Like the little man, people in Oklahoma see things differently from people in New England. Once I was eating tortillas in a cafe in Antlers. It was family style and a bunch of us sat around the table. One fellow who did some commercial traveling in that part of Oklahoma began to describe the famous bees over at Idabel. The bees, he said, were as big as turkeys. "What," said a youngster who worked for HEW and had a hairdo that looked like a milking machine had been sucking on it. "What," he said; "how big are their hives then?" "They are the same size as normal," the traveler answered. "Very strange," the young man said with a smirk on his face; "how do they get into their hives?" "That's none of my business," said the traveler, "let them look to that."

And that's the way I feel about New England. Let them that suffer here look to it. Nobody else wants to. I'm taking the night flight to Tulsa. Once I get through the mud to the airport, I'm throwing my L. L. Bean boots into the garbage can and slipping into some new Florsheims. On the airplane I'll be the fellow in the double knit. My necktie will gleam like the sunset. Turned backwards, it will deliver a full-fisted, eyelid bruising message. Sit next to me, and if we get along, I'll invite you to lunch with my Aunt Sally and Sister Rebecca—whose standing in the church is, I hear, not quite what it used to be since she produced a Messiahess instead of a Messiah.

— Summer 1979

Nancy Willard

Close Encounters of the Story Kind

Once upon a time an editor, knowing my fascination with angels, invited me to write a story about one. I thought, "Here's an assignment after my own heart," and I said yes. Then I panicked.

What did I know about angels?

The first angel I saw had a chipped nose. It was blond, male, and lived in a clock, which hung in the parlor of the apartment Mrs. Lear rented in my grandmother's house in Owosso, Michigan. When the hour struck, two doors opened at the top and a tiny platform revolved, bearing the archangel Michael from one door to the next. Such dignity, such beauty—he was a procession of one. Mrs. Lear's husband had fought in the first world war and brought it from Germany, along with a Luger and some empty shells. A local jeweler who repaired it told him that it must have once held other figures, probably Adam and Eve being driven from the garden. Time had taken the archangel's sword, the fugitives, and the tip of his holy nose. Nevertheless, when I knew the hour was preparing to strike, I would knock on Mrs. Lear's door and ask to see the angel, moving from darkness into darkness. When the novelty wore off and I no longer asked, Mrs. Lear would knock on my grandmother's apartment to announce the angel was marching and did I want to watch it?

An angel marching from darkness into darkness—such an event should not go unnoticed.

The second angel I saw was a picture from an old insurance calendar that my grandmother had saved long after the year was out. A young woman in a white nightgown was standing with arms outstretched over two children playing at the edge of a cliff. There was a large asterisk of apple butter on her wings, as if someone had hurled a full jar during an argument, and the angel had taken a blow intended for someone else. The calendar hung in my grandfather's treatment room, where patients with rheumatism and asthma came to avail themselves of the wonders of osteopathy. Only the angel and our family knew that the treatment room had once been a pantry and the waiting room doubled as the doctor's bedroom; my grandfather unfolded the sofa at night to sleep and in the morning folded it up again before the office opened. Grandmother, who managed the renting of the other rooms, had her own quarters off the kitchen.

Though I have seen many pictures of angels since these two, they seem the real ones, the standard by which all others should be measured.

Two days after I'd agreed to write a book about angels, my sister, Kirsten, called from Ann Arbor with bad news.

"Mother fell and broke her hip," she said, "so I grabbed the first plane out of Pittsburgh last night. The doctor said he wants to give her a new one."

"A new hip? At 83?"

"He said it's her only chance of walking. And it's manmade, so it's even better than her old one. It will last forever."

"Is she conscious?"

"She's right here. I'll put her on the phone."

I pressed my ear to the receiver and heard nothing.

"Mother? How are you feeling?"

She did not answer for a long time, and when she did, she sounded far off, as if she were speaking from a different room.

"Isn't it the limit I should have to go through this?" she whispered.

A long silence, broken by Kirsten's voice.

"I found Mother's purse. It's been missing for two months. And now we can't find her teeth. They've simply vanished for good and all."

"How long will she be in the hospital?"

"A week. They like to get you out early here. But we'll need round-the-clock care when she moves home."

"What about bringing her to Shady Park?" I asked. "Can they keep her?"

From the house she'd lived in for fifty years my mother moved to a single large room in Shady Park Manor, a convalescent home in Pittsburgh five blocks from my sister and her husband. She had a room of her own. Kirsten made sure of that. On its bare surfaces my sister put spindles of snapshots; on its white walls she hung the brass filigree frames that kept us all in line: me in my cap and gown standing beside Daddy in the cap and gown he only wore when pressed into marching at commencement; my sister in her wedding dress, rising from a swirl of lace; the grandchildren, who had long outgrown their school portraits; Mother's diploma from Michigan, its blue and gold ribbon faded but intact. The bureau held her lavender underwear, her nylons, her purple shoes. The closet held all ten of her best purple dresses.

This was the room I saw when I arrived from New York. My classes at Vassar were finished, Kirsten and John would be gone for two weeks. The note in the kitchen laid out my duties.

"Please take in the mail, water the plants in the dining room, and feed the tortoise. He only eats scraped carrots. Scraper is on sink. Please take Mother's dresses to the laundromat and wash them on DELICATE. They wash everything in hot water at the home."

Every morning I walked the five blocks to Shady Park past the Fourth Presbyterian Church and the synagogue, past the Greek restaurant, the Café de Sol, the Korean Grocer who hangs strings of jade beads in the window among the melons. Past Eat 'n' Park, where families carry heaping plates from the salad bar and single men sit at the counter, drinking coffee and smoking. Past Jacov's Vegetarian Deli and Tucker's Secondhand Books.

Shady Park Manor stands over all, at the top of a steep hill. I hurry through the lobby, beautifully decorated in silver and blue wallpaper, up the stairs past the nurse's station. When I arrive at my mother's room she is sitting up in her chair, asleep, belted in, like a passenger in a plane about to land—but somewhere deep in the body of the plane, the fatigued metal has given way and sent this one woman, still strapped to her seat, hurtling through space.

Over my mother's bed, someone has taped a list of instructions.

7:30: *Get Mrs. W. up to eat breakfast. Be sure dentures are in with fast-teeth powder.*

8:00–2:00: *Keep Mrs. W. up once she is in chair. She will fight to go back to bed, but she needs to be kept active.*

"Mom," I say, "wake up!"

She opens her eyes.

"What is this place?"

"A condominium," I lie. "Come on, Ma, let's get the wheelchair and go for a spin around the block."

"Why can't I walk? What's the matter with me?"

"You broke your hip."

I unfold the wheelchair and lift her into it. She is staring at my feet.

"You need new shoes," she says.

We both gaze down at my scuffed loafers. Miles of pavement have pared the heels away and loosened the stitching.

"Promise me you'll buy a new pair. Take some money from my purse. Where is my purse?"

I hand it to her. She opens it and peers in and twitches up a five dollar bill.

"Didn't I have more money than this when I started?"

"Oh, Mother, you don't need any money here."

"Is this an old people's home?"

"It's a condominium, Ma."

"It's a home. I never thought my children would put me in a home."

"Ma, you need twenty-four-hour care."

"What did people do in the old days?"

What *did* they do? Dutiful daughters struggled with lifting, feeding, and changing their aged parents. I thought of my mother under the stress of caring for her own mother, who lived with us when I was growing up. Does my mother remember the night she got up to go to the bathroom and passed out from exhaustion? She landed against the radiator. Now, at the edge of her short sleeve I can see the long scar on my mother's arm, deep as a knife wound, where the flesh burned slowly away as she lay numb to the pain. These dutiful women—caregivers is the current term for them— did not go off to jobs in the morning. And they certainly were not writers.

We pass the nurse's station and the board which lists the day's activities. Talking Book Club, Pet Therapy, Monday Night Movie, Bingo, Current Events, Sensory Stimulation, this month's birthdays. In the all-purpose room, the physical therapist is tossing a beach ball to a group of men and women in wheelchairs. None of them raise their arms. As I wheel Mother outside into the sunshine, she raises a pleading face to mine.

"Can't you find a little corner in your house for me?"

In the evening, when I unlock the door of my sister's house, the tortoise creeps out of his shell and crosses the kitchen floor to meet me. His ancient eyes blink when I scrape his carrots, letting the shavings pile up on the plate like golden pages. The bedroom is suffocating. I carry my sheet and pillow downstairs and make a bed on the living room floor. I read another chapter in John Gardner's *The Art of Fiction* and underline a sentence that sounds like good advice, if only I knew how to follow it: "Fiction does its work by creating a dream in the reader's mind." The last sound I hear before falling asleep is the tortoise taking his constitutional, the faint scraping of his claws along the floor.

Have I told you everything? No. I have not told you how every evening I sat down at my brother-in-law's electric portable and worked on my story. A story about an angel.

The hardest part of writing a story or a novel is beginning it. A letter that arrived recently from a friend of mine whose first novel got rave reviews opens with these words: "So painful coming into possession of a new novel. There is a deep agenda, and I sometimes think I haven't the faintest clue what it is. Still, every day, here I am, at my table, facing it and struggling with lethargy." The material of a story offers itself to the writer like a house in which all the doors and windows are locked. Whose story is it? Whose voice does it belong to? The opening sentence is the key, the way into the house. It may let you in at the front door like a homeowner or at the window like a thief, but it lets you in.

For my angel story, I had no opening sentence. But I had a great many notes on angels, particularly those I deemed useful to writers. Uriel the angel of poetry and Raphael the angel of healing led the list. And how many angels there are, for every problem and purpose! There is an angel who presides over memory and an angel who presides over time, even an angel who presides over Monday. There is an angel for small birds and an angel for tame beasts, an angel for solitude and an angel for patience and an angel for hope. The angel who watches over footstools can offer you a pillar of light to support you, a gift that Hemingway and Virginia Woolf would have appreciated since both wrote standing up.

I also noted the angels who presided over conditions that writers pray to be spared. Barakiel is the angel of chance, Michael the angel of chaos and insomnia, Harbonah the angel of Annihilation, and Abaddon the angel of the abyss.

But among the angels, who can really tell which are for us and which are against us? There is an angel who presides over hidden things. Forgotten names, lost notes, misplaced drafts—does he hide them or find them? There is an angel of odd events. Are they gifts or griefs, lucky accidents or lost opportunities?

Notice, I didn't say I wrote my story. I said *worked on it*. What did I really know about angels? How do we come to know things as a writer? I looked at my notes but no story came. What was I looking for? I made tea. I thought of how other writers prepared to face the blank page. Balzac drank 50 cups of coffee a day till it killed him, Disraeli put on evening clothes, George Cohan rented a Pullman car drawing room and traveled till he was done with the book or story. Emerson took walks. Colette's husband locked her in her room, and Victor Hugo gave his clothes to his servants with instructions to return them when he was done.

After struggling with the story for three days, I understood the problem. This story had the shape of the one I'd just finished writing. What we've just written lays its shadow on the next work, and it can happen with any length, any genre. A friend who was working on her second novel told me, "It took me two years to break the spell of my first book when I started my second. I kept wanting to repeat what had worked so well. Combinations of characters. Scenes." Writing is like panning for gold. You know the grains of ore are sparkling in front of you, if only you could see them. Knowing this, even when you find nothing but broken stones it's hard to throw them away.

So I wrote a story about angels. I wrote badly. I was on the wrong track, but I didn't have the courage to throw those pages away, for then I'd have nothing. Keats was right. All writing is a form of prayer. Was anybody out there listening?

Let me say right now that I don't think anyone can command the angel to come, though I've known at least one person to try, a nun who told her first graders about the guardian angels they'd received at baptism and then said, "I want you all to move over and make room for your angel." Twenty-five first graders shifted to the right and made room for the incorporeal and the invisible. *That* is perfect faith. The nephew who told me the story takes a more skeptical view of angels now.

None of this would be worth telling if I hadn't promised my sister that I'd wash Mother's clothes at the laundromat, and what shouldn't happen did happen. I had a simple plan. I would sit with Mother till noon. While she ate her lunch in the dining room, I would carry the laundry basket over to the Wash Bored and read *The Art of Fiction* and work on my story while the clothes were spinning. And maybe I could take lunch down the street at Jacov's Vegetarian Deli. It had been closed all week but a sign promised it would be open on Monday.

I arrived at Shady Park around eleven and headed for Mother's room. A thin white-haired woman was walking toward me on crutches, leaning heavily on stout Miss Davidson, the physical therapist. Miss Davidson beckoned me over.

"I've been trying to get your mom to walk. She doesn't try. She won't even stand up for me. See if you can get her to make the effort."

"I'll do my best," I said.

"Now, Beulah here is doing fine," said Miss Davidson.

The woman on crutches nodded.

"I walk every chance I get," she said. "Miss Davidson says, 'Well, how about heading back to your room now?' and I say, 'It hurts, but let's go just once more, up and down the corridor.' I can't wait to go home."

Miss Davidson frowned at me.

"Medicare won't pay for your mother's room if she's not taking part in the physical therapy program."

"Is she doing any activities?" I asked hopefully.

"She likes the crafts," said Miss Davidson. "She made a purple flyswatter out of felt yesterday. And she had the kitten on her lap the whole day."

"What kitten?" I asked.

"Pet therapy," said Beulah. "Your mother wouldn't let anyone else have it. Kept it on her lap the whole time."

When I walked into her room, Mother was asleep in her chair.

"Ma," I said, "I hear you had a kitten."

She opened her eyes.

"What kitten?" she said.

"She forgot already," said Beulah, leaning in the doorway. Mother turned to her.

"My husband taught for 47 years at the University of Michigan. We have a total of 22 degrees in our family, all from Michigan."

"Isn't that nice," said Beulah. "Now me, I never went to college. My papa worked in the steel mill, and so did my husband till it shut down. I'm going downstairs in the wheelchair. They have Kool-Aid on the terrace."

We heard her thumping back to her room. Mother gave me an odd look.

"Why are you carrying a box of soap?" she asked.

"I'm going to wash your clothes."

And I heaved the laundry basket onto one hip. Lavender plastic—my sister had picked it especially for her.

"You're a good girl," she said and smiled. "Lord, I'm just an ordinary mother. How did I get two such wonderful daughters?"

I wheeled her downstairs, and we sat on the terrace with Beulah till lunch time. The only other patient was a thin silent man in a wheelchair and a young woman who sat beside him asking, "Grandpa, can you talk? Can you talk, Grandpa?"

"That's Mr. Levine," said Beulah. "He's a hundred and two. The president sent him a telegram." She leaned forward and whispered in my ear, "You ask him how old he is and he shouts 'A hundred and two.' There's not much else he knows. He has Alzheimers. And he still has a full head of hair."

"What disease do I have?" asked Mother.

"You broke your hip," I said.

"I've had lots of broken bones," said Beulah. "Last year I broke my arm."

Mother stared down at her own arm, the scarred one, as if it had just been brought for her approval.

"How old it looks," she said softly.

The Wash Bored was nearly empty. A woman was sitting under the lone hair dryer, reading a magazine from which the cover had been ripped. I threw Mother's clothes in the machine, dialed it to *warm,* and poured in the soap. I put *The Art of Fiction* and my box of Tide in the laundry basket and strolled half a block to Jacov's Vegetarian Deli.

The restaurant was tiny—no more than five tables. A sign on the wall read "TEL AVIV, Jerusalem, Ben Gurion Airport. Discover your Roots!" Only one other customer, an elderly man in a black suit, was waiting at the take-out counter for his order. The two cooks wore yarmulkahs, yet how different the same garment looked on each of them. The older man was clean-shaven and middle-aged. When he chopped the onions, he seemed to be murdering them. He poured coffee as if it were poison; he shoved a plate of dumplings at the elderly man like a punishment. The younger cook had a thick blond beard and kindly blue eyes, and he loped from the stove to the ice box to the counter as if he had not a care in the world.

The menu over the counter listed vegetable soup and vegetarian pizza.

"I'll have soup," I said. "What kind of dumplings did you just give that man?"

"You won't like them," said the sour cook.

"I'll have them anyway," I said.

"Try one first," said the young cook, "and if you like it, I'll give you a plateful."

He handed me a dumpling on a paper plate. It tasted like nothing I'd ever eaten before or would want to eat again. I ordered a plate of them, to spite the sour cook. The elderly gentleman took his paper plate and then paused at a small rack on the wall from which he plucked a greasy page. Out of curiosity, I took one also and found it was a page from the Jewish prayer book, Hebrew on one side, English on the other. There was also a pamphlet, *Thought for the Week,* so I took that as well and read it as I munched my dumplings:

A Thought for the Week: Love your fellow Jew as you love yourself.

Alas, I was not a Jew. They would feed me here but they would not love me. I read on:

Sidra Vayeishev. It is different at home (Part II). Last week we learned that our forefather Jacob did not feel "at home" in the world of material possessions. Knowing that he was only a temporary resident in this physical world he felt that his true "home" was in matters of the Neshama, in Torah and Mitsvos. The world with all its comforts, its palaces and mansions, is nothing more than a tent, erected during the journey of life to sleep over for a night, or rest for a day or two. And on a journey, after all, only the bare necessities of eating and sleeping are required; but when the journey is over and one comes home . . . well, at home it's different.

When I finished the last greasy bite, I put the pamphlet and the prayer sheet in the rack and returned to the laundromat. The lights on the machine were off. The clothes were clean. So was the top of the machine.

The clothes basket, along with *The Art of Fiction* and my manuscript, had vanished.

Though the day was hot, I felt as cold as if I wore the wind for a cloak. A terrible calm washed over me, leaving me lightheaded. Loss had numbed my capacity to rage.

Suddenly, among the *Reader's Digests* on the folding table, I spied *The Art of Fiction.* I snatched it up. With shaking fingers I rifled through all the other magazines, shook them, and waited for my manuscript to come out of hiding like a mischievous child.

Nothing. On this occasion the angel who presides over hidden things was not on my side.

What else was there to do but walk across the street and sit on the bench at the bus stop and consider my life? When the elderly gentleman from Jacov's Deli sat next to me, I was scarcely aware of him till he began to edge closer.

"I notice the subject of your book," he said. "It is a subject dear to my heart. Are you a writer?"

"Yes," I said.

"Stories? You write stories?"

"Stories, a novel, poems," I said.

"I too wrote stories once," he said, "though I am not a writer now. I am a teacher. A teacher of American literature. But I have written stories."

My heart sank. He saw in me a kindred soul. Soon he would press his manuscript upon me. Yet he had used the past tense; perhaps he wrote stories no more. Had his inspiration run dry? Had he lost him memory?

"What kind of stories do you write" he asked, "if I may ask?"

"Short stories," I said.

"Forgive me," he said. "It's like asking the birds what kind of eggs they lay. Blue? Speckled? Large? Small?"

"Look," I said, "I can't really talk about my stories just now. Somebody just stole the only copy of the story I've been working on for weeks."

"You're sure somebody stole it?" he asked, as if such things did not happen in this world.

"I left it in the laundromat while I was eating lunch. And when I came back—"

"Excuse me," he interrupted, "but may I tell you a story? Long ago there lived in a north province of China a man good at interpreting events. This man had a son, and one day the son's best mare ran away and was taken by the nomads across the border. The son was distraught, but his father said, 'What makes you think this isn't a blessing?' Many months later, the horse returned, bringing with her a magnificent stallion. The son was delighted and mounted the horse, but had scarcely set out for a ride when he fell and broke his hip. Again he was distraught, and again his father said, 'What makes you think this isn't a blessing?' Two years later the nomads invaded and every able-bodied man marched to battle. All were lost. Only the lame son and the elderly father survived. What is blessing and what is disaster?"

"Somebody stole my story. That's a disaster," I said.

Two young women joined us on the bench till one murmured to the other, "I can't stand this heat. I'm going to the drugstore."

"What you need in the drugstore?" said the other.

"Nothing. It's air-conditioned," said the first. "We can look at magazines."

I was about to follow them when the elderly gentleman said, "Steinbeck's dog chewed half of the first draft of *Mice and Men*. And Steinbeck forgave him, saying, 'I'm not sure Toby didn't know what he was doing when he ate that first draft. I have promoted Toby-dog to be lieutenant-colonel in charge of literature.' You know, I used to write stories. And I almost wrote a novel. I had three hundred pages written in a big notebook. And then the war came. During the war I lost everything."

"How terrible to lose a novel!" I cried. I meant to say, how terrible to lose everything.

He shook his head.

"Really, in my case, it was a blessing. I wanted to write a family history, a *bildungs-roman*. Thomas Mann was my hero. I had notes, a family tree, plans, hundreds of plans. But in my heart of hearts I knew my novel sounded wooden. A wise man said, 'A writer with a fixed idea is like a goose trying to hatch a stone.' In 1940, I was sent to Ravensbrück. All my life teachers told me not to daydream. Now it was my salvation. Can you outline a dream? Would it be worth dreaming if you could? In that terrible place I let my mind wander, and my characters came back to me, not as I saw them in my notes and plans but as they saw themselves, full of memories and longings. I understood their real story at last. I turned no one away. Does the sea refuse a single river? Have you heard of Van der Post and his explorations to Africa?"

"No," I said. "Sorry."

"Never mind. He tells of the time he traveled to a village where a great hunter lived. When he arrived, he found the hunter sitting motionless. And the villagers said, 'Don't interrupt him. He is doing work of the utmost importance. He is making clouds.'"

"Did you finish your novel?" I asked. I have a weakness for happy endings.

"How could I finish it? We had no paper. No pens. But we had tongues. So I became a storyteller instead of a writer. I no longer thought of plots, only of voice. Of whose story I was telling. When I hear the voice, I know the story will find me. Storytellers do not lose their stories, except when they die. I like to start my stories in the old style, *once upon a time*. Once upon a time is a promise, a promise of a story, and I try to keep my promises. Of course not everyone agrees with me about these methods. My son, for example. He's a TV writer. Weekends, he wants to write the great American novel, but he doesn't know how to get started. One day he calls me from New York, all excited. 'I've just signed a contract to write the bible!' Naturally I'm interested. He goes on to say that this bible is not from God, of course. This is the book TV script writers use when they're doing a new series of shows. It describes characters, it describes place, it describes adventures.

"'And for what show are you writing a bible?' I ask my son.

"'It's a mini-series,' he says. 'It's called *The Further Adventures of Alice in Wonderland*.'

"'How can that be?' I say. 'There is only one Lewis Carroll.'

"'Yes, papa, but there are five script writers. They'll make up the other adventures. But they can write only about what they know. I'm going to write them a detailed description of Wonderland and the characters.' What do you think, fellow-scribbler? Is it a good idea, the further adventures of *Alice in Wonderland*?"

"I don't know," I said. "What happened to your son?"

"My son read the Alice books carefully. He mapped the terrain, noted the architecture, the dangers, the geography, the birds and animals. He wrote out character studies of everyone mentioned in the books. And he got paid well. And suddenly a brilliant idea struck him. Why not write a bible for his great unwritten American novel? How much easier it would be to start his novel if he had a detailed knowledge of his characters. Hadn't his English teachers always said, 'Write about what you know?'"

"My teachers said the same thing," I laughed.

"They all say it," said the elderly gentleman. "I even said it to my students. But I didn't mean my students should write such a bible. If you take everyone's advice, you'll build a crazy house. My son wrote out descriptions of all his characters and their locale. Then he wrote the first two chapters and showed them to me. 'Aaron,' I said, 'how can I tell you? This is from your head, not your heart. It's predictable. No surprises. Even God is surprised by the actions of his creatures.'

"'I've put a lot of time into this,' he said.

"'The nest is done but the bird is dead,' I told him. 'You should take a lesson from your Lewis Carroll. He was a storyteller. I know for a fact that when he sent his Alice down the rabbit hole, he didn't know what would happen next. That white rabbit was a gift from Providence! We should follow Providence, not force it.' He's intelligent, my Aaron, but he thinks too much. He needs intelligence to keep him from hindering himself so he is free to do amazing things. I tell him to watch Charlie Chaplin. You have seen his great film, 'Modern Times?'"

"A long time ago," I said, hoping he wouldn't quiz me on it.

"Maybe you remember, near the end, Charlie has to go on the stage and sing a song. And now he can't remember the words. So Paulette Goddard writes the words on his cuff. He goes onstage, he tries to read them, he's hopeless. Not a sound out of him. He's paralyzed. And then Paulette Goddard calls out, 'Never mind the words. Just sing!'"

"I think that kind of thing happens only when you tell stories," I said, "not when you write them."

"It can also happen when you write them," he said. "You have two choices. You can arrange the material, with outlines. Or you can arrange yourself. I see you looking at the laundromat. You have business there?"

"I forgot to put my mom's clothes in the dryer."

"And you want to see if the thief returned your manuscript," he added.

"Yes," I agreed.

Suddenly I remembered my promise.

"Excuse me," I said, rising. "Do you know a good shoe store?"

"From writing to shoes!" he said, and laughed.

"I have to run. I promised my mother I'd buy some new shoes."

"Are you in such a hurry?" he exclaimed. "Let me tell you about a man who set out to buy himself shoes. He measured his foot and put the measurements away. When he got to the market, he found he'd left the measurements at home. He chose a pair of shoes and hurried home for the measurements, but when he returned the market was closed. He never got the shoes, of course. And that night he dreamed his feet asked him, 'Why didn't you trust us? Why did you trust the measurements more than your own feet?'"

We stood up in unison.

"There's a department store one street over," he said. "But all shoe stores are good if you need shoes."

I didn't go shopping for shoes, and I didn't find my manuscript. When I arrived at Shady Park, Mother was not in her room. She had been wheeled into the TV room. She was asleep, her head nearly on her chest; she had been left at a long empty table with her back to the TV. Probably she had told the attendant that she didn't like television. The other chairs were all facing the set, as if their occupants were worshiping it.

I rushed in and turned her chair around.

"Wake up, Ma. We're going back to your room."

But Mr. Levine's chair was stuck in the doorway, blocking it. He was making helpless swoops with his hands, trying to move the wheels.

"Let me help you," I said, and pushed him through.

Instantly a ripple of movement started behind me, as if I had waked the very walls.

"Lady, can you help me?"

"Miss, can you get me out of here? Miss!"

Heads lifted, hands waved.

"Miss!"

I can't help them all, I thought.

"Mother, do you want to look at the box of photographs with me?"

"I want to lie down," she said.

What angel was present in the room with us that evening? The angel of chance or the angel of memory? The angel of time or the angel of hidden things? After I'd put away her dresses, clean but crumpled from being carried in my arms, I sat on the edge of her bed and flipped through the box of snapshots. Tucked in among the pictures were Christmas cards. Mother never threw away a Christmas card that had a photograph on it. I held up a picture of an elderly couple standing in front of the Taj Mahal.

"Who in thunder are they?" exclaimed Mother.

"I don't know," I said. "Let me read you the writing on the back. 'We visited fourteen countries and had a wonderful time. Love, Dorothy and Jack.'"

"Are both my parents dead?" asked Mother.

"Oh, Ma, you know they died a long time ago. If they were alive, they'd be a hundred and twenty."

I pulled out another and held it up. It showed a middle-aged woman standing on what appeared to be a cistern and smiling. I turned the photograph over and read the scrawled inscription.

"'This is your old Aunt Velda standing by the well. Clark covered it over for me and put in running water, hot and cold. He also made the driveway you can see behind me, to the left.'"

Mother's face brightened.

"I remember that well," she said. "There was a pump on Grandpa's farm in Iowa. Oh, he had acres and acres of the best farmland in the country. And when the men were working in the fields, Grandma would fill a bucket of water from that pump. And she'd send me out with the bucket and dipper to give the men a drink. And it seemed like such a long walk coming and going. I was dying of thirst by the time I got back to the house. And Grandma wouldn't let me pour myself a drink from the pump right off. No. She made me hold my wrists under the spout, and she'd pump the water over them. To cool my blood, she said, so the cold drink wouldn't give me a stomach ache. Lord, how good that cold water felt. And how good it tasted."

I'd never heard her tell that story. How many other stories lay hidden in her heart, waiting for a listener to wake them?

Suddenly I understood my real task. I would lay my angel story aside and forget about it for awhile. Tomorrow I would bring a notebook and start writing down her memories. I would have to be patient. Memory has nothing to do with outlines and everything to do with accidents.

On my way home I stopped once more at the Wash Bored and couldn't believe my eyes. There on top of the fateful washing machine stood the clothes basket. And safe in its plastic lavender embrace nestled my story.

I pulled it out and turned the pages, checking them for bruises. I counted the pages. I pulled up a chair and reread them. Was the angel of hope responsible for what happened next?

I threw the entire manuscript in the wastebasket. I would take Rilke's advice: "If the angel deigns to come, it will be because you have convinced him, not by tears, but by your horrible resolve to be a beginner."

Voices. Voices. That night, before I fell asleep, I heard the voices of my characters, though faintly, like a conversation accidently picked up on a long distance line. I did not let them know I was listening.

The next morning I set out for Shady Park Manor with a light heart and was pleasantly surprised to meet my storyteller coming out of the synagogue at the end of the block.

"You are going to visit your mother? May I walk with you as far as Jerry's Good and Used?"

"What's Jerry's Good and Used?"

"Jerry has this and that of everything. His speciality is baseball cards. He calls last night and says, 'I have a treasure. Something you want very much, a card of the great Japanese ballplayer, Sadaharu Oh.' He asks me why I want a card of Sadaharu Oh. I tell him that I want a picture of the man who wrote in his autobiography not about winning but about waiting. Waiting, he says in that book, is the most active state of all. It is the beginning of all action. Did you find your manuscript?"

"I found it. And I threw it away. I'm starting over. This time I'll wait for the story to find me. Like you said yesterday."

I expected my new acquaintance to offer his congratulations, but he did not.

"The freedom of the dream doesn't mean doing nothing. You still have to sit down every day and write. What if the angel came and you were out shopping for shoes? God helps the drowning sailor, but he must row. You have a long journey ahead of you. And it starts with one footstep."

"It feels more like an ending than a beginning," I said.

"Endings and beginnings—are they so far from each other? When I was in Ravensbrück I was chosen to die. Only because someone among the killers recognized me was I saved. Now when I tell my stories, I remember that moment. It makes the telling more urgent. How is your mother?"

"Fine, I guess. Just very tired."

"You know, when I was little, my mother would put me to sleep by describing rooms in all the houses she'd lived in. And so many things happened in those rooms. Now you can hardly find a house in which someone has died or been born. It all happens away from us, in big hospitals."

"My mother told me a story yesterday," I said. And I described to him my mother's journey to the harvest fields with the bucket of water, and the journey back to the well, and the cold water on her wrists.

He was silent for so long that I felt I had said something foolish.

"The cold water—it's such an unimportant detail," I remarked.

"Unimportant?" he exclaimed. "That is why it's worth remembering. When I was young I fell in love with a girl named Hilda who happened to be a twin. I asked her to go out with me. She agreed to go, but only if I could tell her apart from her sister. I studied her face for several minutes. Then she ran and got her twin. Hilda had a blue vein on the bridge of her nose. Unimportant, a blue vein, but when I spied it, I knew I was saved."

"I'll save that detail about the cold water for my next story," I assured him.

He wagged a finger at me.

"Don't save it. Use it, use it now. You just threw out your life savings. This is no time for prudence."

We passed Jerry's Good and Used. My storyteller did not go in. Instead he kept pace with me, up the hill to Shady Park Manor.

"May I tell you a story as we take this little walk together? Long ago, when wizards still walked the length and breadth of the earth, there arrived in the world of the dead a great magician.

"'Why have you come here?' asked the Mistress of the Dead.

"The magician explained that when he was building his boat he found he could not finish it without four magic words, and that he had not been able to find them, however far he traveled.

"'The Lord of the Dead will never teach you his spells,' answered the Mistress of the Dead.

"But the magician could not give up the task of finishing his boat. He wandered here and there until one day he met a shepherd who told him to seek out the giant.

"'In his vast mouth there are a hundred magic words. You will have to go down into his enormous belly and there you will learn marvels. But it's not easy to get there. You must go along a path leaping on the points of women's needles, and over a crossroad paved with sharp swords, and down a third road made of blades of heroes' axes.'

"But the magician was determined to try it. He would do anything to find those four words and finish his boat. Four words! Marvelous words! Would you believe I once bought a photography book because of a single sentence? I was standing in Tucker's—it's a block down the street from us—and I opened up a book and read the epigraph on the first page. It was the beginning and the ending of *Finnegan's Wake*.

A way a long a last a loved
      along the riverrun,
         past Eve and Adam's

Right away I wanted to read *Finnegan's Wake*. But Tucker's didn't have it. And the library was closed for a week. But how could I live without those words? So I bought the photography book. I bought it for those words."

We arrived at Shady Park.

"It is good you are listening to your mother."

"I'm going to write her memories down. I don't want to forget them."

"If you forget a few, don't worry. What you need will come back to you. We don't really understand something until we have forgotten it. Live in your roots, not in your branches."

I took the elevator to the second floor. When I stepped out a nurse hurried up to me.

"Your mother had a seizure last night. We phoned for the ambulance just an hour ago. Call Dr. Rubin right away—you can use the phone at the nurse's station."

The voice of medical authority at the other end of the phone named the problem: staxis epilepsicus. Dr. Rubin explained he had given her valium and phenobarbital.

"It took us over an hour to stop her seizures. Now she's asleep."

"Did she have a stroke?"

"This morning I thought yes. When I looked at the CAT-scan, I thought no. Her brain is shrunken, and there's an abnormal pattern of electric ions. It's probably caused by the little strokes she's had earlier."

"I'll be right over."

I hung up and the nurse touched my arm.

"I'm so sorry," she said. "Let me call you a cab."

I waited downstairs for the cab. The receptionist was changing the bulletin board, posting the new activities. Bingo, Sensory Stimulation, Current Events, Patio Outing.

A way a long a last a loved along the riverrun.

Dr. Rubin and I are standing by my mother's bed in the intensive care section. Mother is sleeping under the watchful gaze of the IV and the blood pressure basket hanging over her bed, its black tubes coiled into a nest. Over the basket a large plastic bottle bubbles and quakes. This is not the first time I have seen Mother in intensive care.

"When do you think she'll wake up?" I ask.

The doctor shrugs.

"Who knows? It could be tomorrow. It could be in ten minutes. Or it could be never."

I reach out and touch her hair, still soft and wavy, and the translucent skin on her temple: pale freckled silk. The doctor pulls away the plastic respirator that covers the center of her face with a clear green beak, and her sunken cheeks flutter in and out like the throat of a frightened bird. A tube snakes out of her nose, ready for her next feeding. Her mouth is a small black hole. The doctor leans close to her face, as if he might kiss her. Then he pries open her eyelids and looks deeply into her pupils and calls, "Mrs. Williams! Mrs. Williams!"

Two green-gray coins stare back at him, as cold and indifferent as the eyes of a fish. I feel my knees growing weak and I sit down fast on the edge of her bed.

"Can she hear us now?"

"Possibly. There's no way of knowing for sure."

When he leaves us alone together, I take her hand, frail as the claw of a wren. The IV has left a deep bruise on her arm. How old it looks, this arm, limp when I lift it, a mottled mineral brown, across which white scars move like the shapes of ancient beasts.

I know I will never see her alive again. I do not know if she can hear me. I put my mouth close to her ear and tell her I love her. I thank her for telling me about the cold water. I tell that I lost my story in Pittsburgh, a story about angels. I lost it at the laundromat, and I met a man who told me how to find it again. Maybe he wasn't a man at all, maybe he was the story angel? He did not have wings, but who needs wings in Pittsburgh? Though my mouth is touching her ear, I feel my mother going farther and farther away. I want to talk to her till she is out of earshot. Though she is traveling with empty hands, I do not want my mother, who has given me so much, to leave with an empty heart. I give her an angel, a daughter, and herself. And I give her my promise to save them: *once upon a time*.

—Fall 1991

UNIVERSITY PRESS OF NEW ENGLAND publishes books under its own imprint and is the publisher for Brandeis University Press, Brown University Press, University of Connecticut, Dartmouth College, Middlebury College Press, University of New Hampshire, University of Rhode Island, Tufts University, University of Vermont, and Wesleyan University Press.

Library of Congress Cataloging-in-Publication Data

The Unfeigned word : fifteen years of New England review / edited by
    T.R Hummer and Devon Jersild.
        p.   cm.
    Contains works published in the New England review since 1978.
    ISBN 0-87451-619-6
    1. Literature, Modern—20th century.   I. Hummer, T. R.
II. Jersild, Devon. III. New England review (Middlebury, Vt.)
PN6014.U45   1993
808.8'004—dc20   92-56906